Forensic Medicolegal Injury and Death Investigation

Forensic Medicolegal Injury and Death Investigation

Mary H. Dudley, MD

CRC Press
Taylor & Francis Group
Boca Raton London New York

CRC Press is an imprint of the
Taylor & Francis Group, an **informa** business

CRC Press
Taylor & Francis Group
6000 Broken Sound Parkway NW, Suite 300
Boca Raton, FL 33487-2742

© 2017 by Mary H. Dudley, M.D.
CRC Press is an imprint of Taylor & Francis Group, an Informa business

No claim to original U.S. Government works

Printed on acid-free paper
Version Date: 20160720

International Standard Book Number-13: 978-1-4987-3488-2 (Hardback)

Library of Congress Cataloging-in-Publication Data

Names: Dudley, Mary H., author.
Title: Forensic medicolegal injury and death investigation / Mary H. Dudley.
Description: Boca Raton : Taylor & Francis, 2017. | Includes bibliographical references and index.
Identifiers: LCCN 2016013149 | ISBN 9781498734882 (hardback : alk. paper)
Subjects: | MESH: Forensic Medicine--methods | Wounds and Injuries | Cause of Death
Classification: LCC RA1063.4 | NLM W 700 | DDC 614/.1--dc23
LC record available at http://lccn.loc.gov/2016013149

Visit the Taylor & Francis Web site at
http://www.taylorandfrancis.com

and the CRC Press Web site at
http://www.crcpress.com

Contents

Section I

INTRODUCTION TO FORENSIC INVESTIGATION

4 Postmortem Changes   39

5 Death Scene Investigation   45

6   Mass Fatality Management   61

7   Forensic Legal Issues and Expert Witness Testimony   69

ROBERT J. McWHIRTER

Section II
INJURY RECOGNITION

Section III
NATURAL AND ACCIDENTAL DEATHS

Preface

Forensic Medicolegal Injury and Death Investigation is the basic text for forensic medical investigation. It is written for both beginning students and experienced practitioners in fields that involve investigation of human injury or death. Death or injury can result from a predictable or unpredictable accident, or, in cases of homicide and suicide, a planned or unplanned event. Insurance companies, estate heirs, health-care providers, governmental regulatory agencies, and survivors frequently use the resources of private and public forensic specialists in injury and death investigations.

Forensic Medicolegal Injury and Death Investigation introduces basic concepts of clinical forensic medicine and death investigation. The forensic team involved in the overall medicolegal process includes nurses, physicians, attorneys, law enforcement investigators, dentists, death investigators, and other highly skilled specialists. Anyone who has direct contact with death, crime, and the medicolegal system will find *Forensic Medicolegal Injury and Death Investigation* necessary for understanding his or her own role as well as the roles of other professionals as they collaborate for a solution to an initially unexplained death.

Forensic Medicolegal Injury and Death Investigation covers six main areas of forensic investigation including introduction to forensic science, injury recognition, natural disease, accidental death, child fatalities, and domestic violence.

Mary H. Dudley, MD

Acknowledgments

I thank the contributing authors for providing their expertise, current knowledge, and assistance to specific sections in my book including Dr. James L. Caruso (Drowning Fatalities), Dr. Lauren E. Dvorscak (Chapter 14 [Natural Deaths], Chapter 17 [Fire Deaths], and Chapter 24 [Sudden Unexpected Infant Deaths]), Robert J. McWhirter (Chapter 7 [Forensic Legal Issues and Expert Witness Testimony]), Cheryl L. Pozzi (First Responder System and Chapter 20 [Workplace Deaths]), and Dr. Ross E. Zumwalt (Chapter 25 [Elder Abuse]).

I especially thank Dr. Kurt Nolte and the Office of the Medical Investigator (OMI) at the University of New Mexico in Albuquerque, New Mexico, for their permission to use current digital photos and images to support the narrative in the manuscript.

I also thank my research assistant, Megha Garg, from Kansas City, Missouri, for her many hours of help in updating the manuscript format and for early submission to the editors.

I am extremely grateful to Dr. Lauren E. Dvorscak for her time and assistance during her busy forensic fellowship year at the OMI. She was instrumental in updating current statistical data and references in preparing the manuscript for final submission for publication. She also contributed to writing three sections of the book as listed earlier. Her help was vital in selecting appropriate digital images and providing captions to correspond to the written narrative.

Author

Mary H. Dudley, MD is the former chief medical examiner for Jackson County in Kansas City, Missouri. She is board certified in anatomic and forensic pathology by the American Board of Pathology. She completed a 2-year fellowship in forensic pathology at the University of New Mexico in Albuquerque, NM, following a 4-year anatomic and clinical pathology residency at Penrose Hospital in Colorado Springs, Colorado. She has a diploma, BS, and MS in nursing and also founded the first Forensic Nursing Certificate Program in 1994. Dr. Dudley originated the first Forensic Medical Investigation Course in 1996.

Dr. Dudley is a fellow member of both the National Association of Medical Examiners, and the American Academy of Forensic Science. She served as co-chair of the Medical Examiner Advisory Board for the Musculotissue Foundation, member of the Missouri Child Fatality Review Board, and member of the National Disaster Medical Systems (Disaster Mortuary Operations Response Team). She also held appointment as associate professor of Clinical Pathology at the University of Missouri, Kansas City, MO, and the University of Kansas, Kansas City, KS.

Contributors

James L. Caruso, MD is the chief medical examiner and coroner for Denver, Colorado. He completed 30 years in the U.S. Navy where he served as an Armed Forces Medical Examiner, forensic pathologist, Diving Medical Officer, and Flight Surgeon and retired in January 2014 to take the Denver position. Dr. Caruso's research interests include water-related deaths and forensic toxicology. He has authored numerous book chapters, peer-reviewed publications, and scientific presentations.

Lauren E. Dvorscak, MD is currently a fellow in forensic pathology at the Office of the Medical Investigator for the State of New Mexico. She completed her medical education at Indiana University School of Medicine, Indianapolis, Indiana. She then completed a pathology residency at the University of New Mexico Hospitals, Albuquerque, New Mexico, and is board certified in both anatomic and clinical pathology. She is a member of the National Association of Medical Examiners, American Academy of Forensic Sciences, and Alpha Omega Alpha Medical Honor Society. She has authored several peer-reviewed publications and presented at national conferences regarding her research interest, sudden infant death.

Robert J. McWhirter, certified specialist in criminal law, supervising attorney, ASU Alumni Law Group is a nationally and internationally known speaker and author on trial advocacy, immigration law, and the history of the bill of rights. He is a certified specialist in criminal law with the State Bar of Arizona and first chair qualified to defend capital cases by the Arizona Supreme Court.

McWhirter has extensively taught in Latin America on comparative criminal procedure and trial advocacy in Venezuela, Colombia, Mexico, Nicaragua, Ecuador, and Uruguay. He has been a visiting professor at the Catholic University of Chile and the University of Chile. In 2010–2011, McWhirter served in El Salvador administering an $11 million USAID project to reform the justice system where he successfully developed and oversaw programs and training for the Salvadoran courts, police, prosecutors, and public defenders.

In 2009, McWhirter was named a Southwest Super Lawyer, a rare instance for a public defender. McWhirter is also the 2009 recipient of the Phoenix Saint Thomas More Award and the immediate past president of Arizona Attorneys for Criminal Justice.

McWhirter is the supervising criminal attorney at the ASU Alumni Law Group, a teaching law firm.

Cheryl L. Pozzi, RN, BSN, MS, BCFN is a health professional with over 35 years of progressive and accomplished nursing responsibilities in safety. Pozzi's extensive experience brings a unique perspective and one of the strongest with a combination of investigative, emergency, behavioral, and safety-oriented skill sets.

Pozzi has worked in emergency medicine, occupational nursing, correctional nursing, and forensic nursing and has flown as a medivac flight nurse. She has a master's degree in industrial safety management, postgraduate certificate in forensic nursing, and postgraduate certificate in animal-assisted therapy. Pozzi has worked extensively performing research on the incidence of violence in prehospital providers and was one of the first to document and publish the studies. She developed an educational program for the State of Alaska managing behavioral emergencies for Emergency Medical Services (EMS). Pozzi is currently employed as a nurse case manager for a worker's compensation claims company.

Ross E. Zumwalt, MD is a medical investigator and professor of pathology at the Office of the Medical Investigator for the State of New Mexico. He received a BA from Wabash College in Crawfordsville, Indiana, and an MD from the University of Illinois College of Medicine in Chicago, Illinois. He completed an internship and residency at the Mary Imogene Bassett Hospital in Cooperstown, New York, and a pathology residency at the Southwestern Medical School in Dallas, Texas. He received forensic fellowship training at the Dallas County Medical Examiner's Office. He additionally served in the military as director of laboratories at the Navy Regional Medical Center in Camp Lejeune, North Carolina. After 2 years as deputy coroner in Cleveland, Ohio, and 6 years as deputy coroner in Cincinnati, Ohio, he came to the New Mexico Office of the Medical Investigator in 1987. Dr. Zumwalt is certified in anatomic and forensic pathology by the American Board of Pathology. He was a trustee of the American Board of Pathology from 1993 to 2004. Dr. Zumwalt served as chief medical investigator of the State of New Mexico from 1991 through 2014.

Dr. Zumwalt has served as president of the National Association of Medical Examiners and is a member of the following professional organizations: the National Association of Medical Examiners, the American Academy of Forensic Sciences, College of American Pathologists, American Society of Clinical Pathologists, U.S. and Canadian Academy of Pathology, American Medical Association, and the American Association for the Advancement of Science. He served on a National Academy of Sciences Committee on identifying the needs of the Forensic Science Community from 2007 to 2009.

Introduction
To Forensic
Investigation

I

1

Introduction
To Forensic
Investigation

Forensic Investigative Systems

1

OBJECTIVES

Upon completion of this chapter and the corresponding reference material, the reader will be able to

- Describe roles and responsibilities of specialists within forensic investigative systems
- Describe a psychological autopsy and a forensic autopsy
- Explain how his or her particular role interacts with those of other specialists described in this chapter
- Discuss how local resources differ from state to state, from county to county, from urban areas to rural areas
- Describe how first responders to a death scene can interact with the forensic investigators

Introduction

Forensic investigative systems provide important contributions for medicolegal analysis to the criminal justice system. Many professional and technical specialists are necessary to make the forensic investigative system operate smoothly. Depending on statutes and ordinances, differences exist for reporting deaths within states, counties, and cities. Differences also occur among coroner systems, medical examiner systems, and combined systems. Additionally, the number and responsibilities of individuals within each type of system vary. The overall goal of each system, however, is to determine the identity of the decedent and the cause, mechanism, and manner of death.

Guidelines as to what constitutes a case for the medical examiner (ME)/coroner are based on types of death, reporting procedures, and state statutes. Some states have a "24 hour rule" that requires a report of death be made to the ME/coroner in the case of a presumed natural death that occurs during the first day of a hospital admission. Other states do not have this rule unless the circumstances are covered under state statute.

Most states require report of certain deaths to a law enforcement officer and the ME/coroner by any person having knowledge of the death of a human being. Generally, failure to report such death is classified as a misdemeanor, punishable by a fine or imprisonment.

Categories of death that require a law enforcement or ME/coroner report include

- Death that occurs when not under the care of a physician
- Death that occurs when an attending physician is not available to sign the death certificate
- Death from violence
- Sudden death in an otherwise healthy individual
- Death in prison
- Death of a prisoner or while in custody
- Death that occurs in a suspicious, unusual, or unnatural manner
- Death related to accident or disease associated with the decedent's occupation
- Death that is believed to have presented a public health hazard
- Death that occurs during surgery or while under anesthesia

Examples of Reportable Deaths

- Falls
- Blunt force or crushing injuries
- Stabbing or sharp force injuries
- Fatal gunshot wounds
- Fatal electric shocks or lightning strikes
- Fatal explosions
- Strangulations or asphyxial deaths
- Fatal motor vehicle accidents
- Drug overdoses or poisonings
- Fatal burns or fires
- Stillborns or newborn deaths if associated with trauma or illicit drug abuse
- Rapid fatal illnesses
- Occupational deaths
- Persons found dead
- Clustering of undiagnosed infectious disease

Legal Issues Regarding Death

Numerous legal issues are associated with a death including notification of the next of kin, death certification, estate transfers, worker's compensation claims, criminal and civil investigations, insurance claims, and settlements. The key to all of the above issues is proper identification of the decedent. Identification may require assistance from multiple forensic specialists including forensic pathologists, police agencies for fingerprints, forensic anthropologists for skeletal examination and comparison, forensic odontologists for dental identification, DNA experts, and a host of other types of experts, depending on the case. Use of forensic team experts is especially needed if the individual cannot be visually identified in circumstances such as fire deaths, decomposition, aircraft accidents, or skeletal remains.

Notification of the next of kin is most properly done in person rather than by telephone. It should be accomplished by law enforcement personnel or the forensic medical investigator.

Proper determination of the manner of death is important for both criminal and civil investigations as well as for insurance claims. A careful ME/coroner examination and scene investigation are required to determine whether the death was by accident or by suicide. For example, some insurance policies will compensate the next of kin with "double indemnity" in an accidental manner of death but will pay nothing in a suicide manner of death. The manner of death is determined by investigation of the circumstances of death determined at the death scene.

Transplantation (Organ and Tissue Donation)

Permission to transplant organs or tissue is requested of and granted by the next of kin of the decedent. In addition, the ME/coroner must grant permission for donation in a medicolegal case prior to donation.

Specialties in Forensic Medical Investigation

Forensic Pathology

Pathology is the study of injury or natural disease; forensic pathology is the interface between pathology and the law. Forensic pathology became a recognized medical specialty in 1959.

The forensic pathologist is a medical doctor with 4 or 5 years of residency training in anatomic and clinical pathology as well as 1 year of fellowship training in forensic pathology. The forensic pathologist is generally appointed as an ME or may be elected to the ME/coroner's office. Forensic pathologists may also contract with the ME/coroner's office to provide forensic autopsy services. Forensic pathologists determine the cause, mechanism, and manner of death for cases that are under their jurisdiction. The forensic pathologist may be called to the scene of death. Rarely, the forensic pathologist may be the one who pronounces the victim dead. The forensic pathologist performs the forensic autopsy, issues an autopsy report, preserves tissue samples as required by state law, and creates a death certificate. As ME/coroner, the forensic pathologist also will grant permission for cremation and will provide court testimony as an expert witness. The forensic pathologist generally coordinates the involvement of forensic specialist consultants. Forensic pathologists are board certified by the American Board of Pathology.

Forensic Medical Investigation

Scene investigation is of paramount importance in any medicolegal inquiry of a death. As in clinical medicine where a comprehensive medical history provides 50%–75% of the information necessary for a diagnosis, a properly conducted scene investigation can provide the majority of information significant to a particular case for the forensic pathologist. The forensic medical investigator functions as the "eyes and ears" of the forensic pathologist and relays pertinent information to the forensic pathologist prior to autopsy. Authority and primary responsibility of crime scene investigation remain with the law enforcement agency whereas the forensic pathologist/ME/coroner has state statutory authority and responsibility to conduct a medicolegal investigation and has jurisdiction of the body at the scene.

The forensic medical investigator has a basic knowledge of medicolegal death investigation and clinical forensic investigation (the "living" forensic cases). Medicolegal death investigators are nationally certified by the American Board of Medicolegal Death Investigators. Forensic medical investigators are generally full-time employees of the ME/coroner's office and function under the direction and supervision of the ME.

Forensic Odontology

Forensically trained, licensed dentists who work for the ME/coroner system are known as forensic odontologists. Depending on the size and structure of the ME/coroner department, the dentist may be employed in forensics on a full-time basis or as a consultant on a contractual basis.

The scope of the forensic odontologist's responsibilities generally involves the identification of victims based on dental comparison in individual situations such as fire deaths and decomposition or in mass disasters such as explosions, building collapses, or aircraft accidents. One major aspect of forensic odontology is the comparison of antemortem and postmortem dental x-rays to make confirmed identities. Forensic odontologists are also called upon to identify and match characteristics of bite marks that may be related to a death. Forensic odontologists can identify evidence of child abuse from oral soft tissue or dental injuries such as a torn frenulum or avulsed tooth sustained from a blow to the mouth of a child. Additionally, as with forensic pathologists, the forensic odontologist may be called upon to testify about his or her findings in a court of law. Forensic odontologists are board certified by the American Board of Forensic Odontology.

Forensic Anthropology

Forensic anthropology involves the study of skeletal remains associated with forensic issues including human identification and trauma. Forensic anthropologists can distinguish between human and nonhuman bones and can determine the age, sex, race, and stature from human skeletal analysis. The forensic anthropologist assists the medical examiner in scene recovery of buried or burnt remains. Forensic anthropologists are board certified by the American Board of Forensic Anthropology.

Forensic Psychology

Forensic psychologists who work with the ME/coroner's office to investigate deaths generally focus on the psychological autopsy of the deceased. The psychological autopsy is a document obtained by interviewing next of kin and friends of the deceased and by reviewing psychiatric history to determine the mental state of the individual at the time of death to help in determination of the manner of death, for example, suicide vs. accident. Within the realm of criminalistics and law enforcement, the forensic psychologist consults on the previous mental health of the decedent as well as that of the assailant. Psychological profiles of the perpetrators offer valuable clues regarding mental state at the time of the crime and/or competency to testify. The forensic psychologist may also be called upon to offer testimony for the defense and/or prosecution in a court of law.

Forensic psychologists have obtained an advanced university degree. Licensure for this specialty is required by some states but not all. The roles of a psychologist and psychiatrist (medical doctor) may overlap in the field of forensic investigation. The psychologist generally reports the results of psychological tests and measurements, which may be valuable in victim or assailant records, whereas the psychiatrist generally deals with modalities of therapy for mental illness in the historical records of the victim and those of the suspect including medication, electric shock, and hospitalization.

Forensic Toxicology

Forensic toxicologists are PhD chemists and/or toxicologists who specialize in the investigation of drugs and other substances found in the body of the deceased. Like other highly specialized individuals on the forensic investigation team, forensic toxicologists may be employed on a full-time or part-time basis for the ME/coroner's office. They are experts in the examination of tissue, blood, urine, gastric contents, bile, vitreous humor, and other bodily fluids for the presence of toxic substances in the body that may result in death or contribute to the death.

Forensic toxicologists also test for blood alcohol levels; levels of illicit drugs such as cocaine, heroin, "designer" drugs, and household chemicals that have become lethal due to high doses; as well as levels of prescription medications. The forensic toxicologist's role also includes maintaining a chain of custody of specimens, preserving samples for a required period of time, and supervising a technical staff to support his or her overall role. As with other specialists on the forensic investigation team, the toxicologist may be called upon to report laboratory findings in court and to testify as to the significance of such findings. Forensic toxicologists are board certified by the Society of Forensic Toxicologists.

Forensic Radiology

Radiographs of the deceased are frequently necessary to determine identity and the cause, mechanism, and manner of death. In addition to the verification of bone fractures, x-ray studies can detect the presence of metal such as shrapnel, knife blade parts, bullets, or other artifacts in the body. X-rays are routinely obtained in all unidentified bodies, skeletal remains, fire deaths, airplane crashes, pipe bomb victims, decomposed bodies, child abuse deaths, and homicides.

Forensic Nursing

Forensic nurses are nurses with specialized training in forensic medical science, criminalistics, and legal issues. Completion of special courses in forensic science, forensic medical investigation, and death investigation is required to prepare forensic nurses for extended forensic nursing roles. In addition to obtaining a state license to practice as a registered nurse, a forensic nurse may also be required to obtain certification in this specialty.

The American Nurses Association has recognized forensic nursing as the newest subspecialty in nursing since critical care nursing. Nurse death investigator, sexual assault nurse examiner, correctional nurse, and trauma nursing are some of the growing subspecialties available to forensic nurses. Several forensic nursing certificate programs are available in the United States and Canada.

Forensic Entomology

Forensic entomology involves study of insect species associated with postmortem decomposition. These studies assist the ME/coroner in determining time of death of the decedent. The forensic entomologist studies insects present on a dead body and can estimate the time of death based on knowledge of that species' growth cycle. Some insects are collected alive and some are preserved in alcohol at the crime scene before being sent to the entomologist's laboratory for evaluation.

Determination of the life stage of an insect is helpful in determining the postmortem time interval. For example, flies are the most common insect associated with decomposing bodies. They tend to lay their eggs in moist orifices of bodies and in areas of open injury or tissue destruction. When only fly eggs are present on a body, the forensic entomologist can generally assume that the time of death was within 1–2 days. However, this can be quite variable depending on temperature, humidity, and specific species. After eggs hatch, maggots grow until they reach the pupal stage—approximately 6–10 days under ordinary conditions. Adult flies emerge in 12–18 days. If cocaine is present in a body, the growth cycle of flies is expedited.

Forensic entomologists are also able to detect the presence of drugs in a body through their studies of insects. Maggots collected from a body can be subjected to toxicological analysis. Because maggots feed upon the tissues of a decomposed body, they can reveal the presence of various drugs in a body. By liquefying the maggots in a blender, an adequate sample can be produced for toxicological testing.

Clinical Forensic Medicine ("Living Forensic Cases")

Clinical forensic medicine is a relatively new specialty field in the United States. This specialty is defined as the application of medical and scientific knowledge of questions of the law and the civil and criminal investigations of trauma. Clinical forensic medicine residency training requires both emergency medicine and forensic medicine training. In England, clinical forensic medicine is an old specialty; the "police surgeon" has existed in England for over 100 years.

Trauma ranks higher than cancer or heart disease as the reason for hospital admission. Clinical "living" forensic medical cases encompass all violence cases including abuse of children and the elderly, sexual assault, drug and alcohol addiction, suicide attempts, gunshot wounds, stab wounds, traffic accidents, occupational injuries, medical malpractice, therapeutic misadventures, and environmental hazards.

Most emergency department visits have potential medicolegal aspects. It is crucial that injuries are properly recognized, documented, and photographed prior to medical intervention or surgical alteration wounds. Proper collection of evidence and clothing as well as maintenance of the chain of custody and transfer of responsibility to law enforcement requires special knowledge by physicians, nurses, and emergency medical technicians (EMTs).

Mortuary Science

The roles of morticians, undertakers, and funeral directors are often overlooked in the forensic investigative system. However, bodies are frequently delivered for embalming or cremation with a death certificate that does not coincide with the findings on the body. Cooperation between individuals in the mortuary sciences, ME/coroner's office, and law enforcement agencies increases when each recognizes the other's role in the investigative process.

Mortuary science is a university major. Other workers in the funeral industry, such as cosmetologists who prepare the body for viewing, may attend to many of the technical aspects. Recognition of unusual circumstances can trigger an investigation from the ME/coroner's office.

Coroner System

History

The word coroner originates from Ferndale, England (circa 1194), when the coroner was actually appointed by the king and had various responsibilities. Coroner also means crowner; the coroner was keeper of the crown. The coroner would also appraise and safeguard lands and goods for the king. The coroner would go to the scene when a person dies, collect what was left behind, and take it to the king. In death investigations, the coroner inspected wounds and reported accusations. The coroner could arrest suspects—he could even arrest a sheriff. As a representative of the crown, he had immense power to investigate deaths.

Coroner Systems

The coroner system was eventually adopted in the United States. Initially, every state had a coroner system and process for an elected coroner to hold a 4-year term. In some states, the coroner had to be 18 years of age and live in the state for 1 or 2 years; otherwise, there were few requirements for the office. In some locales, a mortician or local grocer may be elected coroner. If an autopsy is requested or required, the coroner contacts a pathologist to perform the autopsy. The coroner may or may not be knowledgeable about forensic science or forensic processes.

A coroner may be a medical doctor and is usually a county-elected or appointed individual. However, in most coroner states, the coroner is not required to have medical knowledge, and in some states, they may not be required to have a high school education. The coroner determines the cause and manner of death and signs the death certificate.

Medical Examiner Systems

Several states have instituted statewide medical examiner systems (Figure 1.1). Some of the ME states appoint a forensic pathologist as ME. A pathologist trained in forensics has graduated from medical school followed by 2 years of anatomic and 2 years of clinical pathology as well as 1 year of forensic pathology fellowship. In states with a statewide ME system, state laws dictate specific types of death that must be referred to an ME. For example, any death that is considered to be violent, unwitnessed, unnatural, or under questionable circumstances automatically comes under the ME's jurisdiction. In such circumstances, bodies from anywhere in the state are transported to a central or regional office for autopsy. Field investigators throughout the state are trained to make decisions and notify the central office as to whether or not an autopsy should be performed.

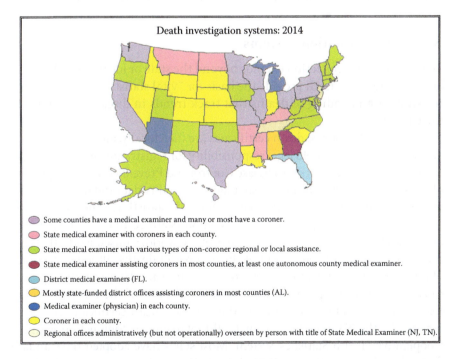

Figure 1.1 Current map of the United States showing the states with medical examiners, coroner systems, and mixed systems.

The central office has a staff of full-time board-certified forensic pathologists, forensic investigators, forensic assistants, and office staff.

The statewide medical examiner system is an ideal system because of the availability of specialty resources at a central location. These specialties can include criminalistics, toxicology, forensic anthropology, and forensic odontology.

Mixed Medical Examiner/Coroner System

The ME/coroner is required to determine the cause and manner of death under many situations. These situations include deaths that have occurred as a result of occupation or violence, in-custody deaths, unexplained deaths, deaths under suspicious circumstances, sudden deaths while apparently in good health, deaths where there was no physician in attendance, and deaths where the attending physician was unable to certify the cause of death. As an example, if an elderly person with a 40-year history of heart disease was seen by his doctor a week prior to dying at home, then the physician who managed the heart problem authorizes and signs the death certificate. However, if a 40-year old person with no medical history was only seen, for example, once or twice by an ophthalmologist for an isolated problem, then that ophthalmologist cannot sign the cause of death if the patient suddenly dies.

National Information Systems

The need for data collection extends beyond the state or local level. The numbers and causes of death provide the basis for "vital statistics" of the ongoing registration and coding of deaths that track trends in disease and injury in the United States.

In the United States, death certificates are filed locally, although each state and some major cities hold legal responsibility for registration and reporting of "vital" events. The Centers for Disease Control and Prevention collects epidemiological data from state health departments. Mortality data and morbidity data provide the frequency of health events. Mortality statistics are generally based on the number of deaths and causes listed on death certificates. Registration of deaths is required by law in most parts of the world. Consequently, this data provides a fairly complete record of the number of deaths, although accuracy of reported causes of deaths varies from place to place. However, the reported causes of deaths are probably an adequate indicator of the mortality count for major causes of death. A standard format for death certificates is recommended by the National Center for Health Statistics in conjunction with the Cooperative Health Statistics System. Most states have adopted the standard forms, but the amount of available information varies since each state determines the format and content of its own certificate. International comparisons of mortality are facilitated through the use of the International Statistical Classifications of Diseases, Injuries, and Causes of Death.

Mortality rates serve as an index of community health and are reported per 100,000 population. Crude death rates, cause-specific death rates, age-specific death rates, infant mortality rates, and fetal death rates are often cited by organizations and public policy planners.

The National Institute of Justice (NIJ) maintains a centralized repository and resource center for missing persons and unidentified decedent records called the National Missing and Unidentified Persons System (NaMus).

First Responder System

Cheryl L. Pozzi

Emergency Medical Systems

Emergency medical systems (EMSs) encompass all those who respond to any medical problem outside of an established hospital or clinic setting. These include the following:

- Emergency medical technicians (EMTs)
- Paramedics
- Firemen personnel
- Physicians
- Physician assistants (PAs)
- Registered nurses
- Nurse practitioners
- Home health care aides
- Social workers (occasionally)

During an emergency or medical need, the primary goal is to render care to the person(s) in need of medical attention. The information presented in this section is not to take precedence over that goal. However, the goal of forensic investigation is to raise a level of awareness such that in the treatment delivery process, forensic evidence is less likely to be destroyed.

In the case of an accident or death, there is almost always a first responder. The first responder may plan to be at the scene or may simply happen to be there at the time of the incident. First responders are trained either formally or on-the-job to assist victims of accident or injury. An organized EMS is expected to be first on the scene, but untrained citizens often appear first and notify the EMS. Regardless of the level of training of the first responder, the goal is to maintain life and prevent further injury to the victim(s). All other goals are secondary to this.

Every city and county has some type of identified first responder. Care may be given by a person with Red Cross training in first aid or rescue breathing and cardiopulmonary resuscitation (CPR). Other areas may have fire departments or an EMS with PAs, EMTs, or nurses competent with trauma and highly technical equipment and in constant contact with trauma physicians. Regardless of the sophistication of EMS responders, few are trained to preserve or collect specific types of evidence that may be valuable in determining cause of death.

First responders have received varying levels of training. A first responder may include anyone from a volunteer who attends an 8-hour basic Red Cross course to a paid paramedic with a degree in a science area. Paramedics have completed a course of approximately 1000 hours with an internship; this can be extended to 2000 hours in training or the equivalent of a full-time job for 1 year. An EMT course is at least 80 clock hours with an internship commonly served in an emergency department; it is essentially the basic preparation for a paid (professional) position in an ambulance crew or fire department.

Chain of command at an accident scene usually follows level of training and whoever is first on the scene. It is customary that the first responder on a scene starts appropriate care and continues that care. The exception is when someone with greater training arrives after care has begun or the victim is transferred to a transport team.

Many systems use a military ranking system, which may correspond to training and additional levels of experience in emergency care. At the scene of an accident, however, there is usually too little time to identify roles and what level of training is held by whom. Within a city or county, people often know one another from experience and exposure. Ultimately, with many responders on a scene, a medical director coordinates all activities.

Types of Systems

Most cities or fire districts have a paid fire department that employs EMTs and paramedics. This is where a 911 call is usually answered. However, some counties use a different telephone number that is routed through the sheriff's office. The system may be governmental, private, or a combination of both with some services contracted by the government.

A two-tier regional system is one in which the fire department responds to 911 calls with a truck or rescue squad but does not transport the victim. A private ambulance company is called to transport the patient to the nearest emergency medical care facility. Private ambulance companies monitor police calls and often appear on the scene quickly, saving time in the response. In a two-tier system, all firefighters are usually trained as both EMTs and firefighters.

A one-tier system has specialty units within the fire department which respond and subsequently transport victims to hospitals. These departments are large and staffed by personnel who respond to medical emergencies; they are not required to respond to other types of emergencies such as fires unless it is reported that people have been injured.

Counties that overlap major cities often have their own fire-rescue system. In areas where the boundaries are uncertain (such as a field or park rather than a street or fence), service may overlap. County systems might have a professional or volunteer available at all times at the fire department. In small communities, volunteers respond to calls from their homes. From home, they may go immediately to the emergency or to a central fire station to pick up a rescue vehicle.

Collaboration between EMS and Investigators

There are few mechanisms, if any, for feedback to EMS about investigations related to an accident or injury. First responders are generally not trained in evidence collection. However, evidence destruction or preservation affects many people and agencies who follow on the scene. Once the "rescue" is complete, the EMS is out of the picture unless the investigation also involves their efforts.

EMS Specialists

The following types of investigators may follow the first responder.

Medical Examiner
The ME develops an understanding of the cause, mechanism, and manner of death based on available facts. Some may believe that the ME needs only a body to complete his or her work. However, MEs also collect evidence as necessary from clothing or the scene to identify potential causes of death and to determine the manner of death.

Police
Police investigators need items such as clothing, materials from the scene, photographs, and exact positions of people and objects at the scene in order to conduct their investigation. Their training provides for proper collection and preservation of evidence. Evidence that is missing or altered may cause confusion and jeopardize a criminal case.

Insurance Representative or Investigator
Life insurance companies only need to establish that a person has died, the time of death, and the cause and manner of death (for example, accident, suicide, or natural). Other insurance companies need to make decisions as to the

cause of injury or death and potential liability involved. Altered evidence may give a false implication, and the company may ultimately adjust insurance rates based on cumulative information. Part of the information used in the investigation is obtained from the medical record that begins with the EMS.

Private Investigator

Private investigators look at evidence long after the accident has occurred. Either a government agency, such as a police or fire department, or a private citizen may hire a private investigator to research the findings in a death or disability. Motorcycle helmets, clothing, contents left inside an accident vehicle, broken roadway signs, and broken automotive parts from the scene can provide a multitude of information at later dates.

Accident Reconstructionists

Accident reconstructionists reconstruct accident scenes and events preceding and following injury or death. Preservation of evidence and good charting frequently play a role in cases long after the fact. The availability of accurate information assists these professionals in recreating an accurate scenario of the occurrence. Their work, in turn, may assist insurance companies, police departments, or attorneys in civil litigation cases.

Biomechanical Engineers

Biomechanical engineers use information in the same manner as accident reconstructionists; however, more emphasis is placed on the mechanism of how injuries occur. They use evidence found on the exterior of the victim, objects involved in the death, and injuries identified by physicians or MEs. They also use automotive pieces, paint smears on solid highway poles, vehicle interiors, helmets, brakes, and other equipment to duplicate the types of injuries that were caused and to help understand the biomechanics involved in the accident.

Safety Investigators

Major companies need information from the scene to determine causes of work-related accidents. Occupational injuries are not always paid for by worker's compensation insurance. If the employee did not follow company procedure, was behaving in a negligent manner, or did not act "like a reasonable and prudent" person, then the individual may be at fault. On the other hand, if faulty equipment was involved or company representatives did not follow procedures, then the company may be liable. In any case, prevention of further accidents relies on the investigation of the safety investigator. New procedures or safety devices can emerge from in-depth inquiry and assist in the prevention of work-related deaths.

Documentation

Each agency has its own report form. Forms use "fill in the blank" and "circle the most appropriate" formats for quick and easy use. A section on the back of the form is also available for a narrative response. However, narrative notes tend to be hastily written and usually offer little detail.

Any EMS must ensure quality documentation—a narrative, diagram, photograph, taped voice recording, checklist, or any combination thereof that provides quick and accurate recording during a response. An audit of flight responses showed a great diversity and inconsistency in record-keeping. Many medical personnel have stated they are afraid to say too much about a death in case it would "pin them into a position at a later date" or come across as if "they know it all" or are commenting about things that are "not relevant." However, lack of information at a later date could cause more difficulty for the person who recorded the information if they are called to trial and need to recall details about the incident. Good charting can help paint an accurate picture for those who may be called upon to put everything together at a later date. Reports should be factual and objective.

One should make it part of his or her regular documentation to note all surroundings, all items on and around the person, and how the person was found on arrival. If anything at the scene is moved or changed in any manner, document it and notify investigators. Do not assume that because you notified the investigator or police that they documented the changes. The best consequence is multiple forms of documentation from different persons and professionals for future comparison.

EMS Procedures

The following are steps that EMS workers can take to facilitate an injury or death investigation. By integrating these steps into a quick response, first responders can contribute to their own "risk management" and minimize potential liability.

- Label anything that is removed from an accident scene or victim's body with the exact location as to where the article was found.
- If assistance is available at an accident scene, assign someone to take photographs. Photographs are one of the most valuable pieces of information for all concerned parties including EMS. Digital photographs should indicate how the victim(s) and/or patient(s) was found and include all injuries from various angles, all pertinent items around the scene and/or body, all vehicles involved from various angles, etc. Photographs of bruises that EMS may not consider significant may assist a reconstructionist or biomechanical engineer

in understanding what body parts hit what objects to create certain injuries. Photographs of various aspects of vehicles at the scene may be very useful at a later time when the vehicles are unavailable or may have been destroyed after the accident. These should include both interior and exterior shots, close-up, and distance shots. Photographs indicating details such as blood stains on the ground where people were found if they were thrown from the vehicle, how they were found initially, whether the seatbelt was in use, or whether the front seat driver was found in the back seat provide very useful information and can also be used in defense of EMS if necessary.

- Leave as much as possible of the accident or injury scene intact while still providing care to the victim(s). Police and investigators follow the EMS and need to document and photograph clothing, materials, body positions, papers or letters, medical supplies, mechanisms, or other items about the person.

- Ensure that any statements obtained from the subject, bystanders, or witnesses identify the speaker such that the reader of a report can separate EMS' observations from a third-party's reporting.

- Do not alter any evidence at the scene. Pay attention to surroundings and do not disturb evidence. Whether one is in a house or at an accident scene outdoors, there may be valuable evidence all around.

- Use appropriate terminology. Review any records at the end of a shift or promptly the next day to ensure that there will be no confusion as to the meaning of any recording. The only abbreviations used in a record should be from a standard list of abbreviations. This list can contain selective codes as long as these are routinely used and widely accepted by the EMS.

- List all personal items removed from the scene such as a motorcycle helmet, clothing, or wallets. List and describe any contents left inside an accident vehicle, such as "clothing cut from victim, including brown loafer-style shoe left in back seat of automobile."

- Specialists may use EMS records as part of an accident or crime reconstruction. Be specific and note time sequences in the record; use exact time, numerals, or letters to indicate sequence.

- Avoid cutting through holes in clothing. Start another entrance to cut clothing from the victim. If clothing falls to the side at the scene or in the transport vehicle, assign someone to bag the clothing and label it with the victim's name. Loss of clothing may equate to evidence being discarded. The clothing becomes part of the chain of evidence and should only be given to a person responsible for such evidence at the destination. Evidence that can be obtained from clothing varies and may include the sizes of holes in clothing, gunpowder residue, hair, blood, body tissue, semen, body fluid spatters, and fibers from objects that have been hit or that have been used to hit the victim.

- Save any blood from injuries to EMS personnel—to differentiate from that of the victim(s).
- Move about carefully to avoid stepping on evidence or moving objects to another location.
- Notify the police or fire person in command if the victim is moved for more convenient access. There are cases where one must move rescue efforts from one place to another. Movement is not a problem as long as the move is documented in EMS notes.
- Communication—both written and verbal—is essential. Photographs are encouraged and provide useful information for many agencies. Communication with other agencies is also important. Different views are shared through communication. However, the intent is not for one agency to influence the perspective of another. Small pieces of information from one individual may assist another in making more sense of another small piece of information that does not seem to fit. Communication can also offer insight into the effectiveness of collaborative efforts and potential need for improvement.
- In cases where the victim is already deceased, it may be necessary to review company policies regarding requirements for performing rescue procedures. In such cases as homicide, suicide, sexual assault, abuse, sudden infant death syndrome, and automotive and airline deaths, there are situation-specific details that require special attention. The various forms of evidence that can be found on or around a person vary from case to case. If a person is already deceased, notations about the surroundings, body position, and artifacts around the body as well as calling the death investigators are important. If death must first be determined but is highly suspicious, rescue procedures can still be performed without disturbing evidence.
- Sudden unexpected infant death is a delicate area. While one's instinct may be to perform rescue procedures on the dead child, those efforts may prevent accurate death analysis. EMS training provides the rescuer with the knowledge to determine signs of death. Rigor mortis, livor mortis, and cold skin are good indications of death. Parents or those who called rescuers to the scene may be expecting "child-saving procedures." In some cases where there are obvious signs of death, one is far more prudent to be upfront and honest with the family and offer support rather that attempt to perform heroic techniques that will give them false hope. Leave the body as it is and call the investigative team to conduct a more accurate analysis if that is the policy in one's jurisdiction.

The EMS person may have to check with company policies regarding termination of CPR procedures. Some EMS systems do not allow EMTs to make the decision as to when rescue efforts should not be performed. Such policies should be discussed and reviewed.

Activities during EMS care can change the direction of any investigation. Clear and concise evidence presentation and documentation provides important information for the emergency department or other agencies trying to understand the cause, mechanism, and manner of death. A "forensicwise" rescue worker is an asset to any community and department. EMS personnel may not be aware that forensic professionals rely on all pieces of evidence after the "rescue" itself is completed and that they plat and important role as members of the forensic team.

Bibliography

Clark, S, Ernst, M, Haglund, W, and Jetzen, J. 1996. *Medicolegal Death Investigator: A Systematic Training Program for the Professional Death Investigator.* Big Rapids, MI: Occupational Research and Assessment, Inc.

DiMaio, DJ and DiMaio, VJM. 2001. *Forensic Pathology,* 2nd ed. Boca Raton, FL: CRC Press.

Dolinak, D, Matshes, E, and Lew, E. 2006. *Forensic Pathology: Principles and Practice.* Burlington, MA: Elsevier.

Kumar, V, Abbas, A, Fausto, N, Robbins, S, and Cotran, R. 2005. *Robbins and Cotran Pathologic Basis of Disease.* Philadelphia, PA: Elsevier Saunders.

Spitz, W and Fischer, R. 1993. *Medicolegal Investigation of Death: Guidelines for the Application of Pathology to Crime Investigation.* Springfield, IL: Charles C. Thomas Press.

Cause, Mechanism, and Manner of Death

2

OBJECTIVES

Upon completion of this chapter and the corresponding reference material, the reader will be able to

- Differentiate between cause, mechanism, and manner of death
- Describe the need for accurate information on a death certificate
- List circumstances that require investigation by the medical examiner/coroner's office
- List some common myths about suicide victims

Introduction

Cause, mechanism, and manner of death are sometimes redundant or confusing as written on a death certificate. When information is erroneously recorded, reviewers for a State Office of Vital Statistics refer the death certificate to the ME/coroner for reissue prior to burial or cremation. Precise identification of cause, mechanism, and manner of death is also required as it relates to liability issues and insurance claims. Attention to the definitions of cause, mechanism, and manner of death assists in completion and interpretation of death certificates.

Definitions

The cause of death is the disease or injury responsible for initiating the lethal sequence of events that results in death. A competent cause of death should be etiologically specific. The underlying or proximate cause of death is that which, in a natural and continuous sequence unbroken by sufficient intervening cause, produces the fatality and without which the end result would not have occurred; it is the cause of death and should be recorded as such on the death certificate. The immediate cause of death, on the other hand, is the event or sequence of events in the underlying cause that immediately precedes the death. There may be one or more immediate causes, and they may occur over a prolonged interval, but none absolves the underlying cause of its ultimate responsibility. For example, the underlying proximate cause of death may be a fractured femur with the immediate cause of death as pneumonia. In completing a death certification, the forensic pathologist would list under Part I of the death certificate, "pneumonia due to fractured right femur." The manner of death would be checked as "accident."

The mechanism of death is altered physiology and biochemistry whereby the cause exerts its lethal effect. Mechanisms of death lack etiological specificity and are unacceptable as substitutes for causes of death. Common mechanisms of death include congestive heart failure, cardiac arrhythmias, sepsis, exsanguination, renal failure, and hepatic failure. The term "cardiorespiratory arrest" ordinarily is meaningless for purposes of death certification; it is a description of being dead—not a cause of death.

Manner of death explains how the cause arose, whether natural or violent. A death must be only one of five classifications with regard to manner— natural, accident, homicide, suicide, or undetermined. Any physician may sign a death certificate for a natural death. However, an ME/coroner is the only individual legally authorized to sign a death certificate if the manner of death is accident, homicide, suicide, or undetermined.

Determinations

The ME/coroner determines the cause and manner of death. Because the cause and manner of death are opinions, judgment is required to formulate both for reporting on the death certificate. The degree of certainty required to classify the manner of death depends on the circumstances of the death. Although such issues will be discussed in further detail below, a general scheme of incremental "degrees of certainty" is as follows (Hanzlick, 2002)

- Undetermined (less than 50% certainty)
- Reasonable medical or investigative probability (greater than a 50:50 chance; more likely than not)
- Preponderance of medical/investigative evidence (about 70% or greater certainty)
- Clear and convincing medical/investigative evidence (90% or greater certainty)
- Beyond any reasonable doubt (essentially 100% certainty)

In most ME/coroner jurisdictions, the classifications of death show that the greatest number is attributed to natural deaths where people died at home (60%); the remaining are attributed to accidental deaths (20%), homicides (10%), and suicides (10%).

All agencies have cases that are undetermined, and sometimes it is impossible to determine the manner of death. It is better for the ME/coroner to leave these cases open as undetermined in the event they are reopened for investigation in the future. Most undetermined cases involve skeletal remains or decomposed bodies. However, sometimes circumstances surrounding a death are unclear and one must rule the manner as undetermined—even after complete scene investigation, autopsy, and review of toxicology results have been performed.

Death Certification

The death certificate is a legal document certifying the identification of the decedent, date and time of death, and the cause and manner of death. The mechanism of death should not be included on the death certificate. Medical treatment often attempts to modify or ameliorate mechanisms rather than causes of illness, thereby focusing clinical attention on mechanisms to the exclusion of causes. For example, digitalis is appropriate treatment for congestive heart failure but does not do anything for coronary atherosclerosis. It is appropriate for autopsies to attempt to clarify and elucidate pathophysiological mechanisms, but the underlying or proximate cause of death should not be lost in the process and thereby be omitted on the death certificate.

There may be one or more immediate causes of death, and they may occur over a prolonged interval, but none absolves the underlying cause of its ultimate responsibility. For example, a man sustains a transabdominal gunshot wound with perforation of the colon. Despite treatment over a period of 3 months, he develops peritonitis, septicemia, disseminated intravascular coagulation, hepatic and renal failure, bronchopneumonia, and adult respiratory distress syndrome. Gunshot wound of the abdomen is the underlying or proximate cause of death listed in Part I of the death certificate.

Part II of the death certificate includes "other significant conditions" and should only be used for those conditions that contribute to death but are unrelated to the cause(s) listed in Part I of the death certificate. "Other significant conditions" is not a repository for medically interesting or curious findings that do not offer a pathophysiological contribution to death.

The following types of death require a report and investigation from the ME/coroner's office, completion of the death certificate, and the ME/coroner's signature on the death certificate:

- Violent, unnatural, unattended deaths
- A result from an accident
- A result from a homicide
- A result from a suicide
- In custody
- Occupational
- Unexpected

Legal Issues Surrounding Death

Death can result in a number of legal issues. If the individual has life insurance, the insurance company must have proof of the death in order to pay the claimant. Accident or health insurance companies require that the cause of death is known to ensure that another party is not responsible for the payment of treatment or liable expenses. Wills that are based on successive inheritance need proof of the date and time of death. In situations where many people die as a result of the victim's actions, the time of death of all victims may be important to establish charges. Proper identity of the decedent is vital and of first priority. Other legal issues include notification of next-of-kin and workman's compensation claims.

The investigation of cause and manner of death is a priority of the medical investigative team. Civil and criminal actions often depend on the results of these findings. Documentation of findings and correct information on death certificates facilitate the processing of insurance information, workman's compensation claims, and legal disputes. The manner of death is important to surviving relatives as some insurance policies pay "double" indemnity of accidental manners of death and may not pay at all with suicides.

Medicolegal Investigation of Suicide

Suicide is the deliberate termination of one's life. Approximately 41,000 individuals commit suicide each year in the United States (Heron, 2015). Age varies by sex; peak age for males is over 75 years, whereas peak age for females is 45–54 years (Heron, 2015). Males are four times more successful in their suicide attempts than females. However, females make three times more attempts (Heron, 2015).

Among adolescents and young adults aged 15–24 in the United States, suicide is the second leading manner of death. An increased risk of suicidal thoughts are reported in young adults aged 18–29 (Heron, 2015).

Signs of Risk

A sudden, unexpected mood change—particularly a change from a frantic or agitated state to one of calm deliberation—is often a clue. Other personality changes and signs of suicide risk include the following:

- Increased depression/exalted mood or "mood swings"
- Increased fatigue or listlessness
- Sudden increase in alcohol use
- Giving away one's treasured possessions
- Making peace with family members and oneself

Elements of Suicide

Two elements are required to cite suicide as a manner of death:

1. An intent to commit suicide
2. A specific act that carries out that intent

Proof of suicide may be demonstrated from one or more of the following:

- A suicide note in the victim's handwriting (however, fewer than half of all suicidal individuals actually write a note).
- Audio/video tape recording.
- Body in a locked room, possibly with deadbolt and/or chain in place.
- Firearm residue on hands.
- Evidence of prior rehearsal.
- Flag folded into a triangle and placed near suicidal veterans or patriots.
- Presence of the book *Final Exit* or use of any of its recommended suicide methods (*Final Exit* is a book about and for persons who want to end their lives because of age or sickness; it serves as an instruction manual on how to commit suicide).
- Recent membership or interest in the Hemlock Society, a national group that supports euthanasia, assisted suicide, or suicide. The mode of suicide is asphyxia with a plastic bag and/or overdose of a sleeping pill or sedative (Seconal [secobarbital] is often the drug of choice).

Probable Suicide

An ME/coroner's office often has to make some difficult decisions. Characteristics of wounds or overdose of ingested drugs suggest suicide. Locations of wounds, contact gunshot wounds, practice or hesitation marks (numerous superficial incised wounds on wrists or neck), or coexistence of multiple sublethal and/or lethal wounds may or may not indicate suicide. Drug ingestion can be validated by high stomach concentration of legal or illegal drugs, as distinguished from low or absent drug metabolite in body fluid. The investigation of death usually reveals related indications of suicidal intent.

Suspicion of Suicide

When suicide is a suspicion, the decedent's present and past situations must be considered. For example, grief caused by recent losses or threats of losses can create feelings of hopelessness that prompt suicide. Grieving occurs not only from loss of a loved one through death or divorce but also from loss of one's professional reputation, personal reputation, financial security, or political position. A history of emotional illness (particularly depression), change of habits, and record of substance abuse can also raise suspicion of suicide. Physical findings supported by behavioral clues may be the only evidence available to an ME/coroner for a suicidal intent.

In addition, recent purchase of weapons or prior suicide attempt strongly supports suspicion of suicide. In fact, one suicide occurs for every 25 attempts (Vitiello et al., 2009). Among those who made an initial attempt, a second attempt occurred within 3 months.

Death Investigation of Suicide

Death investigation often begins with the victim's prior history. Interviews with relatives and friends create a "psychological autopsy" of the person and his or her life. Medical records are reviewed for physical or mental illness. The body is searched for signs of previous attempts or "hesitation marks" such as wrist scars, neck scars, or forearm scars. Tracheotomy scars, surgical cutdown scars, or other scars may indicate prior attempts or treatment.

Suicidal behavior can be subtle or overt. Teenagers or adults who play Russian roulette are generally aware of the chances to live or die if they put a loaded gun to their head and pull the trigger. The manner of death in Russian roulette is suicide. Reckless acts such as "chicken," drug abuse, or volunteering for hazardous duty may indicate a conscious or unconscious desire for death.

Concealment of suicide by family members is a frequent behavior when the body is discovered. Concealment is often motivated by financial gain, religion, social stigmas, insurance, and fear. Families or friends may alter the body or scene or misinterpret events when they want to hide a suicide. Ways of altering the body include concealing a wound, cleaning the body, or taking down a hanging body.

A variety of methods are frequently employed in efforts to remove evidence or alter the scene or investigation. These include

- Removal of any notes, weapons, or drug containers
- Planting a gun cleaning kit
- Emphasizing an illness of the deceased
- Withholding the actual story
- Introducing evidence of struggle to the scene
- Sanitizing the scene

Suicide Methods

Gunshot Wounds

The majority of suicidal deaths occur as a result of gunshot wounds. A gunshot either in contact or at close range to an easily accessible body area often indicates a self-inflicted injury. A working knowledge of both suicide patterns and gunshot wounds is necessary when treating patients in the emergency department or evaluating a body at a death scene in order to determine whether a homicide, suicide, or accident was the manner of death. In many instances, it is difficult to discern one from the other.

Suicide by firearms has traditionally been a male technique for suicide. The purchase of a firearm increased the risk of suicide greatly, by up to 57 times the expected suicide rate, which is most apparent in the first week (Romero and Wintemute, 2002). The rates for women committing suicide by firearms have actually modestly decreased from 1980 to 1998; however, the rates among the elderly population have increased (Romero and Wintemute, 2002). The ME/coroner needs to consider suicide when dealing with contact gunshot wounds to the head (particularly the forehead or temporal area) or mouth (intraoral).

Contact entry gunshot wounds can be identified by gunshot residue or soot surrounding the wound. The size and shape of a gunshot wound are unreliable indicators as to whether a wound is an entry or exit wound. However, if soot is present, it is an entry wound; residue is never associated with exit wounds. An intermediate range wound shows the deposit of burnt and unburnt gunpowder stippling or tattooing surrounding the entrance wound. The circumference of gunpowder stippling relates to the range of fire—the closer to the skin that the barrel of the weapon is at the time of firing, the smaller the circumference of gunpowder stippling. The range of fire is determined by the firearms examiner firing the weapon with similar ammunition.

Stellate splitting of the skin, particularly over bone, also indicates a close contact gunshot wound. The in-rushing propellant gases that accompany a bullet through the skull and into the brain blow back and are trapped between the skull and skin, ripping and tearing the skin in a stellate manner.

Blow-back and gunshot residue will also remain on the hand of the individual who pulls the trigger. Thus, the victim's hands should be protected with paper bags until the ME/coroner can examine them for residue.

Drugs

Suicide by drug overdose is more common among females. Multiple drugs and/or alcohol may be involved. Scene investigators should be alert for empty prescription bottles; those bottles may have patient names other than the victim's on the label. Thorough background investigation and complete toxicology analysis are indicated in suspicious cases. All medication bottles should be collected at the scene and documented on the medication log brought back to the ME/ coroner's office.

Hanging

Suicide by hanging does not require total suspension. The victim's position at time of death is variable—the body can be kneeling, sitting, or lying. If the body is hanging, it is frequently cut down by the person who discovers the body. Ligatures used are variable and a noose can be a T-shirt, sheet, shoestring, or even braided dental floss. Anything that can constrict the carotid arteries is sufficient to cause death. For example, the weight of the head alone is approximately 8–10 pounds; the pressure of the weight of the head against the neck ligature is sufficient to constrict the carotid arteries and cause death.

In a hanging case, the noose is the most valuable piece of evidence to the investigation. The investigator should preserve the noose without disturbing the knot. To do this, remove the noose by making a cut away from the knot.

Asphyxia

A plastic bag found over the victim's head may indicate suicide by asphyxia or suffocation but not conclusively. Often, an overdose of a sedative in addition to the plastic bag and a history of chronic illness indicate individual or assisted suicide.

Cutting or Stabbing

Suicide by cutting or stabbing is recognized by multiple incised wounds or hesitation marks. Favored sites are the neck, wrists, and chest. The nondominant wrist and forearm are frequently involved. Suicide by stabbing or wounds that cause exsanguination are more prevalent in countries where firearms are banned.

Electrocution

As with suicides by cutting or stabbing, suicides by electrocution are more prevalent in countries where firearms are banned. For example, firearms are banned in Australia; thus, a popular way to commit suicide is by electrical death. Electrical wires are separated and put onto the wrists; then the electrical cord is plugged into an outlet.

References

Hanzlick, R, Hunsaker, J, and Davis, G. 2002. *A Guide for Manner if Death Classification*, 1st ed. Atlanta, GA: National Association of Medical Examiners.

Heron, M. 2015. National vital statistics report for 2012, Vol. 64, pp. 10. Atlanta, GA: Centers for Disease Control and Statistics.

Romero, M and Wintemute, G. 2002. Epidemiology of firearm suicide in the US. *J Urban Health* 79:1.

Vitiello, B, Silva, SG, Rohde, P, Kratochvil, CJ, Kennard, BD, Reinecke, MA, Mayes, TL, Posner, K, May, DE, and March, JS. 2009. Suicidal events in Treatment of Adolescents with Depression Study (TADS). *J Clin Psych* 70(5):941–947.

Bibliography

Clark, S, Ersnt, M, Haglund, W, and Jetzen, J. 1996. *Medicolegal Death Investigator: A Systematic Training Program for the Professional Death Investigator.* Big Rapids, MI: Occupational Research and Assessment, Inc.

Forensic Pathology

3

OBJECTIVES

Upon completion of this chapter and corresponding reference material, the reader will be able to

- Discuss the role and function of the forensic pathologist in forensic medical investigation
- Discuss the investigative role of the forensic pathologist—the expert witness role
- List training opportunities for physicians to enter the forensic field and describe the purpose of a forensic autopsy
- Explain the general procedure of a forensic autopsy
- Discuss types of information available following an autopsy

Introduction

Scene investigation is of paramount importance in any medicolegal inquiry of death. As in clinical medicine where a comprehensive medical history provides 50%–75% of the information necessary for a diagnosis, scene investigation provides the forensic pathologist with the majority of information about a particular case. Authority and primary responsibility for crime scene investigation remain with law enforcement agencies. However, the ME/coroner has legal authority and responsibility to conduct a medicolegal investigation and to secure the remains of any victims.

The forensic pathologist and/or designee (forensic medical investigator) attends the death scene for various purposes. For example, information and evidence from the scene are necessary to

- Estimate time of death
- Assess and interpret wounds
- Determine extent of injuries and estimated amount of bleeding at the scene
- Determine cause and manner of death

31

- Correlate scene findings with circumstances of death, medical history, and autopsy findings
- Provide clues to distinguish between antemortem and postmortem artifacts
- To reconstruct events thereby assisting law enforcement agencies in formulating questions related to the death

Duties of the forensic pathologist or forensic medical investigator at the crime scene include

- Verifying that death has occurred and officially pronouncing the victim dead
- Collecting information about circumstances of the death and background information including medical history about the decedent
- Assuming jurisdiction of the body, clothing, and physical evidence associated with the body
- Observing and documenting observations about the scene with photographs, sketches, diagrams, and videos
- Examining the body
- Preventing alteration, contamination, destruction, or concealment of evidence
- Preserving clothing, personal effects, and trace evidence and recognizing extraneous materials at the scene that might have been used for attempts at resuscitation or treatment of the victim
- Preventing postmortem injury
- Ensuring the body is wrapped in a clean sheet and the victim's hands are protected with paper bags
- Establishing and maintaining chain of custody for the body, clothing, and physical evidence associated with the body

A scene investigation kit should always be ready to take to a scene of investigation. Minimal contents for an investigation kit include

- Notebook, pen, pencil, clipboard, blank ME forms and diagrams, measuring tapes (10 and 25 feet), and flashlight
- Digital camera with flash and extra batteries
- Ruler (American Board of Forensic Odontology) and color chart
- Thermometer (range 0°F–120°F) – to check ambient temperature
- Latex gloves (many pairs)
- Forceps, scissors, scalpel with blades, syringes (5 mL) with 18-gauge needles, and magnifying lens
- Assorted zip-seal plastic bags and waterproof marker
- Shoe covers or rubber boots

- Handheld tape recorder, extra tapes, extra batteries, and video recorder
- Saline solution, cotton swabs, filter paper, and envelopes
- Sexual assault kit (ME) and foot covers
- Plastic bag for trash

Medical Quality Control

The issue of quality assurance/quality control (QA/QC) is a popular management concept of the last two decades. QA/QC is primarily directed toward self-monitoring and self-correcting activities. Risk management of professional activities is important for individuals or agencies to reduce liability and costs. QA/QC committees review standards of care to assess preventability of morbidity and mortality and to improve patient care.

The forensic pathologist plays an active role in medicolegal problems related to expected and unexpected deaths in hospitals and nursing care facilities. The forensic pathologist often participates with medical or trauma review teams or acts as a consultant to "in-house" investigators. Injuries sustained while under medical care, such as a fall within a hospital or nursing home or asphyxial injuries from restraints or hospital treatment, are examples of need for a forensic investigation. Assaults on patients or professional staff by other patients or professional staff occur and require confirmation as to cause of death or injury.

Institutional investigations may be conducted when a number of deaths occur by the same methods in the same or similar surroundings. Disconnection of life-support machinery and mass murders by nursing staff are examples of such circumstances.

Other QA/QC settings within the institution may relate to diagnostic or therapeutic procedures and drug-related injuries and/or deaths. Examples include surgical complications, complications from indwelling or temporary catheters, use of medical equipment, blood transfusions, radiation therapy, and anesthesia. Drug side effects, hypersensitivity reactions, over- or underdosage, and wrongly administered drugs may be causes for review of circumstances and deaths.

Individual and group practices are common subjects for QA/QC reviews. Malpractice can apply to any professional health-care providers within an agency, but the physician is the most common legal target. Neglect; misdiagnosis; uninformed consent; refusal of treatment; and incorrect, inadequate, or outdated treatment are all types of malpractice.

Medicolegal problems that may involve the forensic pathologist also encompass chronic industrial or agricultural exposure that leads to carcinogenesis and disability. The effects of remote trauma that contribute or do not contribute to death are within the realm of the medicolegal problems that may relate to QA/QC.

Forensic Autopsy

Purpose of the Forensic Autopsy

Forensic autopsy is conducted to answer medicolegal questions regarding cause and manner of death. The primary difference between a forensic autopsy and a hospital autopsy is that a forensic autopsy is more oriented toward the external examination than toward the internal examination and organ systems. Findings are reported to families, juries, and law enforcement personnel in layman terms rather than to physicians in medical terms.

Objectives for Medicolegal Autopsy

The purpose of the forensic autopsy differs from hospital autopsies. The forensic autopsy attempts to accomplish the following:

- Determine cause, manner, and time of death and recover, identify, and preserve evidentiary material
- Provide interpretation and correlation of facts and circumstances related to death
- Provide a factual, objective medical report for law enforcement, prosecution, and defense agencies
- Separate death due to disease from death due to external causes for protection of the innocent
- Identify unknown remains

External Examination

External examination begins with a head-to-toe examination. This includes notations about eye color, height, weight, hair color, gender, and presence or absence of rigor mortis. Abrasions, contusions, scars, or puncture wounds are carefully documented. Injection marks from drug use can be found almost anywhere on the body including between the toes. With cocaine overdoses, a purple contusion (bruise) with a whitish center might be found.

The insides of the wrists are examined for the possibility of prior suicide attempts; these are usually seen as linear scars (hesitation marks). Surgical incisions help document prior medical conditions or surgical history. This is particularly helpful if no medical records are available. Photographs can be taken to document any significant findings related to the cause or manner of death. X-rays are taken on all homicides, decomposed bodies, gunshot wound cases, and unidentified bodies. Stab wounds may also require an x-ray to determine if the tip of the blade remains embedded in the body.

X-rays are recommended for all child fatalities to identify injury or to detect signs of child abuse such as previous trauma or healing fractures.

Internal Examination

After the initial Y-shaped tissue incision over the chest, the rib cage is removed first. Samples for toxicological analysis are collected from heart blood, peripheral blood, body fluids, solid organs, and vitreous fluid as standard procedure. Vitreous fluid is clear and may be used to detect ethyl alcohol or may be used in other biochemistry tests. Samples taken for toxicology also include brain and liver tissue, urine, stomach contents, and bile. Other samples required depend on suspected cause and/or manner of death. Samples are analyzed in the toxicology laboratory.

All internal organs are eviscerated in one block or through organ-by-organ dissection. Block removal, in which the chest and abdominal contents form one continuous block, allows for close examination of the relationships between organs. The proximity of organs is helpful in some instances to follow the path of penetrating injuries. All organs are examined grossly for injury and/or natural disease. Upon removal, all organs are weighed and the weight is recorded.

The small bowel is tied off at the second part of the duodenum. A ligature around the sigmoid colon prevents spillage of contents when the bowel is cut. The large and small intestines are cut away from the major blood vessels and their attachments at the back of the abdomen. The femoral and carotid arteries may be tied off to assist the funeral directors for embalming purposes.

The rib cage and spinal column can be seen from the base of the brain down through the pelvis after the internal organs are removed. The ribs and vertebrae are examined for fractures, hemorrhage, or hidden injuries.

The heart is examined for natural disease or injury by external and internal inspection. The coronary arteries are serially horizontally sectioned at 5 mm intervals to check for narrowing by atherosclerotic plaque prior to cross-sectioning the heart starting at the apex and ending at the papillary muscles at 1 cm sections. The heart is then opened along the right posterior and anterior septums, left lateral wall, and left anterior septum to inspect the heart chambers and valves. The aorta, vena cava, and branches of the aorta to the kidneys, stomach, and intestines are examined.

The lungs, pulmonary arteries, and bronchi are examined. Black carbon pigment that often marks the surfaces of both lungs in adults is due to smoking, secondhand smoke, or environmental or industrial pollution. The bronchial tree is examined for foreign material such as aspirated food, soot from smoke inhalation, tumors, or pus from pneumonia. The pulmonary arteries may be occluded by emboli (blood clots from leg veins). The lungs normally have a spongy character due to the mixture of air and fluids that is usually present. After death, the back of the lungs becomes darker and heavier as a result of blood pooling if the body had been lying supine.

The adrenal glands lie within fat on either side of the aorta directly above the kidneys. The central medulla of the adrenals produces adrenaline and noradrenaline (epinephrine and norepinephrine) while the outer cortex produces steroids such as cortisone. The kidney filters blood and produces urine that is carried to the bladder through a small tube called the ureter. The kidneys are also padded in fat and encased within a thin capsule; the fat and capsule can be peeled away from a normal kidney surface for further examination.

Just beneath the left hemidiaphragm lies the spleen. The spleen functions as a filter of old red and white blood cells and platelets.

The stomach lies roughly in front of and to the right side of the spleen and drains into the small bowel or duodenum. The stomach contents are collected and saved for analysis. Gastric contents can show partially digested food, drugs, or liquids and are analyzed for toxicology. Sometimes odors such as alcohol can be detected during dissection.

The biliary tract begins with the gallbladder that looks like a green sack attached to the liver. It has a duct that drains into the duodenum through the head of the pancreas. The same duct is shared with the pancreas that lies behind the stomach and produces insulin and digestive enzymes.

The liver appears spongy and dark purple and is one of the largest body organs. The liver functions to help break down fat, carbohydrates, and protein into usable forms. The liver also produces bile to aid digestion. Fatty changes in the liver are most commonly due to alcohol abuse. Liver samples are saved for toxicology.

The pelvic organs include the uterus, ovaries, and fallopian tubes in the female and the prostate gland, testicles, and spermatic cord in the male. Both genders have a bladder and urethra. In the male, the prostate appears as a firm rubbery gland at the base of the bladder.

The head is examined following removal of the thoracic and abdominal organs. A coronal incision is made over the top of the head behind the ears. When the scalp is reflected forward and backward from this central incision, the pathologist examines the internal surfaces of the scalp and surfaces of the skull. Examination for subscalpular or subgaleal hemorrhages is completed. The skullcap is removed with a bone saw to reveal the brain. Further examination of the brain includes a view of the brain surface to examine the cerebral hemispheres including the frontal, temporal, parietal, and occipital lobes. At the posterior and base of the brain, the cerebellum surrounds the brainstem that includes the midbrain, pons, and medulla. The brain receives its blood supply from the vertebral arteries and carotid arteries. The cerebellum and brainstem are dissected from the internal cerebral hemispheres at the midbrain and are serially sectioned and examined.

After examination for epidural or subdural hemorrhages, the dura (skull covering) is removed from the skull, and the skull is examined for fractures. The cerebral hemispheres are composed of gray matter and white matter that are responsible for higher mental functions. The brain is serially sectioned and examined for tumors, trauma, or other abnormalities. Within the deeper structures of the brain are the lateral ventricles that become narrowed with cerebral edema or brain swelling.

The neck block including the tongue, trachea, larynx, thyroid gland, hyoid bone, epiglottis, and esophagus is removed last. Careful layered dissection of the neck strap muscles will demonstrate any possible bruises or fractures that might relate to such actions as strangulation or hanging. The hyoid bone is removed from the thyroid cartilage. The hyoid bone is horseshoe shaped and is examined for fractures. Beneath the hyoid is the epiglottis that closes down over the opening to the airway in the larynx. Beneath the epiglottis are the vocal cords, and posterior to the larynx is the opening to the esophagus. The larynx is opened posteriorly to inspect for a lodged food bolus or any other abnormalities.

With a suspected seizure, the tongue should be examined for injury. The tongue is sectioned to ensure that there are no contusions or lacerations.

Tissue Processing

When dissection is complete, organs are separated and weighed individually. Each organ weight is recorded. The organs are dissected, and a small tissue sample is put into formaldehyde. These tissue samples are used to make histology slides for examination under microscope. Sections are also saved for future use. State statutes determine the length of time tissue samples must be saved.

Autopsy Report

The forensic pathologist summarizes the autopsy findings in a report along with body diagrams. The final report is issued when the toxicology results, microscopic exam, and other studies are completed and a final diagnosis has been reached. The ME/coroner issues a death certificate that states the cause and manner of death. A copy of the autopsy report is part of the permanent case file and may be sent to the investigating office and family upon request. The death certificate is filed with the State Bureau of Vital Statistics.

Misconceptions about the Medicolegal Autopsy

Common misconceptions about the forensic autopsy include the following:

- Time of death can be precisely determined. Autopsy always yields the cause of death.
- Autopsy can be properly performed without a history. Embalming will not obscure examination.
- Only true and suspected homicide victims require examination.
- Cause and manner of death are the only determinations of an autopsy.
- Any pathologist is qualified to perform an autopsy.
- Poisons are always detected by the toxicologist.
- All physicians are good death investigators.
- Autopsy must be performed immediately.
- Medicolegal autopsy is oriented toward criminal prosecution.

Bibliography

Kumar, V, Abbas, A, Fausto, N, Robbins, S, and Cotran, R. 2005. *Robbins and Cotran Pathologic Basis of Disease*. Philadelphia, PA: Elsevier Saunders.

Postmortem Changes

4

OBJECTIVES

Upon completion of this chapter and corresponding reference material, the reader will be able to

- Describe three methods for determining time of death or injury
- List situations where body position and postmortem findings may indicate that the body was moved after death
- Discuss the significance of establishing time of death
- Define a list of terms that describe signs of death
- Describe actions of insects on a body

Introduction

The ME/coroner is responsible for establishing the time of death or injury. Changes in body temperature, stiffness of the body, or color changes at the time of the scene investigation can help establish the time a person died. Terminology frequently used to describe signs of death tends to range greatly. The use of standardized descriptive terms will help to clarify observations about the appearance of the body. This chapter discusses frequently used terms that describe postmortem changes and factors that help establish time of death or injury.

Rigor Mortis

Rigor mortis means rigidity of the body. Rigidity of the muscles is triggered by a chemical reaction due to the depletion of adenosine triphosphate (ATP). Rigor mortis begins almost immediately after death starting in the small muscles—mainly those around the eyes, face, and fingers—and extending to the larger muscle groups as time passes. Rigor mortis peaks in about 12 hours and then begins to disappear at 24 hours. Temperature affects muscle tension; if the area is warm, rigor speeds up and then begins to disappear earlier or in approximately 8 hours. The rigor response can be interrupted when muscles are manipulated. For example, rigor can be broken when clothing is removed. Consequently, the progression of rigor mortis should be evaluated prior to moving a body's position or clothing and prior to long bone donation.

The following conditions imitate or mimic rigor mortis:

- Cadaveric spasm or instant rigidity, which occurs at the moment of death. This can occur during violent deaths or exercise. The mechanism relates to rapid depletion of ATP.
- Freezing. Frozen muscles may mimic rigor.
- Heat stiffening. Heat coagulates muscle and causes shortening of the muscle and flexion at the joint.
- Fusion of bones. Abnormalities of the skeleton may cause deformity of the bones at the joints that mimics rigor mortis.

Livor Mortis

Livor mortis is a red-purple discoloration of the body that occurs in dependent parts of the body—those parts closest to the floor—by gravitational pooling of blood, except in areas exposed to pressure. Livor mortis begins when blood circulation ceases. For example, a person who dies in a supine (face up) position should show lividity in the backs of the arms, legs, and trunk. If the person is sitting at the time of death, lividity appears along the buttocks, lower legs, feet, and possibly hands. It becomes noticeable in 30–40 minutes in dependent areas but not in pressure areas where the blood is pushed to the side (Figure 4.1).

Accentuated livor mortis may mimic bruising. Tardieu spots, red or purple patches on the body, refer to actual bleeding into areas of intense livor mortis. Tardieu spots are sometimes seen in asphyxial deaths and hangings. Other bleeding such as mucosal bleeding may occur from the nose because of intense livor mortis.

Cherry-red lividity is seen instead of purple blotchy discoloration in three situations:

1. Carbon monoxide poisoning
2. Cold (as when the body is refrigerated)
3. Cyanide poisoning

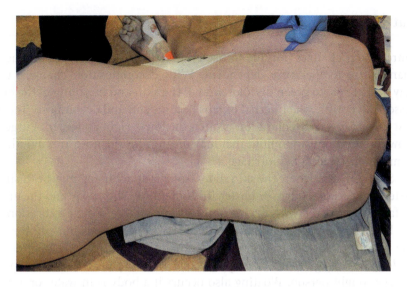

Figure 4.1 Photograph of livor mortis with blanching.

Algor Mortis

Algor mortis is the cooling of the body as temperature is lost from the body. There is no decrease in temperature during the first hour after death; after the first hour, temperature decreases at a rate of 1.5°F per hour. Early rectal or core temperature taken at the scene may be helpful in establishing the time of death as the body eventually equalizes with the room or environmental temperature. However, this is not standard practice in most medical examiners' offices.

Postmortem Drying Artifacts

The body begins to dehydrate after death, but the extent and rate of drying depend on climate and humidity. For example, dry, arid climates can cause mummification. In these climates, the fingers and hands are the first to become extremely dehydrated.

Some signs of postmortem drying may be misinterpreted as signs of injury. For example, mucous membranes around the lips dry to a dark red or purple color; these may appear to be bruises or abrasions. Tache noire refers to drying of the conjunctiva when the eyelids are left open after death. These markings are red to brown, horizontally situated, and sharply circumscribed and show midbulbar discoloration; tache noire may be mistaken as a trauma injury. The dark red color of a dry scrotum or dried diaper rash may appear to be abrasions.

Putrefaction

Putrefaction changes are due to bacterial activity after death. Putrefaction changes are temperature dependent. With decomposition changes, there may be a purple to green discoloration of the skin and marbling of the blood vessels. Over time, the internal organs become soft and decompose. The earliest area of green discoloration is often the lower right abdomen. Purge is a browned decomposition fluid that may drain from the nose and mouth and be misinterpreted as hemorrhage.

Skin slippage, where the skin slides from its attachment, may be misinterpreted as an injury, burn, or blister. The outer layer slips away and the undersurface becomes red with drying and may appear similar to an abrasion.

Bloating results from gas produced by microorganisms in the gut. The abdomen, face, scrotum, and eventually the entire body become distended. Bloating gives the false appearance of obesity in an otherwise thin or average-weight person. Bloating also occurs if a body is in water or a damp climate.

Insect and Animal Activity

The age of insect larvae on a body can be used to estimate time of death. Forensic entomologists say that "critters" are the first to arrive at the scene because they seek damp, moist areas such as the nose, mouth, eyes, or areas of injury in which to lay their eggs. An entomologist can judge the time interval based on the stage of insect development from egg to pupa, to larvae, to "critter," or to adult flies. Other insects such as beetles or other animals are often next to arrive at the scene depending on geographic region.

During the immediate postmortem period, ants and roaches may cause damage to the body that mimics injury. Maggot activity may also alter preexisting injuries or create defects in the soft tissue that can be confused as injuries.

Worms, bugs, and insects are collected from around the body and kept alive as well as preserved in alcohol. Later, they are examined by a forensic entomologist. Studies on cocaine overdoses have found that larvae and maggots can be used to register cocaine levels when very little tissue remains.

Animals can affect postmortem conditions both indoors and outdoors. For example, rats may chew on exposed features of a body indoors. Domestic cats and dogs may also feed on a body if there is no other food available. In the outdoors, wild animals may skeletonize body remains within 1 week.

Postmortem Injuries

Contusions, lacerations, abrasions, fractures, and burns may be incurred after death. Injuries after death are indistinguishable from those formed shortly before death or at the time of death. With lacerations, tears of the skin caused by blunt force can "bleed" if they are made after death when blood is still in a liquid state in the vessels. Scratches or abrasions, on the other hand, may appear yellow or orange in areas where livor mortis has not developed. Postmortem burns are also indistinguishable from antemortem thermal injuries.

Postmortem Medical, Surgical, and Embalming Artifacts

Cardiopulmonary resuscitation can cause broken ribs and bruises to the chest. Patterned burns on the chest may result from defibrillator paddles. Bruises and abrasions of the face and mouth may result from mouth-to-mouth resuscitation. Surgical incisions from advanced efforts at resuscitation may mimic stab wounds or other antemortem injuries.

Body preparations for transport or embalming can also result in artifacts. For example, bindings or wrappings used to prepare a body for transport after pronouncement of death may create artifacts that suggest premortem injury. Embalming artifacts left from arterial and trocar embalming can create defects that may be confused with antemortem injuries. In addition, cosmetic preparations for funeral viewing mask premortem bruises.

Other Factors Useful in Establishing Time of Death

Time of death is based on many observations before the ME/coroner performs an autopsy. The first people to arrive at the scene must document the condition of the body. As others arrive, documentation may change as the appearance of the body changes over time. Scene investigation and interviews are also useful in establishing time of death. Presence of mold on the body, state of vegetation beneath a body, and chemical changes in body fat can all be used to establish time of death. Occasionally, weather affects the stages of decomposition. For instance, if someone dies outside in October and a snowfall occurs, the body may be well preserved by the cold weather if not found until spring. Patterned animal artifacts are generally localized and show little hemorrhagic reaction to underlying tissue.

Changes in body fluids may be useful in establishing time of death. For example, vitreous electrolytes may be useful to establish time of death during the first 24 hours. Vitreous potassium levels increase on a linear rise, although time of death may vary up to 4 hours. Stomach contents reflect the character of the last meal; food remains undigested for up to 2 hours after eating and may provide useful clues to the time of death and whereabouts of the decedent prior to death.

Bibliography

Clark, S, Ernst, M, Haglund, W, and Jetzen, J. 1996. *Medicolegal Death Investigator: A Systematic Training Program for the Professional Death Investigator.* Big Rapids, MI: Occupational Research and Assessment, Inc.

Spitz, W and Fischer, R. 1993. *Medicolegal Investigation of Death: Guidelines for the Application of Pathology to Crime Investigation.* Springfield, IL: Charles C. Thomas Press.

Death Scene Investigation

5

Physical Evidence at the Crime Scene

Physical refers to as those characteristics of or relating to tangible items or the result of natural law—as opposed to those relating to mental, moral, spiritual, or imaginary concepts. It relates to those areas dictated by natural science. Evidence refers to something that furnishes proof and can be legally submitted to a tribunal to ascertain the truth of a matter. It can also arise from information provided by one who bears witness or voluntarily confesses to a crime and testifies for the prosecution against his or her accomplices.

Without physical evidence, the attempt to prove a case is extremely difficult. One cannot fully depend on eyewitness reports since people have different perceptions as to what they see. For example, sociologists have found that when several witnesses are asked to report what they saw regarding an automobile collision, they report several versions of what may have actually occurred. Some may see an opportunity to gain notoriety if they are asked to serve as a witness to a crime. These situations can result in inaccurate and/ or exaggerated accounts of what occurred or be disregarded as "hearsay." Identification of physical evidence can provide irrefutable information that can be used in a court of law.

Death Scene Photography

One of the most critical aspects of any death scene investigation is successful and proper photography. With regard to death scene information, it is certainly true that a picture is worth a thousand words. Photographs provide invaluable information to the investigation team. High-quality equipment facilitates the job, but there is no substitute for careful, conscientious work by the investigator. The death scene should be photographed immediately upon its discovery before anything is disturbed or moved. All angles should be considered during death scene photography. Photographs should include overall views, midrange views, and close-ups of the scene and victims. Too many photographs are always better than too few.

Purpose

The purpose for death scene photography is to visually record the scene as it was found. Those photographs will then be used by police investigators and prosecution and defense attorneys to present their cases to a judge and jury in a court of law. For that reason, it is important to ensure that police equipment (camera cases, briefcases, clipboards, etc.) and investigative personnel are not included in the photographs. The investigation team depends, to a large extent, on professional quality in its death scene photography; photographs that are not taken properly render loss of important information and may jeopardize the case.

It is important to remember that, if one has never been to the death scene, it is often difficult to accurately visualize through photographs only how the scene actually appeared and where things were in relation to each other. Thus, careful attention to detail by the photographer is essential to ensure that the photographs are of value.

Three Stages of Death Scene Photography

When photographing a death scene, the photographer must keep in mind that the camera has a limited field of view. In order to compensate for this limitation, the scene must be photographed in three stages.

Stage One: Overall Photographs

The purpose of the overall photographs is to include in one photograph as much information about a death scene as possible. These photographs should be taken before anything at the scene is disturbed or moved. They should serve as a record of how the scene was found (Figure 5.1a).

The goal of the photographer should be to ensure that every single item within the death scene appears in at least one photograph. This is extremely important as investigators do not always know what is important during the initial death scene search. Something initially overlooked will hopefully be preserved in an overall photograph.

Overall photographs should be composed such that the person viewing them will see the scene as a whole rather than focus on one particular aspect or detail. The overall photographs also serve as references for midrange and close-up photographs.

In taking overall death scene photographs, the photographer moves as far back as possible to encompass the entire scene. This may require a position across the street or atop an automobile or building. If a building is being photographed, photographs should be taken of all sides of the building as well as the business sign and address. Photographs of nearby street signs, cross streets, etc., should also be taken. If the scene is in an isolated area, one should attempt to locate a recognizable landmark such as a nearby hill, unusual tree, or power line pole. If the scene is indoors, stop inside the doorway and photograph the room panoramically in overlapping segments starting at one corner of the room and moving to the opposite side. Follow the same procedure for each corner of the room and in other relevant rooms. A normal 50 mm lens can usually be used for outdoor overalls; however, a wide-angle 35 mm lens is preferable for both indoor and outdoor overall photographs.

Helpful hint: Turn the camera sideways for indoor overalls. This will allow for a ceiling-to-floor photograph that provides more information. The use of a wide-angle lens can also produce a considerable amount of distortion in an image; if so, a normal 50 mm lens should be used instead. Film is relatively cheap. Therefore, many photographs are encouraged. Remember, too many photographs is always better than too few!

Stage Two: Midrange Photographs

The purpose of a midrange photograph is to focus the attention of the viewer on a particular object. However, it should still be taken from a position far enough away that the overall surroundings remain important. Midrange photographs should be free of distortion. Therefore, the normal 50 mm lens is recommended (Figure 5.1b).

(a)

(b)

(c)

Figure 5.1 (a) Overall photograph of a hotel room; (b) Midrange photograph of cut ligature and body; (c) Close-up photograph of body.

Indicator Cards When it has been determined what evidence will be collected and the overall photographs have been taken, indicator cards or evidence markers should be placed with the evidence and photographed again. Thus, there are two sets of photographs for the scene—one to show the scene undisturbed (as it was found) and a second to show the scene with the evidence cards in place. Indicator cards serve as easy references for everyone involved.

Use of Scales When a scale is used, relationships are more clearly defined. The addition of a scale to a photograph of evidence that is not to be collected such as a bullet graze, fingerprint, bloodstain, shoe print, or tire track is essential. The placement of an L-shaped ruler or two ruled scales at 90 degrees to each other to frame an impression or stain allows for any distortion in the photograph to be detected and potentially corrected at the printing stage. The camera should be placed at a 90-degree angle to the subject matter and the scales. Pens, coins, and paper clips are not recommended as scales unless as a final resort. A clearly legible ruler or scale is best. Without an appropriate scale, many photographs are rendered worthless.

Helpful hint: American Board of Forensic Odontology #2 scales have two scales set at 90 degrees to each other. In addition, circle indicators are printed on the scale and can be used to correct distortion during printing. When photographing injuries such as bruises, photograph them with and without scales and color charts.

Lighting and Flash Considerations The photographer should always be aware of the amount and source(s) of light available in order to determine when a flash is necessary. The flash should be positioned properly in order to maintain appropriate lighting in the photograph. The creation of shadows can obliterate areas of a photograph, which may be vital to the investigation. For example, the photographer should be aware of doorjambs and other objects that might create unwanted shadows. Footprints and tire tracks should be photographed with oblique lighting from all four sides of the print to create shadows that highlight the individual characteristics of the print.

Helpful hint: The photographer should check the camera settings every two or three frames (especially when using flash). One erroneous setting could ruin the remaining exposures.

Following is the checklist for using a flash:

- Is the flash turned on?
- Is the flash set to "manual" or "auto" mode?
- Is the ASA/ISO setting correct?
- Is the flash charging fully between flashes?

Following is the checklist for the camera:

- Is the shutter speed properly set to be synchronized with the flash?
- Is the f-stop properly set for the flash setting (auto or manual)?
- Is the thru-the-lens light meter functioning properly?

A word of caution: One should not take a picture of anything he or she does not want anybody to see. All pictures taken at a death scene are evidence and can be used in court by the defense or prosecution.

Stage Three: Close-Up Photographs

Every piece of evidence present at a death scene does not necessarily need to be photographed close up. Close-ups should be taken when important aspects of a piece of evidence are not depicted in the overall or midrange photographs (Figure 5.1c). Good close-up photographs show direction of travel or pattern of injury. An example of when close-up photography might not be necessary is where multiple cartridge casings of the same brand are on the ground in a group; a close-up of each casing does not reveal any new information. If, on the other hand, the casings are different brands, then close-ups would have more value. Close-ups can be taken from a distance with a telephoto lens or up close with a macro lens. In some instances, the telephoto is preferred because it is easier to light the subject with a flash positioned away from the subject.

Helpful hint: Use the smallest f-stop possible to improve the depth of field, particularly with extreme close-ups.

As a general note about death scene photography, photographs are not necessarily taken in the order of all overalls, then all midranges, then all close-ups. Usually all overalls are taken upon discovery of the death scene, and then midranges and close-ups are taken in sequence as evidence is discovered.

Video   Videotape is an excellent method for recording a death scene. Video, in combination with still photographs, can provide a jury with a better sense of the death scene and the relationships between pieces of evidence. The microphone should not be used as it can record unwanted comments from others at the scene. Narration of the videotape is also not recommended; comments made at the scene may later prove incorrect. If narration is desired, it should be dubbed in later from a prepared script. When taping a scene, one should pan *very slowly* and hold the camera as steadily as possible. Do not move too fast since vital information might be overlooked (it can also make viewers motion sick). Use the zoom sparingly; overuse is distracting and can contribute to nausea.

Pearls of Photography
- Always check your equipment; carry a back-up camera, flash, and extra batteries.
- Avoid undershooting. Bracket the photographs.
- Remember that batteries are sensitive to temperature extremes.

Legal Aspects of Photography   The photograph is considered one of the best methods of documentation. Photographs are extensively used in establishing four major categories of discovery of evidence:

1. To establish that a crime was committed
2. To discover how a crime was committed
3. To help prove the identity of a suspect
4. To collectively connect a suspect or suspects to a crime

Photographs can prolong evidence that otherwise may deteriorate with time. They must be taken as soon as possible particularly when dealing with perishable evidence.

Photographs again can depict a scene more cleverly than perhaps a witness can articulate it. They may be used to "jog" a witness' memory. A photograph may also contain elements that were initially overlooked by investigators or that may have been forgotten by witnesses.

Most importantly, photographs lend credibility to testimony and help jurors actually visualize rather than imagine the variables of the crime, lending to more objectivity.

Admissibility of Photographs   Photographs cannot prejudice or mislead the jury; therefore, factual photographs are better than those that are overdramatized. Photographs must be authenticated by a witness who was present during the shoot. The photographer is responsible for identifying evidence in a photograph and testifying to the accurate portrayal of its content and to the fact that it was not subject to tamper.

Identifying the Photograph   Hundreds of photographs are often taken—perhaps at different times and by different photographers. Therefore, it is recommended that a log be kept to detail the following:

- Date and time the photograph was taken.
- Name of photographer and title.
- Type of equipment used.
- Description of the angle at which the photograph was taken in relation to subject (e.g., "bullet hole in SW wall").
- Clarifying comments (e.g., rain equipment, probes, hot or cold conditions).

Chain of Accountability Photographs are considered as important as physical evidence. Therefore, a chain of accountability is necessary—from photographers to crime laboratory (lags in time, person submitting the disc (chip), time, and date). The laboratory also logs the number of prints made, who received them (Federal Bureau of Investigation, police department, etc.), and each time a photograph is released, returned, moved, or handled. A disruption in chain of accountability could discredit the validity of the photograph.

Evidence Identification: Documentation and Collection

Evidence collection is important since it represents materials that may have to be presented in a court of law. Because of that possibility, certain procedures must be followed in the collection of evidence to ensure that it can be admitted into the court case.

The following guidelines should be considered during the process of evidence collection:

- All major investigations must first have one person to lead the investigation. That person must first decide the type of crime that exists. Once that is determined, the necessary resources must be considered including the types of experts required from various disciplines (ME/coroner, forensic odontologist, forensic anthropologist, criminologist, hazardous materials team, Federal Aviation Association, National Transportation Safety Board, bomb technician, etc.), crime scene processing equipment, and manpower.
- To ensure an orderly process, the lead investigator must know who has been at the crime scene (first responders, rescue personnel, initial law enforcement personnel, photographers, witnesses, etc.). All traffic patterns should be ascertained in order to know potential contributions or deletions made by previous investigative personnel. After a briefing on all known facts, the lead investigator makes an assessment of the crime scene, which enables him or her to develop an organized plan as to how to approach and sequentially process the scene. A good initial step minimizes any chance of destroying evidence or overlooking valuable information. It is also critical to minimize the number of personnel permitted at the crime scene.
- The best way to approach a crime scene is to work inward toward the body from the outside scene perimeter. Avoid initial focus on the body as this may create a "tunnel vision" approach to the study of the overall situation thereby overlooking important forensic evidence surrounding the body. The scene may hold clues as to the cause of death by thermal injury, drugs, firearms, etc.

- If blood has been shed at the scene, all investigative personnel must utilize appropriate personal protective equipment (PPE). This may include gowns, masks, gloves, goggles, or eye shields, shoe and head covers, and respirators. If at any point during the investigation any blood or biological matter is transferred to the protective wear of anyone involved, a new piece of PPE must replace the affected garment. The contaminated piece of PPE must be discarded in containers placed at appropriate locations near the crime scene.
- A complete rough diagram of the structure or area can be created during the initial overview of the scene; this provides the opportunity to note positions of significant items within the scene. A more detailed sketch of the primary scene should also note evidence items and their positions, orientations, and relationships to the body. Good methods for diagramming include
  - A general overall approach with dimensions of structures, rooms, furniture, etc.
  - A specific diagram for the death scene (bedroom, living room, kitchen, etc.)
  - A series of diagrams to document locations of evidence items or to indicate bloodstain patterns

The process of evidence collection is one of the most important steps during crime scene investigation. When evidence is properly collected, valuable information contained in or with the evidence can be preserved for presentation in court. If evidence is mishandled, that same information can be lost or ruled as inadmissible by the court.

Packaging Evidence

Prior to actual collection of the evidence, the investigator must decide what containers are needed for the various types of evidence to be seized. That decision should be based on the need to

- Provide proper evidence preservation (protection)
- Prevent evidence from being compromised, contaminated, destroyed, damaged, or altered

Among the types of protective containers are

- *Paper bags*: New paper bags are one of the most universally accepted containers for most evidence collected. Since they can be readily purchased almost anywhere in bulk and in various sizes from large "shopping bag" size to small "lunch bag" size, they remain popular among investigators. They provide an excellent container for clothing, bedding, shoes, numerous articles from a home or office, beer cans, bottles, and hats and for protecting trace evidence on the hands of the deceased. Unlike most plastic containers, paper bags are not airtight; therefore, biological evidence will not degrade.

- *Envelopes*: Like paper bags, new envelopes can be purchased almost anywhere and in various sizes from large document size to small coin envelope size. Envelopes can be used for small items.
- *Butcher paper rolls*: This type of paper is excellent for viewing, photographing, and packaging evidence. Pieces of butcher paper can also be laid between folds of clothing or other large cloth items to separate and help prevent cross-contamination of biological evidence.
- *Pharmacy fold paper*: These small 6- or 8-inch sheets of paper are useful for packaging small forensic evidence. Pharmacy fold paper can be formed into a small package. This is an ideal method for collecting fibers, hairs, paint chips, and samples of dried blood; this helps prevent damage or degradation to the sample.
- *Vials*: Plastic vials are useful for containing various types of evidence that are not biological in nature. This may include bullet casings, matches, cigarette butts, soil samples, paint chips, and debris.

Glass vials are useful for containing various types of liquids that could potentially react chemically to plastic (such as through melting or dissolution). Unlike plastic vials, glass vials have screw-on lids that prevent leakage. Glass vials can be used for corrosive chemicals, loose pills, alcohol samples, liquid samples found in drinking glasses, etc. (Note: The main drawback to using glass evidence containers is the potential for breakage; glass vials must be packaged carefully to avoid damage.)

- *New metal paint cans*: Cans can also be purchased in various sizes (from one gallon to one pint). Most fire stations maintain a ready supply of these for their use in collecting evidence in arson cases. These are excellent for collecting flammable liquids, accelerants, and volatiles. These containers are excellent for collecting samples of glass, fine clay, soil, and sharp items.
- *Syringe holders*: These are required for packaging hypodermic needles. Use of syringe holders also ensures that syringes remain in the same condition as when they are found. Investigators at a crime scene as well as those who have to handle evidence at a later date (evidence custodian, criminalist, officers of the court, etc.) must be protected from accidental punctures when they handle evidence.

- *Cardboard boxes:* These can be used to secure knives, guns, and other sharp instruments. Various sizes are easily obtained. Suspected weapons should be tied/secured to the bottom of the box to avoid slippage of the item.
- *Indelible ink marking pens:* These are essential for investigators. All containers that hold evidence items must be labeled with permanent marker identification. Containers must be sealed with evidence tape and documented as to proper chain of custody information.

Fingerprints

Fingerprints (when available) are the best evidence for identification because the individual characteristics of fingerprints remain constant throughout a person's life. Individual characteristics make each print unique and allow for specific identification of individuals. Fingerprints can be entered into a national database Automated Fingerprint Identification System (AFIS) for comparison. In general, the most latent fingerprint processing is done at the scene. Exceptions are items such as tape or paper prints that require chemical processing. Some items require a laboratory environment in order for experts to utilize controlled testing techniques to obtain optimum results. Some items may require enhancement through specialized lighting to capture additional ridge detail. Circumstances such as these also require photography of the latent print. Consideration should be given to careful transport of small items, items with difficult surfaces from which to obtain prints, or any items requested by the latent print examiner.

Biological Evidence

The collection of biological samples is important to the forensic investigation. Information that can be ascertained from biological samples includes

- Blood spatter pattern
- Blood stain patterns
- Semen or saliva stains
- DNA information

Before collecting any biological samples, one must determine whether the samples offer any value to the investigation. A photograph of the sample in situ can help the investigator determine the importance of the sample. Exercise caution when collecting samples; latex gloves should be worn. After the sample is collected, it must be protected through drying and refrigeration as soon as possible.

Clothing

It is important to collect clothing in nearly every homicide, assault, fire death, firearms death, electrical death, or motor vehicle accident. Evidence from clothing of those involved can provide important information. The victim's clothing can provide

- Bloodstains, burns, or tire-mark patterns that help with reconstruction of the situation that led to the death
- Type and size of weapon used such as width of a knife blade and range of fire of a firearm
- Trace evidence including samples of
  - The suspect's blood, body fluids, hair, and clothing fibers
  - Paint chips from a hit-and-run vehicle or accelerants on clothing from arson

The suspect's clothing can provide

- Trace evidence including samples of the victim's blood, body fluids, hair, and clothing fibers
- Bloodstain patterns that help with reconstruction of the situation, which led to the death

Prior to packaging bloodstained clothing, one must ensure that the stains are dry and patterns are not destroyed during the packaging process. In situations where proximity testing of gunshot residue is required, extremely careful handling of the clothing must be ensured since residues can be easily dislodged. The ideal method of packaging bloodstained clothing is to place a paper towel over the gunshot area and fold the clothing carefully over it. Again, the value of good photographs cannot be overstated.

Fibers and Hairs

When fibers or hairs are found at a crime scene, they should be collected as they are found since they can easily be lost. An examination of hair can indicate

- Whether it is human or animal
- Body region from which it originated (head, chest, or pubis)
- Whether it was forcibly removed or fell out
- Whether it was burned, cut, crushed, dried, or bleached
- Blood groups if the root is attached
- Racial groups
- Information provided through DNA analysis

DNA Analysis

DNA contains the genetic blueprint. DNA strands in the shape of a "twisted ladder" or double helix can be mapped by genetic patterns. Since each person's DNA differs, DNA mapping provides a unique identity marker.

Extraction

Police and scientists use any available cell tissue found at a crime scene—blood, semen, tissue, bone marrow, hair, urine, saliva, wood pulp, cheek scrapings, fingernails—for DNA typing to compare with a suspect's genetic coding.

Fragmentation

A DNA strand from a sample is dissolved in a "restriction enzyme" that breaks the DNA molecule, or double helix, into thousands of pieces. Laboratory scientists know which fragments have specific DNA coding signifying unique traits for comparison.

Lining Up the Fragments

The chosen DNA fragments are placed in an electrically charged gel. The negatively charged DNA drifts toward the positive pole on the gel slab with smaller fragments moving faster. This process of electrophoresis leaves DNA fragments arranged according to length.

Radioactive Probe

These bands are transferred to a nylon membrane. Radioactive DNA fragments containing specific coding that varies greatly from person to person are applied as "probes." These special radioactive probes bind with complementary DNA fragment landmarks on the fragments.

Comparative Analysis

An x-ray film is laid over the nylon membranes and reveals the size of each piece upon which each landmark falls; the process may take 1 or 2 days or much longer due to a backlog of cases. The DNA bands (DNA fingerprint), which by now resemble a Universal Product Code symbol, are transferred onto the file as a result of the radioactivity. The bars are lined up. If those from the crime scene evidence line up with those from the suspect, prosecutors use the band patterns in court to claim that a coincidental match would be extremely rare—the probability of a match is one in 100 million.

DNA Evidence in Forensic Cases

Since first introduced into the United States courts in 1987, DNA evidence is now generally accepted in most courts. DNA evidence is used in current and cold cases to include or exclude suspects. The proper collection and preservation of biological evidence at the scene is extremely important for future investigation. DNA can be entered into the national DNA database, Combined DNA Index System (CODIS), for comparison.

The power of DNA prints comes from its precision, which is immensely greater than standard analysis of blood, semen, or hair. Although DNA fingerprinting has attained mythic status in the public mind—one critic calls it "a fist on the scales of justice"—outweighing all other evidence, it is not an infallible crime solver. It is problematic enough that the very term "DNA fingerprinting" is not allowed in some courts and is replaced by DNA typing or DNA profiling in order to not dazzle jurors into thinking that DNA evidence is as unambiguous as an ordinary fingerprint. That is because DNA tests do not compare each of the 3 billion chemical units of a person's heredity. (If they did, there would be no dispute that a match is a match; DNA is unique to every individual except identical twins.) Instead, the tests compare only three to six regions of DNA—up to 13 core loci.

Firearms

Before a weapon is touched or moved at the scene of a crime, notations should be made regarding its position and placement, hammer position, safety position, visible blood, hairs, dust, etc. The weapon should be handled on its knurled or serrated surfaces. Common sense can help ensure that personal safety is addressed and that fingerprints are not added or removed.

Ammunition

When cartridges, fired cases, and projectiles are found at a crime scene, special attention is required to document their locations. Occasionally, the shooter's and/or victim's positions can be determined. Bullets and casings need to be handled with a gloved hand (not metal forceps), packaged separately, and preferably wrapped in tissue to prevent the possibility of scratching or otherwise damaging the items. Care must be taken to avoid any introduced marks or imprints to ensure the evidence remains in the exact condition in which it was found. Once packaged, the container should be sealed and marked.

Casings and projectiles can reveal the type and brand of ammunition, and comparisons can be made to determine whether a bullet or casing was fired from a specific weapon by the firearms examiner. A national database, National Integrated Ballistics Information Network (NIBIN) can link projectiles and casings to those used in other crimes.

Toolmarks

Toolmarks are often left behind when a forced entry is made into a building. If tools are recovered from the scene, they can be subjected to tests and comparisons similar to those applied to bullet analyses. Recovery of tool-marks may require the entire piece to be removed and sent to the laboratory for analysis. If that is not possible, silicone casts can be made. Beyond that, scale graphs should be obtained.

Shoe and Tire Prints

Nearly every shoe and tire print has individual characteristics that could make it unique and identifiable. Photographs of these items are generally taken upon arrival at the crime scene as these types of evidence are easily destroyed.

Documents

Documents are collected primarily for

- Content
- Possibility of latent fingerprints

These items should be handled with tweezers or forceps or by the edges to avoid destroying or leaving latent fingerprints. Authorship can often be determined through handwriting analysis.

Organizing Evidence

The lead investigator should establish a central collection point at the scene of the crime where all evidence is initially marked, numbered, and inventoried. As evidence is collected, a written inventory should include the item, indicator number, and location it is found. This master list of all items is retained for later cross-reference. It also serves as a double check of the collection to ensure that all evidence has been collected. Upon finalization of this list and packaging of items to be removed, the investigator should make a final walk-through of the crime scene to ensure that no evidence has been overlooked and that all investigative equipment has been returned to its proper place and secured.

Debriefing

The lead investigator should finalize the crime scene investigation process with a debriefing of all personnel involved. At this time, he or she must ensure that the process has been explored to the fullest extent possible. The lead investigator may also obtain further input from members of the team before offering closure to the process and thanking team members. The chain of communication should be clearly established prior to commencement of the next stage of investigation. The value of this communication contributes to improved procedures when the team reconvenes.

Team Approach

Team approach to crime scene work is essential and works efficiently when every member of the team knows his or her role and carries out individual responsibilities. Most members of such a team are experts in their own realms; the lead investigator should be able to meld the offerings of each expert into the overall process.

Tips for Forensic Investigations

Death Scene

The death scene offers many clues to the time of injury or death:

- Presence or absence of milk, mail, and/or newspapers. Look at postmarks or datelines.
- Are lights on or off? Is the television on or off? Are appliances on or off?
- Clothing worn by the deceased such as street clothes, night wear, or work clothes.
- Kitchen dishes and food on the stove or table.
- With newborn deaths, note the clothes, towels, or newspapers that may provide wrapping.

Time of Death

The following events do not occur after death:

- Exudation of leukocytes (white blood cells)
- Proliferation of fixed tissue cells
- Growth of hair or nails
- Penetration of foreign particulate matter into alveoli
- Formation of significant carboxyhemoglobin
- Significant degree of propulsion of food along the gastrointestinal tract

Bibliography

Clark, S, Ernst, M, Haglund, W, and Jetzen, J. 1996. *Medicolegal Death Investigator: A Systematic Training Program for the Professional Death Investigator*. Big Rapids, MI: Occupational Research and Assessment, Inc.

Fisher, BAJ. 1993. *Techniques of Crime Scene Investigation*, 4th ed. Boca Raton, FL: CRC Press, Inc.

Redsicker, DR. 2000. *The Practical Methodology of Forensic Photography*, 2nd ed. Boca Raton, FL: Taylor & Francis.

Mass Fatality Management

6

OBJECTIVES

Upon completion of this chapter and corresponding reference material, the reader will be able to

- Define three areas of operation for a mass fatality management
- Describe the role of the incident scene investigators
- List the stations of the temporary morgue
- Identify the functions of the team leaders of the morgue stations in collecting information for victim identification
- Discuss the role of personnel at the family assistance center

Introduction

A mass fatality incident is defined as an occurrence of multiple deaths that overwhelms the usual routine capability of an agency. Preplanning and training with community partners are essential goals to prepare for a mass fatality event. It is important to know the resources available at the local, state, and national levels for the three basic activities that follow a disaster, including rescue and treatment of survivors, repair and maintenance of basic services, and the recovery and management of bodies. Many communities have annual mass casualty exercises involving multiple medical, law enforcement, and fire disciplines.

It is important to plan for the various possible types of disasters that may occur in your area of the country, for example, hurricanes along the coast or tornadoes in the Midwest. However, many different types of disasters may occur in any jurisdiction, including natural, terrorist, accident, biological, man-made, or radiation disasters. It is important not only to have a plan, but also to remember that all disasters are unique and, even with preplanning, there will be unexpected events that occur. It is important to have a flexible and adaptable plan in place.

Initial Evaluation

1. An evaluation team consisting of the medical examiner, the chief investigator, and one on-duty investigator will be equipped with cellular phones. The following will be evaluated:
   a. Number of fatalities involved
   b. Condition of the bodies (e.g., burned, dismembered)
   c. Difficulty anticipated in the recovery of the bodies
   d. The personnel and equipment required for the operation (e.g., fire search and rescue, heavy equipment)
   e. The accessibility of the scene to transport vehicles and the difficulties that may be encountered in transporting bodies from the scene
   f. The presence of chemical, radiological, biological, or other environmental hazards
2. Identify the personnel possibly needed to staff the morgue for identification, body examination, evidence collection, and other procedures.
3. Anticipate the type of facility that would be most useful for a family assistance center (FAC). If the victims live in the local area, their families may also be local and housing would not be a critical issue. If the victims are predominately not local, the need for housing the families of victims would have to be anticipated.
4. If the incident is a mass fatality, contact the D-MORT regional coordinator or the national D-MORT organization at 800-USA-NMDS (800-872-6367):
   a. The disaster mortuary unit provided by D-MORT will send an evaluation team to the location and aid in the assessment. They can activate the evaluation team and have experienced, reliable individuals on site within 8–12 hours.
   b. The disaster portable morgue units are caches of highly specialized equipment and supplies prestaged for deployment to a disaster site. One is currently stationed in Maryland, a second in California, and a third in Texas.

Plan of Operation

The plan of operation includes an initial evaluation and three major operations, including the scene, temporary morgue, and FAC. Someone must be in charge of each of the operations. All three need to be set up and coordinated at the same time:

Scene: Body Recovery and Evaluation

1. Select personnel and equipment for scene investigation and body removal:
   a. Communications—Telephones (hard line and cellular), fax machines, etc.
   b. Body bags—D-MORT, airport, state funeral directors association
   c. Refrigerated trucks—Trucks at the scene and morgue
   d. Transportation—For personnel (e.g., cars and vans)
   e. Security—For scene, examination center, and FAC
   f. Identification—I.D. badges for all personnel
2. Select a temporary morgue site: In the event that a disaster occurs, the local county medical examiner facility may not be suitable for disaster operations. This facility will conduct day-to-day business as usual without interruption. Alternate sites for disaster operations for the temporary morgue may be identified at the time of a disaster.
3. Select a location for a FAC: The location of the FAC will depend upon the location of the incident. The center will be selected at the time of the disaster.

Scene: Body Recovery

1. Scene investigation and body recovery
   a. Equipment and supplies—Someone in charge of equipment and supplies
   b. Protective clothing—Gloves, boots, coats, hard hats, rain suits, etc.
   c. Body bags—A good, heavy bag with six handles and c-zipper
   d. Refrigerated trucks—Metal walls and floor
   e. Transportation—For personnel
   f. Transportation for bodies—Funeral homes, contract service, etc.
   g. Tents and trucks—For storage of supplies and equipment
   h. Paint—Contrasting color for numbering body bags
   i. Flags—Stakes for marking location of body, body parts, etc.
   j. Plastic toe tags/bands—Tags with Sharpie permanent ink pens to number them
   k. Biohazard bags and boxes—For safe disposal of biohazard debris
   l. Documentation—Document body location, body parts, and personal effects
   m. Food—Have someone in charge of food services for workers

n. Numbering—All numbers will be assigned at the scene. Use simple numbers (i.e., 1, 2, 3, …). Body numbers should be 1, 2, 3, …. Body part numbers should be P1, P2, P3, …. Personal effect numbers should be E1, E2, E3, ….

Note: Write the number on the body bag 12 inches high with white paint (if using black body bags). Place plastic toe tag on bag and body.

o. Worker safety—Ensure that provisions are in place for the health and safety of the scene workers.

2. Scene body recovery teams and other personnel
   a. Recovery director will coordinate and direct the recovery teams:
      i. Body recovery teams—Comprising one of each of the following:
         A. Team leader—Preferably someone knowledgeable about human remains (e.g., pathologist, anthropologist, medical examiner)
         B. Assistant to team leader—Will assist the team leader and photograph as needed
         C. Scribe—Documentation
         D. Runner
   b. Body moving area—Comprising four people to move bodies out of the scene to the body staging area

3. Evacuation area: Transfer of the bodies/remains from the disaster site to the temporary morgue site. In natural disasters such as tornadoes, floods, etc., recovery teams and evacuation teams may have to be the same. Team members include
   a. One evacuation director
   b. Two transport personnel
   c. One scribe
   d. Staging area assistants (as needed)
   e. Clerks (as needed)

Morgue Operations

1. Logistics:
   a. Get personnel and equipment in place! Put someone in charge of supplies and equipment. Have someone tracking personnel (i.e., who, where they are from, and the hours worked each day).
      i. Security—I.D. badges
      ii. Refrigerated trucks—Ramps into trucks

     iii. Protective clothing—Gloves, scrubs, shoe covers, masks, coveralls, hats, etc.

     iv. Communications—Telephones, cell phones, fax machines, P.A. systems

     v. Computers—Programs, someone in charge of data processing

     vi. Records—Postmortem and antemortem, must have someone in charge

     vii. Office equipment—Copiers, typewriters, fax machine, computers, etc.

     viii. Receiving—The person in charge should be documenting in the log-in book, by date and time received, the person receiving the body, and the person delivering the body. The person in charge of the bodies must know the location and final disposition of bodies at all times.

     ix. Workers—To move bodies, perform lifting, and other tasks

     x. Numbering of bodies—The same numbers are used as marked on the body bag and used on the scene; this number should be used throughout the entire process

     xi. Log books—Three: one for bodies, one for parts, one for effects

     xii. Case file—Initiated with body number. File must stay with body during entire processing. All forms and paperwork used should be available at each station. The case number should be placed on each form as it is used

     xiii. Body trackers—Personnel to escort body and all paperwork from station to station in the order so intended

     xiv. Station processing system—The stations and their order may change with the type of incident

     xv. Worker safety—Ensure that provisions are in place for the health of the examination center workers

     xvi. Critical incident stress debriefing personnel—Will monitor workers' mental health at the morgue site and other locations as needed. Individuals skilled in massage therapy may also be useful

2. Overview: The temporary morgue facility will process all body bags delivered from the disaster site in station-by-station fashion. Data gathered from the examinations will be compiled and entered into a network computer system by clerical staff at the temporary morgue. The remains and other items will be examined in an organized approach by qualified professionals in an attempt to identify remains and to document findings for the purposes of the disaster investigation.

3. Stations of the morgue:

  a. Admitting: This is the first station located inside the temporary morgue. At this station, morgue personnel will assign a body tracker to the decedent. The body tracker's responsibility is to accompany the decedent to all the stations at the morgue. The body tracker will stay with the body until each station has completed its examination. The body tracker will collect all paperwork completed at each station concerning the decedent and after the decedent has been through all stations, the decedent will be taken to the exit and placed into a clean body bag. The paperwork for that decedent will be given back to the admitting station and ultimately taken to the resource center of operations.

  b. X-ray: The second station of the morgue will be x-ray. After admitting, the body tracker will take the decedent to the x-ray station at which time a full body x-ray will be done. The body bag will remain closed during this time to ensure that everything in the body bag has been x-rayed prior to being examined. If, after examination, additional x-rays are requested, the body tracker will accompany the decedent back to the x-ray station for additional x-rays.

  c. Assessment/pathology/photography: The third station will be assessment. At this station, the decedent will be photographed and undressed, and a complete body examination will be completed. All scars, marks, tattoos and distinguishing features will be noted. If any implants are located, such as pacemakers, surgical pins, bone replacements, or breast implants, they can be removed by the pathologist and used for identification.

  d. Personal effects: The fourth station will be personal effects. This station will be given all personal effects taken from the decedent during assessment. All effects will be photographed, logged, and packaged. Jewelry, watches, photo identification, billfold, paperwork, U.S. currency, and clothing will be photographed with the number that has been assigned to the decedent. A handwritten log will be completed indicating what was taken off the decedent. The effects will then be packaged and placed with the decedent prior to being taken to the next station for examination. The body tracker will be responsible for keeping the effects with the decedent. If U.S. currency is located on the decedent, the morgue supervisor will be notified and it will be up to the supervisor whether the currency will be secured in a location other than with the decedent.

  e. Odontology: The fifth station will be forensic dentistry. A complete dental workup examination will be completed by the forensic dentist. After the workup examination has been completed, the forensic dentist will compare antemortem and postmortem x-rays and records for possible identification.

f. Fingerprinting: The sixth station will be fingerprinting. At this station, personnel will make every effort to recover fingerprints from the decedent. Once fingerprints have been obtained, they will be assigned the decedent's case number and will be given to the appropriate agency for comparison and possible identification of the decedent.

g. DNA: The seventh station will be for the recovery of DNA from the decedent. DNA personnel will recover a sample of blood, bone, or muscle from the decedent. The sample will be identified by the decedent's case number and stored. The chief medical examiner will determine where the samples will be sent and analyzed for identification.

h. Anthropology: The eighth station will be for anthropology examination. If needed, a forensic anthropologist will complete a forensic examination of the decedent to determine the race, stature, sex, and age of the decedent.

i. Exit/rebagging: The ninth station will be for rebagging and exiting of the decedent. When the decedent has been through all identification stations of the morgue, the decedent will be placed in a clean body bag. The body tracker will make sure that a tag is placed on the decedent and the body bag indicating the decedent's case number. The body tracker will then return all paperwork gathered from the examinations from the other stations and give the paperwork back to the personnel in admitting. The decedent will then be placed into a refrigerated truck until released to the family for final disposition. All paperwork for the decedent will be taken to the resource center and used for identification.

Family Assistance Center

A representative of the Medical Examiner's Office needs to be in charge during the initial setup of the FAC. Personnel from the National Transportation and Safety Board (NTSB) will be organizing the center and coordinating workers as needed in the event of a transportation disaster. Other personnel may be recruited from the local funeral directors association. The FAC is a multiagency organization and cannot be handled by the medical examiner alone:

1. Site selection—It is extremely important that the site selected be functional for the incident that you are taking care of (e.g., if the families are coming from out of town, the site may be a hotel or motel). If it

is a local incident and the families are local, then housing would not be a consideration and churches, business offices, and such should be considered. The location should not be too close to the actual scene and it should be easily accessible by families. Parking should be a consideration, depending on the number of families expected. Security for the parking lot and the outside, as well as the inside, of the FAC is the number one priority.

2. Medical examiner/general administration—Antemortem records, family information, and death notification.
3. American Red Cross/Salvation Army—Family support, transportation, housing, supplies, equipment, volunteer coordination.
4. Security—Parking, checkpoints, family escorts.
5. Food services—For families and staff.
6. Communications—Telephones and cell phones for workers.
7. Mental health—Family support, staff support, assisting with death notification.
8. Medical—Family care, staff care, assisting with death notification.
9. Religious support—Family support, staff support, assisting with death notification.
10. Site support—Custodial, site maintenance.

The medical examiner/coroner (ME/C) is responsible for several different areas during a mass fatality event, including the initial site or sites of the disaster, the temporary morgue, the Emergency Operations Center (EOC), the Family Assistance Center (FAC), and the day-to-day operation of the Medical Examiner/Coroner's Office. In a mass fatality incident, the ME/C is faced with a host of complex and time-sensitive responsibilities. These include identifying victims, collecting property and evidence, determining cause and manner of death, issuing death certificates, and returning bodies to their families. Both the National Association of Medical Examiners (NAME) accreditation standards and the Federal Emergency Support Function (ESF-8) require a written mass fatality plan. Preplanning and training with community partners are essential goals to adequately prepare for a mass fatality event.

Bibliography

Dudley, MH. 2013. *Mass Fatality Management Concise Field Guide*. Boca Raton, FL: CRC Press.

Forensic Legal Issues and Expert Witness Testimony

7

ROBERT J. McWHIRTER

OBJECTIVES

Upon completion of this chapter and corresponding reference material, the reader will be able to

- List common rules of testifying as an expert witness
- Differentiate between a lay witness and an expert witness
- Describe the role of the expert witness

Introduction

Let's start with the basic rules of testifying:

- Don't be defensive.
- Don't fudge.
- Speak from your knowledge and don't try to use your knowledge as a weapon.
- Do not become an advocate.

Sure, there are other good ideas like have your report ready, don't dress like a slob, testify slowly, and look at the jury while you are testifying. All those things are important, but they generally are not going to land you in great trouble if you somehow violate them. On the other hand, if you are defensive or fudge or speculate or, worst of all, try to become an advocate (in other words, argue), you will not only be ineffective as a witness, but you can also actually get into trouble.

But you may ask, "What about being truthful—isn't that an important rule for testifying?" The answer is, "Of course." Leaving issues of morality aside, any good trial lawyer will tell you that most juries can cut through a lie pretty quickly. And there is always that nasty little crime of perjury (telling a lie under oath) looming. The point is that telling the truth goes without saying and if you intend to lie, nothing in this chapter will change that.

With that said, let's cover some preliminaries before discussing the aforementioned rules in greater detail.

To Whom to Talk

In any jurisdiction in the United States, at least 95% of all cases plead out. That means there is no trial, which means you won't testify—at least not in front of a jury. Consequently, as a witness, you should ask yourself, "Why should I be getting adversarial with one side or the other at any stage in the process?" Although you may be on the witness list of one side or another, you are not necessarily "their witness." In fact, if a lawyer tells you not to talk to the other side, he is committing a crime usually called "obstruction of justice." You are there to help either the judge or jury make what we hope is a fair decision. Usually lawyers are just trying to get as many facts as possible—especially at the initial stages of a case. They want to know what you have to say, and they really don't have an interest in attacking you. Good lawyers work with the facts—they don't try to change the facts. What lawyers are trying to do—especially in the initial stages of a case—is to broker some sort of fair and proportioned resolution. This is the heart of "plea bargaining." Thus, they need to talk to you to find out information to help their client—either the government or the accused.

With this in mind, your best policy is to be open with both sides of the lawsuit. And, of course, when you are talking to the lawyer, remember the five rules—don't be defensive, don't fudge, speak from your knowledge, and don't become an advocate.

Reports

Reports are important in your work. Bring all your reports and review them before you are asked questions. This is regardless of whether you are interviewed in a lawyer's office or testify at a deposition, grand jury, or trial. The important rule for reports is don't write them for litigation. In other words, write them because they help you do your job—don't leave out or add things that you think may help or hurt somebody's case later on. For one thing, that might not be a good report for your job. For another, what you may now think will help or hurt one side in a lawsuit may ultimately backfire. Again, write your reports according to the dictates of your profession. And, of course, remember the four rules—don't be defensive, don't fudge, speak from your knowledge, and don't become an advocate.

So You Got a Subpoena

A subpoena is an official looking document that tells you to appear at a certain time and place to testify. Also, it may tell you to bring certain documents and things. A subpoena is nothing more than an order from the court. But again, most criminal cases are resolved well before trial. A subpoena should have the specific time and courtroom where you are supposed to testify and an address and telephone number. In addition, the subpoena should have the name of a specific attorney who asked for the subpoena; call that attorney. Also, call the attorney on the other side or wait until they call you. They can keep you posted as to what is really going on in the case and whether or not you are really going to testify. Attorneys have a responsibility to ask for subpoenas well before trial. Many cases end up settling between the time the subpoena goes out and before trial. Again, the key is communication with both sides of the lawsuit.

For example, you may end up talking to the attorney who did not call you and he may learn some information about your testimony. This may cause him to find a different resolution for the case than going to a trial. Again, more justice is created in the system when all parties have all the information from all witnesses.

What Is a Lay Witness vs. an Expert Witness

According to most rules of evidence including the Federal Rules of Evidence, "Every person is competent to be a witness, except as otherwise provided in these rules" (Federal Rule of Evidence 601). Thus, unless you are somehow "incompetent," there is nothing to bar you from being a witness. Incompetent witnesses are generally people such as very small children or people with mental or psychological defects.

The question then is whether you are going to testify as a lay witness or an expert witness. Generally speaking, a lay witness testifies only about something that he or she perceived with any of the five senses—what he or she saw, heard, touched, felt, or smelled. In fact, the only time a lay witness is supposed to give an opinion is when it is based on perception from the senses. (See Federal Rule of Evidence 701. [A lay witness can testify as to his opinion "rationally based on the perception of the witness, be helpful to a clear understanding of the witness's testimony or determination of a fact or issue, and not based on scientific, technical, or other specialized knowledge…"].)

Conversely, an expert witness can offer opinions based on his or her "specialized knowledge" or a specialized skill, experience, training, or education. Expert's testimony is supposed to help the jury better understand the evidence. (See Federal Rule of Evidence 702.) Thus, even experts are not allowed to give an opinion on the "ultimate issue" as to, for example, whether or not the defendant is guilty. An expert could testify as to cause of death, but not, for example, who caused the death.

Remember "specialized knowledge" does not necessarily mean advanced degrees. Anybody who happens to have a special expertise can qualify as an expert. A great example of this is in the movie *My Cousin Vinny* where he put his girlfriend on to testify about tires.

Once again, whether you testify as a lay witness or an expert, remember the rules—don't be defensive, don't fudge, speak from your knowledge, and don't become an advocate.

Rules

So after all the pretrial negotiations and time, you are going to testify after all. Just remember the rules—don't be defensive, don't fudge, speak from your knowledge, and don't become an advocate.

Don't Be Defensive: It's Not about You

Although you may feel that you are being attacked—and sometimes you actually even are—ultimately, when you are testifying, it is not about you. It is about the evidence that you provide and the presentation; the evidence is what you say and the presentation is the way you say it. An attorney, during questioning, may wish to emphasize a certain point. If you are defensive, even if you feel like you have defended yourself or "won the battle," you may not realize that you are actually emphasizing the very point that the attorney wants to emphasize as the following demonstrates:

Q: You've got laceration of the scalp. We will talk about that. But what you have here is focal hemorrhage of neck muscles, right?
A: That's correct.
Q: Focal, that means focused, correct? Am I right in that?
A: The way I use the word "focal," is it's localized vs. a diffuse thing. And what I mean by focal, it means it's not spread all over. It's got a definite area.
Q: So the answer to my question is yes?
A: Yes.
Q: Thank you.

As you can see, the attorney (in this case, me) wanted to emphasize the small nature of the hemorrhage. By acting defensively, the witness helped the jury understand that. Any juror who was not paying attention at the start was paying attention by the end. All of this could have been avoided if the witness had given a simple "yes" to the question instead of acting defensively.

Don't Fudge: Answer the Question Asked

"Fudging" is when you attempt to avoid answering the specific question. This is different than not understanding a question. In that situation, it's perfectly appropriate to say, "I don't understand your question." Fudging, however, is deliberate. Just remember that any attempts to minimize an answer instead of giving a simple "yes" or "no" might be precisely what the attorney wants:

Q: Very good. I believe—did you say in the area where if you used excessive force, one would expect fractures of the thyroid and hyoid bones? Do you remember saying that?
A: I don't remember saying that. But I, yeah, I can imagine that I might have. It leads me, in my opinion, I've not seen it written anywhere. It's just my opinion that it takes a little bit more force to break a bone than it would if you don't break a bone.
Q: Well, Spitz and Fisher, again, say that fractures of the hyoid, thyroid, and cricoid cartilage are frequently associated with manual strangulation; is that correct?
A: Yes, they can be associated with manual strangulation.
Q: I believe it was said "frequently associated." That's what the book says?
A: That's fine. It can say that.

As you can see, by fudging with the term "frequently," the witness allowed the attorney to ask the same question again and again. This only serves to emphasize the point. Just answer the question and don't fudge even if you don't like the attorney, don't like his client, or you've decided who should win. Once again, remember—it's not about you, it's about the evidence.

Speak from Your Knowledge: But Don't Try to Use Your Knowledge to Beat the Questioner

Attorneys try to emphasize certain points. They may do this by asking questions that appear stupid. In fact, the questions may really be stupid as the attorney has no idea (and does not need to have any idea) of the details of your expertise or knowledge. Again, what the attorney is trying to do is emphasize certain points to the jury—not to prove that he is as smart as or as knowledgeable as you in your subject. Thus, speak from your knowledge, but don't try to use your knowledge to beat the questioner:

Q: I believe, in your autopsy report, you say that there are no other injuries any other place on the scalp, correct?

A: She has just the one tear.

Q: Okay. That is the one laceration?

A: The one laceration.

Q: That means there are no other bruises or cuts, or any other tears, at least on the scalp, correct?

A: Right. When I did the inside part, there was some bruising on what we call the galea or the scalp underneath, there's bruising underneath where the tear was and extended underneath it and around the right and left front.

Q: Well, Doctor, we will get to that. The answer to my question is, yes, there was nothing else on the scalp?

A: You asked me if there were any bruises. That is a bruise in the scalp.

Q: I will try to be more careful. I said a bruise on the exterior portion of the scalp?

A: No, there were no other bruises on the exterior.

Again, the witness went to great efforts to lecture the attorney. The bottom line though was that it emphasized the very point that the attorney wanted the jury to hear. A good attorney's affirmation does not come from proving that he is "right" on any given point. It comes from trying a case well so the jury gets the point. Good attorneys realize that jurors, as all of us, can have very limited attention spans. If the witness spends a lot of time giving a lecture to the attorney and correcting him, the witness may be doing exactly what the attorney wants. On the other hand, if the attorney really is just stupid, you do not need to lecture him to have the jury know it—as we attorneys know only too well, juries don't miss.

Don't Become an Advocate

This is the most important rule. Our system of justice provides for an adversarial process where two attorneys argue about almost everything. Thus, there is absolutely no reason for you to take on the job as well; you are not paid for it. (Of course, many of us, public defenders, do not feel like we are paid enough for that job, but that is a different issue.) In short, answer the questions and do not argue. This is often easier said than done especially in a case involving something like child abuse. However, the point is that you are better evidence if you are objective and not an advocate.

The following comes from a homicide case I tried some years ago. The forensic pathologist had developed an opinion as to the cause of death. I had a different theory. Normally, a juror will believe a trained forensic pathologist over a lawyer trying to defend a specific client about cause of death. This specific doctor, however, violated all of the aforementioned rules by being defensive, fudging, and trying to use knowledge as a weapon. The doctor clearly became an advocate for the prosecution and greatly diminished her effectiveness as a witness:

Q: When a person is throttled, Doctor, they would pass out before they would die, correct?

A: That's the usual progression, yes.

Q: So, they would lose consciousness before they would die?

A: I assume your definition of death is stoppage of heartbeat?

Q: My definition of death is death.

A: Well, there are all different definitions of death. It can be loss of awareness.

Q: Doctor, I don't care.

A: Well…

Q: Loss of heartbeat?

A: Well, you have to define "loss of heartbeat." Her heart would continue to beat after the pressure is applied to the neck, yes.

Q: And a person who passed out from throttling, if that throttling stopped, they would not necessarily die, correct?

A: That's possible, yes.

Q: So a person can be choked, and when the choking stops, the person would not die?

A: It's possible.

Q: And it's possible that they would actually, if they did die, die of something else, that is possible?

A: It's possible.

Q: How long would you have to continue choking somebody after they pass out before they would die?

A: That's hard for me to know. I can't answer that question. I have read that loss of consciousness occurs 2 to 3 minutes and we know that people that have, that arrest without heartbeat, they can die somewhere in the area of 5, longer than 5 minutes, they are dead.

Q: So that means that a person would have to continue, in the normal case, choking for 5 minutes after the person lost consciousness before the person would die?

A: It's possible.

Q: Your report did not speak to bleeding to death, correct?

A: There's a difference between the mechanism of death and the cause of death. My job is to certify the cause of death. Exsanguination or bleeding to death is a mechanism.

Q: Your report did not speak to the issue of bleeding to death, correct?

A: I did not say that. No, I did not say she bled to death.

Q: Your report had no findings on that issue at all?

A: That's not true.

Q: You made no findings as to the amount of blood in her body, correct?

A: That's correct, I did not.

Q: You cannot eliminate the possibility that she died of bleeding to death?

A: I would like to clarify this bleeding to death, if I could.

Q: Doctor, you will have the opportunity. Please answer my question.

A: Will you restate it then, please.

Q: You cannot eliminate the possibility that she died to death—died of bleeding to death?

A: It's possible.

Mr. McWhirter: Thank you.

As you can see, the doctor agreed that it was "possible" that the defense's theory as to cause of death could have happened. If the doctor would have just answered that directly, at the very start, it would have gone nowhere. On redirect examination, the doctor would have said, "Yes, it's possible," but that "possible" would fit into the category of nearly anything being "possible"—like the victim dying from a meteorite. By breaking the rules through defensiveness, fudging, using knowledge as a weapon, and becoming an advocate, it made her final concession, "it's possible," into something much more. Her "it's possible" became a reason to doubt. Given that the standard in a criminal case is proof beyond a reason to doubt, the attorney got far more out of her testimony than if she simply would have answered the question at the start.

Conclusion

Remember, it is not about you. It is about the evidence that you present. Frankly, the best lawyers and judges understand the same thing. It is not about us but a system of criminal procedure that we serve. Indeed, our system can be compared to what Winston Churchill had to say about democracy: "Democracy is the worst form of government conceived of by mankind—with the exception of all the rest."

Injustices occur, but when we all do our job in the system, the most justice results.

Bibliography

Davis, G. 2004. *Pathology and Law: A Practical Guide for the Pathologist.* New York: Springer.

Injury
Recognition

II

Blunt and Sharp Force Injuries

8

OBJECTIVES

Upon completion of this chapter and corresponding reference material, the reader will be able to

- Differentiate between findings of blunt and sharp force injury during examination
- Describe two types of sharp force injury
- Differentiate between antemortem and postmortem injuries
- Describe three types of blunt force injuries and describe differences between hesitation marks and defense-type injuries
- Define patterned injuries and give three examples

Introduction

Wounds to the body can be intentional or accidental. Intentional wounds can be inflicted by self or others. Wounds can also be classified by the type of trauma caused:

- Wounds due to blunt trauma
- Wounds caused by sharp or pointed objects

The significance of such wounds relates to the angle, force, and instrument used to cause the wound and to the appearance of the tissue surrounding the wound. The importance of a precise wound classification is twofold—it allows clarity of communication among forensic investigators and aids in reconstruction of events causing injury.

Blunt Force Injuries

Blunt force injuries are caused by forceful contact (blunt impact) from a broad or dull-surfaced area or object that disrupts the integrity of tissues. In general, the more the force of the impact is spread over a larger body surface, the less severe is the injury. This is because the force of the blow is dissipated over a wider area. Falls, blows from nonsharp instruments, and motor vehicle accidents are often associated with this kind of injury. Blunt force injuries usually occur during accidents or homicides but may also occur with suicides involving falls from great heights.

There are three basic categories of blunt force injury:

1. Abrasions
2. Contusions
3. Lacerations

These may appear alone or in combination such as laceration or tearing of the tissue with one or more abraded margins. Fractures may also result from blunt forces.

Abrasions

Abrasions are superficial injuries that involve only the outer layers of skin or mucosal surfaces (Figure 8.1). They are the traumatic removal of skin layers by forces tangential to the skin surface. The direction of the abrasion may be shown by parallel lines. "Flaps" of skin may be torn from intact tissue when the force is sufficient or the surface of the impact is not smooth. Synonyms frequently used are scratches, scrapes, and friction marks. Scratches are linear abrasions whereas grazes describe wider abrasions. Impact abrasions are also called impressions, patterned abrasions, or imprints. Friction abrasions or brush burns are due to frictional forces. With an abrasion, there is minimal bleeding, rarely scar formation with healing, or disability. Thus, from a medical point of view, abrasions have little, if any, significance.

However, in medicolegal investigations, abrasions are never too small or insignificant. Abrasions may be the only indication of foul play or severe internal injury. For example, abrasions on the abdomen may indicate ruptured visceral organs (such as the liver or pancreas), whereas crescent abrasions on the neck may indicate fingernail marks from manual strangulation. Fingernail marks on the inner aspects of the thighs (particularly on a female) may indicate forcible rape. Abrasions on the nose or mouth of an infant or incapacitated adult direct the examiner to look for other signs of smothering (asphyxiation). Drying effects along the edges of the scrape provide some indication as to when the injury occurred. In addition, abrasions may indicate the direction in which force was applied, especially if flaps of rolled-up epidermis are attached to the terminal end of the wound. These indicate the direction in which scraping occurred. Subtypes and patterns further define and describe

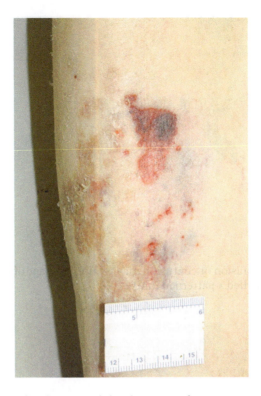

Figure 8.1 A superficial scrape of the skin is an abrasion.

abrasions. The abrasion may reflect a "patterned-type injury" (Figure 8.2) of the instrument used to inflict the wound.

Contusions

Contusions (or bruises) are deep injuries of soft tissue with tearing and rupture of capillaries and hemorrhage beneath an intact epithelium (Figure 8.3). Both the skin and internal organs are subject to contusions. Contusions leave the skin intact, and the object that causes the contusion may leave a patterned shape on the affected skin. Unlike abrasions, contusions do not necessarily lie at the point of impact. A delay often exists between the time of injury and appearance of bruises, and contusions may remain deep-seated without an overlying external bruise. The effects of gravity exaggerate the bruising process and, postmortem, can be mimicked by lividity. The extent and severity of contusions are also influenced by the vascularity, location, and structure of the tissues bruised. Some individuals such as the elderly, alcoholics, or those with blood disorders may be "easy bruisers." "Easy bruising" can mislead the investigator regarding the force and extent of the injury. If bruising

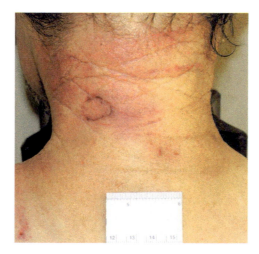

Figure 8.2 An abrasion or contusion may retain the shape of the object that created the injury, called a patterned injury.

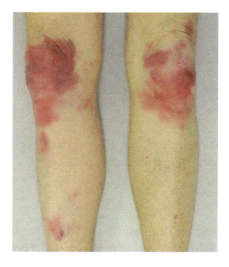

Figure 8.3 Contusions, or bruises, may be of various colors and shapes.

is present on the neck, careful layer by layer dissection and examination of underlying soft tissues of the neck provide evidence of potential force with manual strangulation. Contusions may be "dated" microscopically with the use of an iron stain—positive iron staining indicates a bruise over 3 days in age. Contusions and/or abrasions of the scapulae or spinous processes may indicate firm pressure on the body against the ground or a similar resistant surface. Such an injury may be caused by an assailant kneeling on the subject. Contusions to the thighs, particularly the inner aspects and genitalia, often result from forcible rape.

Lacerations

Lacerations are tearing of the skin and underlying tissue and indicate blunt force injury (Figure 8.4). Features of lacerations include abraded edges; "undercutting" in the direction of the force; and "tissue bridging" of underlying connective tissue fibers, blood vessels, and nerves connecting the sides of the tear. Blunt trauma injury over bony prominences is particularly subject to splitting or laceration. There may also be dirt or trace evidence inside the wound. The laceration may show a distinct pattern of the blunt object used.

Combined injuries are frequent findings and can occur both externally and internally. It is important to identify and describe each injury impact site in sufficient detail to determine if the injury is a combined type. Old accidental injuries and recent traumatic injuries can occur on the same site. Internal findings may not be evident until discovered by medical treatment or by the ME/coroner. These are often more extensive than is evident on external examination.

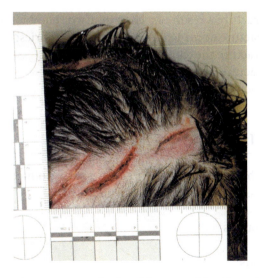

Figure 8.4 Lacerations are tears in the skin caused by blunt forces. The edges are often irregular and contain bridging of the tissue.

Antemortem vs. Postmortem Injury

Initial examination of the body requires differentiation between injuries caused to the victim before death and those that occur postmortem. Abrasions that occur postmortem generally have a tan, brown, dried parchment-like appearance with no vital tissue reactions noted. Antemortem bruises change in color and prominence with time; consequently, recent contusions are usually red or purple and gradually change to blue, green, brown, yellow before fading completely. However, this sequence may vary depending on the location of the bruises, vascularity, etc., and cannot be dated with exact precision. Postmortem bruises are usually small or disproportionate to the degree of force used. Application of considerable force is required to cause a postmortem bruise and must occur near the time of death while the blood is still in fluid state. Postmortem bruises and other deep bruises can be slow to appear postmortem due to gravity and diffusion of blood. Incisions of bruised areas provide evidence of hemorrhages.

Fractures

Fractures are breaks in bone. Classification of fractures in forensics is the same as in medical practice. Considerations of investigation into fractures include the following:

- Was the fracture a result of a chop injury or blunt force trauma?
- Did the fracture occur before or after other injuries?
- Was the fracture the cause of other trauma?
- Did the fracture occur before or after death?
- Are the fractures of different ages?

Sharp Force Injuries

Wounds from sharp forces can be made by sharp, pointed, or edged instruments or objects. Sharp force injuries include

- Incised wounds
- Slashes
- Stab wounds
- Cuts
- Chop wounds
- Surgical wounds
- Puncture wounds

Sharp force injuries include defense-type injuries that are seen on the extensor (outside) surfaces of the arms or legs or palms of the hands where the victim attempted to ward off an assailant during a homicide. Hesitation marks are self-inflicted incised wounds on the wrist or neck during attempted suicide.

Characteristic weapons demonstrable from sharp force injuries include single-edged or double-edged knives such as kitchen, craft, woodworking, hunting, and sport knives. A wound created by a pair of opened scissors indicates a patterned injury of paired puncture wounds. Injuries to cartilage and bone can also occur from sharp, pointed, or edged instruments.

Incised Wounds

Incised wounds are caused by sharp edges drawn across the body surface producing cuts that are longer than they are deep (Figure 8.5). In an incision, edges are not abraded or undermined, there is no bridging, and the edges can be realigned easily. Incised wounds usually begin rather superficially, then get deeper, and end superficially. The wound margins may be straight or jagged depending on the weapon, nature of the target tissue, and amount of force applied.

Therapeutic incised wounds are surgical incisions created by a scalpel whereas accidental wounds are knife, razor, or equipment injuries. The majority of incised wounds seen at autopsy are defensive wounds. Cuts or slashes on the lower extremities of a female suggest sexual assault. On the other hand, incised wounds on the upper extremities—especially the forearms and hands—are probably sustained when the victim raises his or her arms or grabs at the weapon in an effort to ward off the assailant's attack. These types of incised wounds may result in severed ligaments or cut bone. Remember this during investigation of skeletal remains as cuts may be seen on the bones and offer a clue as to cause of death even in a skeletonized body.

Stab Wounds

Characteristically, stab wounds are deeper than they are wide or long (Figure 8.6). As with cuts, tissue "bridges" and undermining are absent. Margins of stab wounds are usually devoid of abrasions or bruises.

Stab wounds are evident on antemortem and postmortem bodies. Entry sites documented at the scene of death may be obscured by clothing or other covers. Consequently, medical examination may not verify prior injury reports. Bruises adjacent to stab wounds may be produced by the impact of a closed fist inflicting the wound.

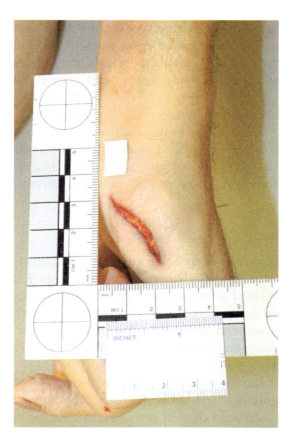

Figure 8.5 An incision is a sharp wound without tissue bridging. Incisions are longer than they are deep.

Stab wounds are rarely inflicted without some cutting that occurs during the thrust and withdrawal of the weapon. Therefore, the length of the external wound is often longer than the width of the blade. Abrasion or bruising of the edges of a stab wound suggest that the blade was completely inserted and the skin surface was in contact with the weapon handle; this is called a hilt mark.

Additional observations during examination include the following:

- Stab wounds of bone, cartilage, and pericardium tend to reflect the dimensions of the inflicting instrument and permit identification of the weapon more precisely than soft tissue wounds.
- Stab wounds may represent the cross section of a weapon—for example, a single-edged knife often produces a stab wound with one sharp extremity and one blunt-edged or squared-off extremity.
- A stab wound that severs the cleavage line of Langer will gape open and distort the wound—for example, a single-edged knife wound may appear as a double-edged knife wound.

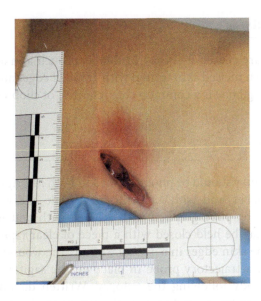

Figure 8.6 A stab wound is a sharp force injury that is deeper than it is long.

- Depth of a stab wound does not depend on length of the blade alone. Due to compression of the body, depth of a knife wound frequently exceeds length of the blade (frequently seen in stab wounds of the abdomen).
- Thickness of the blade can be rather accurately estimated by reapproximating and realigning the wound edges to reconstruct the wound and then measuring the blunt edge width.
- Stab wounds produced by a cylindrical instrument with a pointed end—such as ice picks, screwdrivers, or awls—may resemble small-caliber bullet wounds with an abraded edge.
- A bullet wound exiting the skin in a slit-like pattern may resemble a stab wound.
- Direction and depth of a stab wound can only be determined by examination of the wound track. Notation regarding the trajectory of the wound should indicate the course of the wound—for example, front to back, left to right, or downward.
- Wrinkle wounds are most commonly found in elderly or obese victims. These are inflicted in folded skin, and the defects show multiple wounds arranged linearly with skip areas of uninvolved skin.
- Penetration wounds enter organs or soft tissues.
- Perforation wounds enter and exit organs or soft tissues.
- Serrated knives may also show a patterned abrasion mark if scraped on the skin surface.

Chop Wounds

Chop wounds are caused by heavy instruments such as axes, machetes, or meat cleavers. An incised skin wound with abraded edges and a deep groove in the underlying bone is a common characteristic of chop wounds.

Photography

A blunt force injury should be photographed in both its original and cleaned states, with a label, and with and without a scale and color chart. Stab wounds should be photographed with a label, with and without a scale. Stab wounds may be held closed with a piece of clear tape if necessary to pull together the skin edges in a gaping wound. The wound should be photographed with a trajectory probe in place on the sagittal and horizontal planes of the body following the autopsy. Written documentation must include location of the wound measured from up the heels or gluteal folds, size, shape, color, characteristics, course, trajectory, and correlation to defects in the clothing.

Bibliography

Dolinak, D, Matshes, E, and Lew, E. 2006. *Forensic Pathology: Principles and Practice*. Burlington, MA: Elsevier.

Spitz, W and Fischer, R. 1993. *Medicolegal Investigation of Death: Guidelines for the Application of Pathology to Crime Investigation*. Springfield, IL: Charles C. Thomas Press.

Forensic Radiology

9

OBJECTIVES

Upon completion of this chapter and corresponding reference material, the reader will be able to

- List five applications for forensic radiology to assist the forensic pathologist prior to the autopsy
- Describe the process of comparing antemortem to postmortem x-rays
- Discuss the uses for forensic radiology in blunt and sharp force injury and gunshot wound cases
- Describe how forensic radiology can assist in identifying injuries in child abuse and elder abuse cases
- Identify the role of forensic radiology in a mass fatality incident

Introduction

Forensic radiology is essential to the practice of forensic pathology and is used as a diagnostic tool to accompany the forensic autopsy to recognize fractures, locate projectiles and natural disease. The purpose of the forensic autopsy is to accomplish one or more of the following objectives:

1. To determine the cause of death
2. To describe and interpret any injuries
3. To retrieve trace evidence that may help in the investigation
4. To exclude or discover natural disease that may be relevant
5. To determine the time of death
6. To identify the decedent, when necessary

In several of the objectives mentioned earlier, radiography is helpful or even essential.

Historically, radiology was provided on plain film by contracting hospital radiology services, whereas in today's modern medical examiner's offices, the autopsy suite contains in-house digital radiology equipment for plain film and dental x-rays performed by trained forensic technician staff. Recently, larger jurisdictions also provide in-house CT and MRI services. Forensic radiology is used for identification in cases where the decedent cannot be visually identified due to facial trauma, decompositional changes, skeletal remains, fire, or in mass fatalities. Postmortem x-ray comparison can match available antemortem x-rays to postmortem autopsy x-rays to make a positive identification of an unidentified body. Other applications for forensic radiology include blunt trauma, stab wounds, gunshot wounds (GSW), child abuse, elder abuse, airplane crashes, and explosions. X-ray studies of the decedent are frequently necessary to determine the cause, manner, and mechanism of death.

Identification

Identification is possibly the most important forensic use of radiography. Scientific positive identification is needed for criminal cases, visually unidentified bodies, and to identify victims of a mass disaster, such as an airplane crash. General skeletal classification can be made into species, sex, age, race, and stature. Much of this is determined anatomically and dentally, but age determination is especially aided by radiology. In fetuses, infants, and young adults, age can be determined with great accuracy from knowledge of the appearance of ossification centers and epiphyseal fusion, as well as the development of two sets of dentition. Later in life, aging is more difficult, but work on tooth root rarefaction and remodeling for cancellous bone in the humerus, ribs, and pelvis has proven useful. Specific positive identification is made possible through comparison of a variety of anatomical and artifactual structures by a study of antemortem and postmortem films. Rib patterns, teeth, frontal sinuses, skull parameters, injury, surgical metal appliances, and a range of congenital and acquired abnormalities are of great value but depend upon a short list of potential subjects and also on the availability of antemortem films, usually from clinical medical records.

One means of positive identification is through dental x-ray comparison based upon teeth characteristics, root structure, and restorations. Standard x-ray comparison can also match characteristic features, such as frontal sinus detail, as no two people, not even identical twins, have the same sinus configuration. As the sinuses are usually preserved, even in fire deaths and plane crashes, skull films can prove an absolute identification. X-ray comparison of spinal osteophytes or old healed fractures may also show positive identification. X-rays are helpful for comparison of surgical intervention, such as metal suture similarities, metal prosthesis, and devices, such as hip replacement, metal rods, or pacemakers. Once these metal implants are identified on x-ray, they may be removed at autopsy to obtain the specific identification as to make model and serial numbers to identify the individual. Pacemakers and defibrillators can further be analyzed by the company for final tracings of heart activity and may be able to indicate the exact date and time of death.

Blunt Trauma

Forensic radiology can identify the types and numbers of fractures including those not seen at autopsy including long bones and facial fractures from falls, motor vehicle accidents, and assaults. X-rays can show unique fracture characteristics and distinguish fractures of different ages of injury.

Stab Wounds

Obviously, plain film x-rays cannot show soft tissue injury from a stab wound that may be seen with CT or MRI. However, with a penetrating stab wound injury, the object depth and location can be seen on x-ray prior to autopsy if the knife tip was broken and retained in the body. In that case, it is important from safety reasons to identify the location of the sharp object prior to autopsy and to safely remove it for evidence preservation.

Gunshot Wounds

In a GSW case, it is essential to know where the projectiles are located and to help to identify the type of projectile and evaluate the track of the projectile and fragments. In wounds from rifled weapons, such as revolvers or rifles, the jacket and core or jacketed bullet must be recovered without damage for evaluation by the firearms examiner to match the rifling marks with a test bullet fired from the suspect gun.

All GSW homicide cases must be x-rayed prior to autopsy through the sealed body bag to include the head, chest, and abdomen to identify the presence or absence of projectiles. After the body is undressed and cleaned, more x-rays may be needed including anterior/posterior (A/P) and lateral views and x-rays of the extremities, if GSWs are seen on the external body examination. Projectiles can take extraordinary paths inside the body and may be far away from the entrance wound. X-rays are helpful in identifying the location of the projectile that may be in soft tissue and difficult to locate at autopsy alone for removal. GSW suicides may only need x-rays of the area shot for projectile removal.

Child Abuse

Forensic radiology is important prior to autopsy in cases of sudden unexpected infant death and in suspected or known cases of nonaccidental trauma to ensure that a whole-body skeletal survey is obtained before the autopsy. Because of the disturbance of the thoracic cavity and skull during autopsy, x-ray studies must be completed before the autopsy procedure starts to rule out autopsy artifact from actual injury. Ideally, infant and child radiographs should include a suspected nonaccidental trauma series of x-rays using highly sensitive film and read by a pediatric radiologist to rule out any injury or fractures. Other modalities, such a CT or MRI, are helpful to identify abusive head injuries and timing of injuries, such as fractures or subdural or epidural hemorrhages of different ages.

Head and neck injuries in infants and children are the most common types of fatal child abuse injuries including skull fractures, vertebral fractures, cerebral edema, and subdural, epidural and subarachnoid hemorrhages. CT and MRI findings are helpful in the evaluation of head injury, especially in dating hemorrhages and contusions.

Other common inflicted injuries include multiple rib fractures, long bone fractures, metaphyseal (corner) fractures at the elbow, knee, and ankle joints. Corner fractures may be difficult to recognize if they are not a complete fracture and very small or only ragged appearing on the surface of the periosteum. One of the main characteristics of child abuse is multiple bony injury, often over a period of time, so that both recent fractures and healing lesions with callus may be seen. Previous films must be used to assess old and new fractures. Shearing of the periosteum with subperiosteal calcification on long bones and chipping of the metaphyses around knees and elbows is a characteristic finding. In small babies, multiple fractures of the ribs in the paravertebral gutter due to lateral squeezing by adult hands may leave rows of callus visible radiographically as "strings of pearls." All fractures need to be located, bones removed and decalcified, and injuries dated histologically.

Elder Abuse

Similar to child abuse, fractures are seen in elder abuse and may include injuries of different ages including rib fractures and long bone fractures.

Explosions and Airplane Crashes

Radiology plays an important role in explosions and airplane crashes for victim identification and to recognize the extent of injury. In addition, x-rays help to identify any metal parts of the airplane or explosive device that may be imbedded in the body. These objects are removed by the forensic pathologist, documented, photographed, and released as evidence to the investigating agency of the incident.

Bibliography

Thali, MJ, Viner, MD, and Brogdon, BG. 2010. *Brogdon's Forensic Radiology*, 2nd ed. Boca Raton, FL: CRC Press.

Craniocerebral Injury 10

OBJECTIVES

Upon completion of this chapter and corresponding reference material, the reader will be able to

- Identify the physical findings, mechanisms, and complications involved in craniocerebral injuries
- Describe the characteristics of subdural, subscalpular, subgaleal, epidural, and subarachnoid hemorrhages
- Distinguish by history and examination the different types of craniocerebral injuries
- Discuss the pathological findings related to craniocerebral injuries
- Describe characteristic findings of diffuse axonal injuries, cortical contusions, and cerebral edema

Introduction

Traumatic forces applied to the head can result in injuries to the skull, fractures of the bony vault and injuries to the brain itself. Homicide or accidental circumstances are more common with head injuries as a manner of death than suicide. However, an intentional fall from great height, an intentional motor vehicle accident, or a self-inflicted gunshot wound may result in craniocerebral injuries with a suicidal manner of death. Examination of the victim is complex because of the numerous body systems enclosed in a relatively small space—skeletal, circulatory, and nervous systems.

External Head Injuries

Abrasions, lacerations, and contusions are relatively common external head injuries. However, these blunt force injuries of the head are often associated with fatal internal craniocerebral injuries.

95

Hemorrhage and infection are the primary complications that occur with external injuries. As the face and scalp are quite vascular with blood vessels close to the surface of the skin, they are easily injured. The potential for exsanguination exists if superficial bleeding is not controlled. Infection as a result of exposure to bacteria can bridge the communication between extracranial and intracranial veins. Areas at risk are the ophthalmic and diploic veins. Suppurative phlebitis can progress to leptomeningitis and cavernous sinus thrombosis; both conditions can be fatal.

Internal Head Injuries

Head injuries can involve one or more than one layer of the scalp, skull, and/or brain including the *subscalpular, subgaleal, epidural, subdural,* and *subarachnoid* layers.

Subscalpular/Subgaleal Hemorrhage

Subscalpular hemorrhage is bruising underneath the scalp seen at autopsy when the scalp is reflected away from the skull. *Subgaleal hemorrhage* is bleeding of the *periosteum* (covering over the outer surface of the skull) (Figure 10.1).

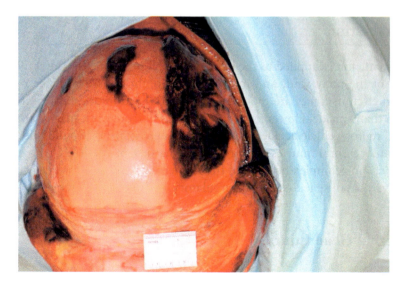

Figure 10.1 Bleeding on the undersurface of the scalp is subscalpular hemorrhage. Bleeding on the surface of the skull is subgaleal hemorrhage.

Skull Fractures

A *skull fracture* indicates that there was sufficient force to break bone. However, the complications of a skull fracture can be deadly.

Significant complications include laceration of the meningeal artery resulting in an epidural hemorrhage, damage to the nerves or arteries that transverse the base of the skull, laceration of the brain, contusion of the brain, and creation of a cerebral-environmental fistula.

Generally, eight types of fractures can be described:

- Open vs. closed
- Complete vs. incomplete
- Linear vs. complex (comminuted)
- Depressed vs. nondepressed

Local deformation of the skull tends to indicate a depressed, comminuted fracture at the site of impact. Fracture lines extend radially from a central impact area and circularly at the periphery of an impact site. Fatal skull fractures are associated with complex fractures and underlying cerebral injury as seen with motor vehicle accidents and child abuse (see Chapters 11 and 23).

General deformation is usually the result of a linear fracture. However, fractures may occur in areas distant from the impact site. Due to the architecture of the skull, broad-based impact forces tend to be diverted to the middle cranial fossae of the central basilar skull. This can be seen externally with a *hinge-type fracture* by observing *Battle's sign* (bruising behind the ears) (Figure 10.2). *Orbital plate fractures* over the eyes also show general deformation and cause *periorbital bruising* (Figure 10.3). *Ring-type fractures* surrounding the *foramen magnum* (opening to the spinal cord) have both a downward force at the vertex and an upward force via the spinal column. This type of basilar fracture is observed in fatalities involving subjects that jump from great heights.

Intracranial Extracerebral Hemorrhage

Intracranial extracerebral hemorrhage often requires differentiation between an *epidural* and a *subdural bleed*, which may be fresh hemorrhage or an older organizing hematoma. *Epidural hemorrhage* originates in the space between the skull and dura (Figure 10.4). This is an arterial bleed that is almost always due to disruption of a meningeal artery secondary to a skull fracture. The hemorrhage presses the dura against the brain. This causes a linear or

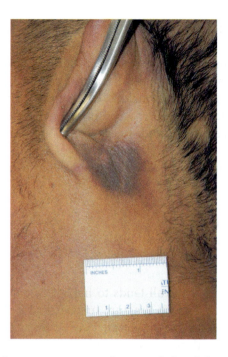

Figure 10.2 A battle sign appears as a bruising behind the ear and is caused by fractures of the skull base.

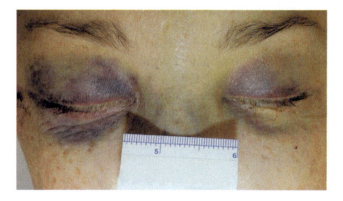

Figure 10.3 A bruised or "black eye" appearance due to fractures of the skull base is commonly referred to as "raccoon eyes."

dish-like flattening and nonuniform displacement of the brain. An epidural hemorrhage is usually fatal unless evacuated.

Subdural hemorrhage is a venous hemorrhage between the dura and leptomeninges (Figure 10.5). Subdural hemorrhage is almost always associated with trauma. Subdural hemorrhage may be associated with skull

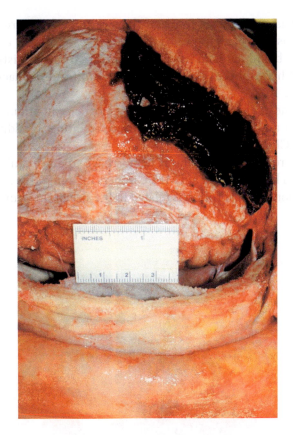

Figure 10.4 An epidural hemorrhage is shown on top of the left parietal dura, inside the skull.

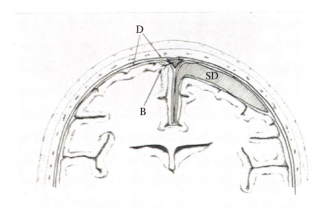

Figure 10.5 A subdural (SD) hemorrhage is located between the brain (B) surface and the dura (D) mater.

fracture but is not a direct result of the fracture. The source of subdural hemorrhage is torn bridging veins or cortical vessels. In an acute subdural hemorrhage, blood tends to have a widespread, uniform distribution over the cerebral hemisphere. There is relatively uniform displacement of the brain (Figure 10.6).

Abusive head injury shows subdural hemorrhage in infants who are violently shaken and may strike a firm surface resulting in additional impact injuries (see Chapter 23).

The progression of a subdural hemorrhage to an organizing subdural hematoma on histology will aid MEs/coroners in "aging" the injury. The rate of organization and resorption is related to the size of the hematoma.

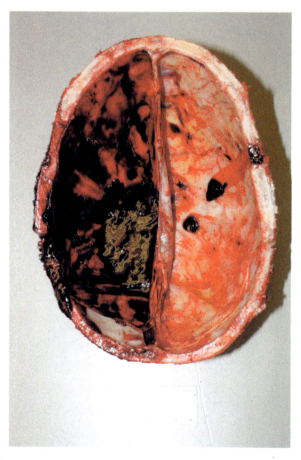

Figure 10.6 Another view of a subdural hemorrhage located between the brain surface and the dura mater.

Histologic changes seen in subdural hematoma over time are the following:

Days 1–4
  Clotting of blood.
  No adherence to the dura.
Day 5
  Multifocal adherence to the dura.
Weeks 1–2
  Degeneration (brown discoloration). Inner membrane starts to form.
  Hemosiderin is obvious. Hematoidin is negative.
Weeks 2–4
  Outer membrane starts to form.
  Hematoma looks like dirty motor oil, grossly. Appearance of
    hematoidin.
  Foci of fresh hemorrhage common.
Months 1–3
  Inner and outer membranes well formed.
Months 3–6
  Fusion of inner and outer membranes. Maturation of collagen.

Chronic subdural hematoma shows new hemorrhage that occurs after encapsulation by membranes. A reexpanding subdural hematoma is similar to an epidural hematoma in that pressure is applied across a membrane in a non-uniform manner.

Subarachnoid Hemorrhage

A *subarachnoid hemorrhage* is a generalized diffuse arterial hemorrhage lying underneath the arachnoid covering (meninges) of the brain. It is caused spontaneously from a ruptured *berry aneurysm* of the basilar arteries or traumatically from a tear of the vertebral arteries associated with displacement of the cervical vertebrae from a blunt force impact to the face, head, or neck.
    Table 10.1 compares the types of hematomas.

Table 10.1 Hematoma Comparisons

	Epidural	Subdural	Subarachnoid
Skull fracture	Yes	Sometimes	Sometimes
Traumatic origin	Almost always	Almost always	Rarely/may be spontaneous
Source	Large arteries	Bridging veins, small arteries	Vertebral or basilar arteries
Development	Rapid (hours)	Slow (days)	Rapid (hours)
Distribution	Circumscribed	Hemispheric	Diffuse

Brain Trauma

Concussions, contusions, lacerations, penetrating injuries, crushing injuries, and *axonal injuries* are associated with head injury and may result in *brain trauma.*

Concussions result in an instantaneous loss of consciousness of variable duration and show no evidence of structural damage to the brain.

Contusions result in rupture of small cortical vessels that causes hemorrhagic necrosis of the brain cortex. Typically, a contusion involves the crests of gyri of the brain. Sometimes contusions may be associated with subarachnoid hemorrhage. Contusions can be independent or dependent relative to motion status of the head. Independent contusions include *fracture contusions* (associated with skull fractures), *herniation contusions* (associated with cerebral edema or brain swelling), or *gliding contusions* (associated with movement of the brain). *Coup contusions* (where the fixed head is struck by a moving object) results in cortical contusions subjacent to the impact site. Conversely, *contrecoup contusions* are caused when a moving head impacts an unyielding or fixed surface resulting in cortical contusions on the side of the brain opposite the impact site. Typically, *contrecoup gliding contusions* involve frontal and temporal lobes. Finally, *intermediate contusions* occur in locations intermediate to coup and contrecoup contusions at the *corpus callosum* (cerebral bridge connecting the right and left cerebral hemispheres), deep cerebral structures, or brainstem. Typically, these occur when the moving head impacts at vertex.

Lacerations of the brain show as gross tears of the brain tissue and are usually associated with fractures or deceleration injuries seen with motor vehicle accidents. Subarachnoid hemorrhage frequently results. Penetrating brain injuries from bullets, knives, axes, shrapnel, or bone also tear brain tissues and may cause complications including hemorrhage and infection. A crushing injury results in extensive fractures and lacerations while contusions are minimal or absent when the head is compressed against an unyielding surface.

Diffuse axonal injury shows widespread shearing of axons caused by excessive force, occasionally from deceleration injuries. The victim is unconscious from the moment of injury and remains permanently in an unconscious, vegetative, or severely disabled state. Axonal injuries are commonly associated with hemorrhagic lesions in the corpus callosum, brainstem, or parasagittal white matter.

Secondary brain lesions result from cerebral edema (brain swelling) causing herniation or hypoxia. Herniation occurs transtentorial either at the brainstem (central) or uncus (lateral). Cerebellar tonsillar and subfalcial (cingulate gyrus) herniation also occur. Brain death occurs when the brain receives inadequate blood supply or oxygen due to compression of the cerebral vessels due to cerebral edema.

Brainstem or spinal cord injuries can be associated with fractures or dislocation of the vertebral column. Typically, contusions and lacerations are associated with cord injury and posttraumatic swelling, leading to secondary necrosis proceeding to death. Subluxation of the head from the first cervical vertebrae is referred to as an atlanto-occipital dislocation and may cause a laceration of the brainstem.

A complete autopsy including opening the head is required to assess for the presence or absence of injury. Careful examination of the skull and dissection of the brain are key to determining the cause and manner of death.

Bibliography

Troncoso, J, Rubio, A, and Fowler, D. 2010. *Essential Forensic Neuropathology.* Baltimore, MD: Lippincott Williams and Wilkins.

Motor Vehicle Accidents

11

Investigating Injury Patterns in Motor Vehicle Accidents

Forensic investigators may be asked to examine the external injuries of motor vehicle accident victims and formulate the cause and manner of death. This is very difficult to do accurately unless obvious severe craniocerebral injury is sustained. Subsequent autopsies frequently reveal unexpected injuries not diagnosed at the scene or in emergency rooms by external examination alone.

To help ensure accuracy of external examination under direction of the ME/coroner:

1. Remove all clothing from the victim.
2. Clean off blood.
3. Examine the body under good light.
4. Record all injuries.
5. Correlate injury to vehicle or ground impact sites to establish primary bumper strike vs. secondary impact site.

If there is insufficient injury to explain death, then an autopsy must be performed. Many forensic pathologists will autopsy all motor vehicle accident victims to photograph and document injuries as criminal or civil litigation may follow.

Motor Vehicle Injuries

Head Injuries

Head injuries are among the largest group of serious injuries and the most important site of fatal injuries sustained in motor vehicle accidents. The primary traumatic lesions include skull fractures; subdural, epidural, or subarachnoid hematomas; or axonal injuries (see Chapter 10). Skull fractures are caused by direct force or transmitted force. Signs of skull fractures include

- Blood/cerebral spinal fluid draining from the ears that indicates a fracture of the basilar skull (middle cranial fossa)
- Bilateral "black" or "raccoon" eyes indicating a fracture of the basilar skull (anterior cranial fossa)
- *Battle's sign* or bruising behind ear indicating a fracture of temporal bone or middle cranial fossa resulting in a skull fracture

The severity of injury varies from mild injury (linear fracture) to moderate to severe (depressed, basilar, or stellate skull fractures).

Subdural hematoma is defined as a hemorrhage between the dura and arachnoid membrane caused by torn bridging veins. Signs include a gradual increase in raised intracranial pressure, for example, bradycardia, gradual loss of consciousness, and fixed dilated pupils. Subdural hematoma is a common fatal injury associated with severe injury that occurs in 30% of serious head injuries. However, 50% occur without skull fractures.

Subarachnoid hemorrhage is defined as hemorrhage between the arachnoid membrane and pia (brain surface) caused by rupture of the vertebral or cerebral arteries associated with moderate to severe injury. Subarachnoid hemorrhage is a common injury with motor vehicle accidents and results in rapid loss of consciousness and cerebral edema.

Epidural hematoma is defined as hemorrhage between the skull and dura associated with extensive head injury, skull fractures, laceration of the middle meningeal artery, and rapid loss of consciousness.

Diffuse head injury or *craniocerebral injury* may include skull fractures, diffuse brain injury, diffuse vascular injury, and/or diffuse axonal injury. The brain is very vulnerable to rotational forces with movement within the cranial vault causing shearing forces within the white matter. The skull may be intact, and the brain often looks extremely normal. Clinically, the victim is unconscious at the scene and never regains consciousness.

Spinal and Brainstem Injuries

High spinal and brainstem injuries include fatal pontomidbrain or pontomedullary junction or high cervical spinal cord injuries (atlanto-occipital dislocation or high cervical fracture) caused by flexion injury and deceleration injuries. These injuries compromise vital respiratory function.

Midcervical fractures and associated spinal cord injuries are usually caused by flexion. Hypermobility of the neck is an unreliable method for diagnosis, especially if the victim is young or rigor is absent.

Thoracic spinal cord injuries are caused by flexion or compression injuries. The severity is mild to moderate. Unlike high cervical spinal cord or brainstem injury, compression of the cord at the thoracic level will not compromise vital respiratory functions.

Lumbar spinal cord injury severity is mild to moderate and is more common in vehicular pedestrian accidents.

Facial Injuries

Facial injuries include maxilla, mandible, and zygomatic bone fractures and cause external bruising of the anterior neck and face, intraoral hemorrhage, and/or avulsed teeth.

Chest Injuries

The chest is the second most important site of fatal injuries. Forty percent of motor vehicle accidents have severe chest injuries but often very little external bruising. Chest injuries include rib fractures resulting in cardiac, pulmonary aortic tears resulting in internal bleeding or pneumothoraces. Cardiac contusions/lacerations are usually fatal injuries and are caused by *deceleration injuries* (heart continues moving forward against fixed sternum) resulting in tearing at the thinnest parts—right ventricle, atria. Associated findings noted at autopsy include fractures of the sternum, bilateral rib fractures, and hemopericardium (blood in the heart sac), which may cause a *cardiac tamponade.*

Aortic laceration is a fatal deceleration injury associated with fractures of the sternum and/or rib fractures. The aorta is relatively fixed at junction with left ventricle and at junction of the arch with left subclavian artery. Lacerations generally occur above aortic valve or just distal to the left subclavian artery resulting in cardiac tamponade or bilateral hemothoraces. Fractures and displacement of the thoracic and lumbar vertebrae often result in laceration or transection of the aorta resulting in a hemothorax or hemoperitoneum.

Hemothorax is defined as blood in pleural cavity caused by aortic, intercostal artery, or pulmonary vessel lacerations.

Pneumothorax is defined as air in chest cavity caused by open chest wounds, torn bronchus, pulmonary laceration, or artificial ventilation. Signs include *subcutaneous emphysema* (bubbles of air under skin of chest, neck, and scrotum) and larynx shift from midline with tension pneumothorax. Severity is moderate to severe and rapid expansion of pneumothorax causes lungs to collapse resulting in a tension pneumothorax, which is rapidly fatal.

Unstable rib fractures (*flail chest*) is defined as multiple ribs broken in more than one place. This creates a segment that collapses on inspiration, interfering with normal respiration. Signs include bruising, palpable rib fractures, and generalized "whiteout" of lungs on chest x-ray. Severity depends on the extent of injury and is more severe if more than four ribs are broken or if ribs are broken in more than one place.

Lung contusions/lacerations are associated with rib fractures and cause hemo-/pneumothoraces. Aspiration of blood or gastric contents occurs with head injuries that bleed and causes a depressed level of consciousness. Aspiration of blood or gastric contents may be the terminal event.

Abdominal Injuries

Severe abdominal injuries may show little or no external bruising. Aspirating the abdominal cavity with a syringe and needle may reveal blood (hemoperitoneum) with abdominal injuries. Severe abdominal injuries often occur in motor vehicle fatalities and often include pelvic fractures and/or lacerations of the liver, spleen, kidneys/bladder, pancreas, or intestines.

Pelvic fractures include anterior/posterior fractures and separation of symphysis pubis and sacroiliac joints. Fractures through sacroiliac joints tear small iliac veins, cause hemorrhage into pelvic soft tissue, and may cause bruising around the groin and instability of the pelvic girdle.

Liver laceration is caused by direct impact and/or rib fractures from steering wheel injury associated with seat belts. Rupture is more likely with a fatty liver; for example, alcohol ingestion resulting in blood in abdominal cavity (hemoperitoneum). Severity depends on the extent of laceration and is moderate to lethal.

Splenic laceration is caused by direct impact and/or rib fractures and is more likely to rupture if enlarged, resulting in internal bleeding. Severity depends on the extent of laceration and is moderate to severe.

Renal/bladder lacerations cause blood in the urine and/or retroperitoneal hemorrhage.

Pancreatic contusion/laceration is caused by direct impact, commonly seen with lap seat belt use and is often associated with duodenal rupture. Lower abdominal seat belt abrasion may be present.

Hollow viscus rupture includes rupture of the colon, duodenum, or stomach and is caused by direct impact. Hollow viscus rupture results in air under the diaphragm seen on x-ray.

Injuries to the Extremities

Injuries to the extremities include femur fractures that may cause severe blood loss, fat emboli, deformity, and bruising.

Crush injuries cause acute blood loss and *rhabdomyolysis* (breakdown of muscle) causing acute renal failure and *disseminated intravascular coagulation* where intravascular microthrombi and bleeding occur concurrently.

Degloving injury (stripping of flap of skin or tissue by abrasions) involves the hands and feet caused by tire tread or road contact and may be worse if vehicle is braking at the time of impact.

Traumatic amputation is caused by direct force and may result in severe blood loss.

Superficial injuries include dicing incisions caused by tempered glass from side windows and may help "place" the occupant in the vehicle (driver vs. passenger) as the injuries occur on the side of the body closest to the side window (Figure 11.1). Parchment abrasions (brown or tan, dry abrasions) occur during the postmortem or perimortem period. Tire tread abrasions are seen in pedestrian or ejected occupant rollover accidents.

Figure 11.1 Cubes of tempered glass.

Motor Vehicles and Trucks

Head-On Collisions

Head-on collisions result in different injuries to the occupants based on position within the vehicle.

Driver

Driver injury occurs when the face hits the windshield and causes facial lacerations (less common now that laminated glass is used in windshields) and/or facial and frontal skull fractures. Injuries from the head striking the steering wheel or roof of the vehicle result in frontal skull fractures (usually bilateral), periorbital contusions (black eyes), subdural and subarachnoid hemorrhages, and frontal and temporal lobe contusions. Contact of chest and abdomen hitting the steering wheel or column results in cardiac contusion and laceration, aortic laceration, fractures at sternum and ribs, liver lacerations, and splenic lacerations. Knees impacting the dashboard cause fractures of femur, tibia, and pelvis and posterior dislocation of femur at the hips. Seat belts reduce but do not prevent these injuries, and air bags reduce injuries caused by steering wheel. (Seat belts must also be worn with air bags.)

Frequently, driver survives the crash and may be subject to charges for death of the passenger, especially if intoxicated. Investigation as to position in the vehicle includes

- Pattern and type of blood in the vehicle or side window
- Trace evidence, hair, and fibers in the vehicle
- Brake or accelerator pedal impression on sole of shoe of driver
- Seat belt abrasions on the body (Figure 11.2)
- Pattern and location of dicing injury

Front Passenger

The front passenger has twice the incidence of serious injuries in motor vehicle accidents. Injury pattern is similar to that of the driver but front passenger does not have steering wheel to hold onto to break forward movement and usually has less warning of the collision. Instead of the head, chest, and abdomen hitting the steering wheel, these body parts tend to hit the dashboard.

Rear Passenger

The rear passenger often sustains less severe injuries as the back of the front seat acts as passive restraint, but often no seat belt or only lap seat belt is worn. However, unrestrained passengers tend to hit their heads on the vehicle roof causing severe injury. Passengers wearing lap seat belts may show typical injuries such as lumbar spine fractures; pelvic fractures; and rupture of the duodenum, liver, and pancreas.

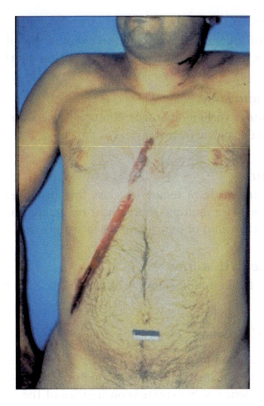

Figure 11.2 Seat belt marks on the chest may indicate the side of the car the decedent was on at the time of injury.

Side Impact Collisions

The modern car is designed for head-on impacts; they are very vulnerable to side impacts because doors and side panels are lighter. There is greater penetration into interior space. Seat belts and front compartment air bags may be less protective in side impacts than in head-on collisions. Side impacts may make front air bags unstable, and they may inflate up to 30 minutes after impact. Side air bags help reduce injuries from side impacts. Injuries tend to be lateralized by direct impact, and the victim may be forced against the door on the side opposite the impact.

Head Injuries

The brain is vulnerable to lateral rotation and may sustain injuries including skull fractures, subdural/subarachnoid hemorrhages, and diffuse closed head injury.

Chest Injuries

Chest injuries include unstable rib fractures on the side of impact, pulmonary contusions, and frequently result in deceleration injuries.

Abdominal Injuries

Abdominal injuries include liver lacerations, splenic lacerations, and often lateral and unstable pelvic fractures.

External Injuries

Side windows are made of tempered glass that produces cuboidal sharp fragments; these cause multiple short linear or squared-off superficial cuts known as *dicing incisions* or injuries on the face and arms.

Injuries to the Extremities

Fractures of the femur and tibia on the impact side are not uncommon.

Rear Impact Collisions

The seat provides good protection to the body in rear impacts provided the vehicle itself is not crushed. The introduction of headrests has significantly reduced the incidence of hyperextension injuries of the cervical spine and whiplash injuries.

Rollover Vehicle Accidents

A complex pattern of injuries occurs with rollover accidents as the victim may come into contact with many surfaces. Collapse of the roof may cause *traumatic asphyxia* due to compression of the chest or head and neck flexion, massive head injuries, fracture of the base of skull, compression fractures of the spine, and chest and abdominal injuries.

Ejection Accidents

Unrestrained, ejected passengers (especially in rollover and head-on impacts) often die of massive head injuries, crush injuries to the chest, unstable rib fractures, or flexion injuries of the spinal cord.

Motorcycle Injuries

Motorcycle helmets decrease death and serious injury by 65%. With head-on impact, the rider is thrown forward over the handle bars striking head and chest and flexing the cervical and thoracic spine. Injuries seen with motorcycle injuries include severe head, spine, chest, abdominal, and leg injuries.

Head Injury

Severe head injuries include

- Skull fractures
- Subdural/subarachnoid hemorrhages
- Contusions
- Laceration of pontomedullary junction of the brainstem

Spinal Injury

Spinal injuries include

- Atlanto-occipital dislocation
- Cervical and thoracic fractures
- Spinal fractures

Chest Injury

Chest injuries often involve

- Multiple rib fractures
- Aortic laceration and cardiac laceration (deceleration injuries)

Abdominal Injury

Abdominal injuries involve

- Liver laceration
- Splenic laceration
- Pelvic fractures

Leg Injury

Leg injuries include

- Extensive abrasion, burns, and bruising of thighs and legs
- Femoral fractures caused by the motorcycle hitting the legs

Pedestrians

Classic Impact Patterns

Primary impact is from the bumper strike as it hits the lower leg resulting in bruising of the calf and fractures of the tibia and fibula. The height of the fracture above the heel reflects the height of the bumper at impact but is often lower because the vehicle is braking at the time of impact. If one foot is raised at the time of impact, fracture may be lower on one leg than on the other. Occasionally, the primary impact site is not obvious without dissection.

Secondary impact results when the body strikes the pavement or hood of the vehicle. Paint transfer or patterned abrasions from impact of the headlight, hood, or windshield may occur. On the buttocks, impact produces an avulsion pocket, a cavity of lacerated adipose tissue, which forms a large deep bruise; often the skin is intact (Figure 11.3).

The head hits

- The windshield if the vehicle is traveling less than 30 miles per hour (mph)
- The top/back of car if the vehicle is traveling faster than 30 mph
- The road behind car if the vehicle is traveling faster than 60 mph

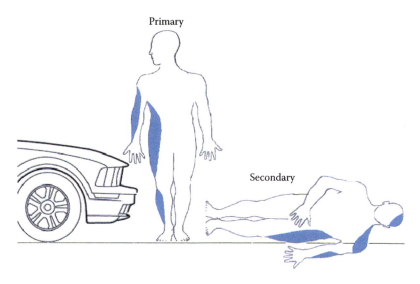

Figure 11.3 Depiction of primary versus secondary impact sites.

Pickup Trucks and Higher Vehicle Accidents

Pickup trucks and higher vehicles tend to push the body under the vehicle rather than throw the body over the vehicle, if primary impact is above the victim's center of gravity. Primary impact is often higher on the body than in an impact from a car. Often a van or truck has vertical or overhung grillwork that causes patterned abrasions.

Secondary impact may involve tire imprints (tire abrasions and "brush" abrasions) as the victim is often run over. "Crush" injuries of head, chest, and abdomen may result in deep lacerations of organs and/or depressed fracture of skull. Protruding objects under the vehicle may produce patterned injuries. Characteristically heavy grease stains may be observed on clothing or body.

Children

Because of their lower centers of gravity, children tend to go under—not over—the car. Children are often hit by pickup trucks and vans backing out of driveways because they cannot be seen.

Children run over by a vehicle sustain crush injuries of the head, chest, and abdomen. Tire mark abrasions are often seen as patterned injuries on the body.

Atypical Pedestrian Patterns

Low-velocity impacts show bruising visible subcutaneously, but no obvious primary impact site on calf is seen.

Unusual pedestrian victim positions include lying, kneeling, or squatting. Individuals lying on the road include intoxicated individuals, suicides, individuals hit by previous car, and already dead or dumped bodies. Kneeling/squatting position shows primary impact site on arms or trunk. These victims have low centers of gravity; therefore, they tend to be run over. Injuries include crush injuries to the head, chest, and abdomen; tire and brush abrasions; and femoral, humeral, and pelvic fractures.

Natural causes of death show no bruising or injury associated with typical motor vehicle pattern injuries. Typically, there is a low-velocity impact or single-vehicle accident with little damage to the vehicle. Autopsy will reveal natural disease to explain death; the manner of death is natural. If the individual has natural disease, but sustained injury from the accident and was alive at the time of the accident, the manner of death is accident (natural disease in a "hostile environment").

Vehicular Homicide

Vehicular homicide involves intentional high acceleration impact of a pedestrian resulting in severe chest and abdominal injuries. Multiple type prints are usually present and manner depends on evidence from the scene and eyewitnesses. "Hit-and-run accidents" are also considered homicides for manner of death.

Accident vs. Natural Causes

Atherosclerotic Cardiovascular Disease

Frequently, the driver is noted to slow down prior to the accident and impact is often very low velocity. In addition, chances are that cause of death is atherosclerotic cardiovascular disease (ASCVD) and manner is natural if there is no good explanation for the crash, collapse was witnessed before the crash, injuries on the body and car are minor and superficial, and driver has severe ASCVD.

However, if there are extensive injuries with abundant bruising and bleeding and evidence of recent heart attack, the manner of death should be accident.

Cerebrovascular Accident

If there is a ruptured berry aneurysm or bleeding vascular malformation, death may be sudden. Often it is difficult to differentiate these natural causes of death from cerebral trauma due to the accident. Old infarcts may predispose to accidents by impairing mobility and visual acuity.

Motor Vehicle Suicide

Accidents with no explanation—for example, a single vehicle hitting a stationary object or driving off a bridge with no evidence of braking—may be a suicidal manner of death. Careful investigative clues may reveal previous suicide threats, previous suicide attempts such as scars on wrists, history of mental illness or antidepression medication, and imprint of acceleration pedal on the sole of the shoe. A psychological autopsy may help sort out the intent and manner of death.

Fatal Pedestrian Investigation*

There are two primary considerations at the scene of an automobile–pedestrian accident:

1. Preservation and security of the area
2. Analysis of the scene, vehicle, body, and circumstance

---

* Adapted from a *1993 Office of the Medical Investigator (OMI) Seminar*, Albuquerque, NM.

Scene Analysis

Scene analysis focuses on determining what happened and how it happened. Most automobile collisions are related to accidents, but some are mechanisms of suicide or homicide. Scene analysis can help the ME/coroner determine whether a death is related to homicide, suicide, or natural causes. Photography preserves the scene for later reanalysis, and photographs provide some of the medicolegal evidence used to determine liability. Sketches and diagrams are also important. The police fill in a standard diagram on the police report. This includes information such as positions of vehicles, traffic light information, damage to vehicles, flow of traffic, and unusual obstructions or obstacles. Perspective sketches of the vehicle from a number of angles relate the vehicle to the scene. Position of the victim and evidence of external injuries can be included in a diagram. Later, the diagrams and photographs can validate one another.

Auto–Pedestrian Collision

When an automobile and pedestrian collide, a complete description of the scene is necessary. This begins with road and weather conditions. The surface material and lighting at the point of collision are noted. The pedestrian's activity at the time of the accident is also described. For example, the pedestrian may be on a scooter, using in-line skates, pushing or pulling a cart or stroller, or carrying materials. Photographs of the scene indicate the items that might have been involved in the collision.

Observations at the scene include skid marks, spills, debris, and personal effects. Skid marks should be measured, photographed, and described. Spills at the scene are usually from the vehicle but might also be from objects that the victim was carrying. Samples of fluids should be either taken or positively identified on site. Automobile coolant, washer fluid, battery acid, and oil are frequently seen. Debris from under the victim's body and the vehicle such as mud, dirt, rust, snow, or other material should be identified as to the location found and type. Other debris might be from the automobile itself such as glass, plastic, chrome, or parts of the vehicle. (One chip of paint will reveal the color, year, make, and model of a vehicle that struck the victim and may have left the scene.) Clothing, shoes, tissue, blood smears, and personal effects are also often strewn about the scene and must be collected and properly preserved.

Driver and Vehicle Investigation

The automobile is photographed, measured, and diagrammed—usually on a standard form. The impact site shows transfer of material and pattern imprints. Hair, tissue, or fibers may be on the vehicle. If the windshield is broken, the patterns of breaks are important. Blood spattered on the automobile is analyzed for spatter pattern.

Driver behaviors contribute to the investigation. Activities in which the driver was involved prior to the crash are researched. The investigator notes the time when the driver first became aware of the pedestrian. A description of evasive actions taken is documented from the driver as well as any witnesses. Also, any obstructions described by the driver that interfered with a clear view of traffic are listed.

The driver and witnesses should describe postcrash actions. In the case of "hit-and-run" accidents, the time of flight related to acknowledgment of impact is important. If the driver began treatment of the pedestrian, all measures taken should be described. Additionally, a determination must be made as to whether or not the victim was moved; if so, how far and by whom? Medical information may be obtained from the driver including blood analysis for alcohol and drugs. The presence or absence of drug paraphernalia at the scene or on the driver is also useful evidence to the investigator.

A psychological autopsy of the decedent adds to other information related to liability issues. Finally, a forensic pathologist presents findings from the autopsy and toxicology results.

Adaptations of standard investigations of motor vehicle–pedestrian collisions can be made to collisions between people on moving sports equipment or large animals. Automobiles frequently collide with deer. In some instances, the driver is injured or killed. Many techniques of investigation can be used to assess damage and driver condition.

Collection and Preservation of Evidence*

Evidence collection from other investigative techniques applies to the scene of a vehicle–pedestrian death. As in other situations, trace evidence from the victim including hair, blood, skin, and clothing fragments is collected. Specific evidence from the vehicle includes paint, vehicle parts, grease, and glass.

The autopsy and examination of evidence in motor vehicle impacts with pedestrians is surely to be included in any litigation surrounding liability. Consequently, the skills of the ME/coroner and death investigators will be challenged.

Motor Vehicle Injuries

Motor vehicles and pedestrians may collide without causing death. Whether the injuries lead to death or recovery, investigations of motor vehicle accident injuries are conducted to determine fault and extent of liability. Settlement of claims related to accidents is generally delayed until all parties to the accident have been satisfied with their independent investigations. In some cases, accidents involve buses, trolleys, or multiple passenger vehicles.

---

* Excerpted from a lecture by Michael Ward, M.D.

Type and Severity of Injuries

Speed, vehicle, and victim size are critical to determining type and severity of injuries. The victim's height, weight, sex, and age are obtained at the beginning of an investigation.

Speed of Vehicle

First, information should be obtained to determine if the vehicle was accelerating or braking. Measurements and configuration of tire marks aid in determination of vehicle activity.

Speeds less than 25 mph

- Little vehicle damage.
- Victim is thrown forward or to the side of a moving car.

Speeds from 25 to 40 mph

- Front impact with victim thrown onto hood and/or windshield.
- Victim then either slides off hood or travels for some distance before falling off.

Speeds greater than 50 mph

- Impact launches victim up and over hood with reimpact to trunk, rear bumper, or pavement.
- Impact by a large truck, van, bus, or semitrailer creates impact site above the victim's center of gravity; victim is launched forward or to the side or held against the grill until the vehicle stops.
- Victim is often run over by vehicle.

Adults

Adult pedestrians sustain *bumper fractures* (fractures caused by front bumpers), pelvic fractures, or a variety of skin and soft tissue injuries (Figure 11.4). Notwithstanding variations in the type of vehicle, bumper height, victim's height, and victim position, one or more types of injury can result. Injuries from the impact of a braking MG Midget differ considerably from those caused by a Lincoln Town Car being driven at the speed limit.

Adult pedestrians who are standing, running, or walking usually have an impact site below the center of gravity—that is, below the waistline at pelvic brim. A pelvic fracture occurs, frequently with a secondary injury where the body hits the edge of the hood. In addition to the fracture, hyperextension of the pelvis with stretch injuries to the groin may be sustained.

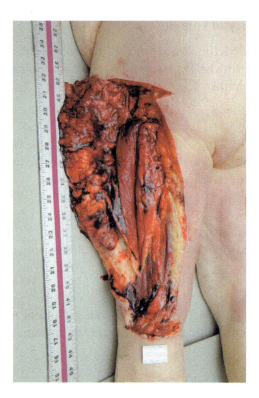

Figure 11.4 Leg injury with ruler measurements to determine impact site in a pedestrian versus motor vehicle injury.

Abrasions and contusions are occasionally absent. Those likely to be seen show patterns that match the vehicle at the impact site. In addition to tire marks, patterns are created by the grill, headlights, mirrors, or emblems.

Bumper fractures are likely. These are wedge-shaped fractures of the tibia, fibula, or femur. Typically, the wedge points in the direction of vehicle travel. The average distance between the ground and fracture is 14–15 inches, including the heel height of the victim's shoes. Bumper fractures of different heights may indicate that the victim was walking or running.

Blunt trauma to the head often results from striking the windshield, windshield support, trunk, or rear bumper. Although few significant chest and abdominal injuries occur, cervical spine injuries are more common. Whiplash injuries can result from a rear strike to the pedestrian. Atlanto-occipital subluxations appear as part of injuries to the cervical spine.

Additional injuries might appear as *avulsion pockets* on body surfaces. Avulsion pockets are pockets of blood and/or liquefied fat beneath the skin at an impact site. That site can represent the impact with the vehicle or ground. Skin overlying the injury is usually intact without external evidence of injury but may be abraded.

Children

Children show impact sites similar to those seen on adults struck by a van or bus—that is, the child is hit above the waist and thrown forward or to the side and run over by the vehicle. Injuries may be more severe with children than adults due to size differences. However, the description, tire imprints, and types of injuries are similar.

Victims Lying in Roadway

Victims of automobile–pedestrian accidents may remain on a road awaiting emergency care or police response. These victims may be hit by a second vehicle. Single-vehicle victims may have an impact site from a "hit-and-run" incident or intoxicated driver. Victims, too, may be intoxicated while lying injured on a roadway.

Injuries to lying victims are commonly blunt injuries from undersurfaces of vehicle, "road rash" abrasions from being dragged, tire imprints, and crush injuries. Tire marks leave a patterned imprint on skin and clothing (Figure 11.5). Photographs of the pattern or tracing the design onto paper

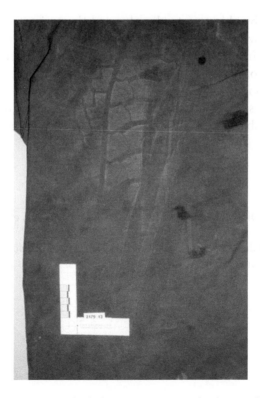

Figure 11.5 Examination of clothing in motor vehicle accidents may reveal clues such as this tire mark on a shirt.

or a plastic transparency can be useful to the investigation. Skin avulsions show tears in the direction of turning wheels, while severe lacerations result from braking tires. Abrasions occur on the skin where the body is dragged or scraped along the ground.

Crush injuries including lacerations to visceral organs and chest compression occur when the victim is run over. There is an "overstretching" of skin (or striae) with resultant superficial tears.

Secondary Impact Injuries

Secondary impact injuries are incurred from striking the ground, other fixed objects, or another vehicle following the initial impact. Brush burns from sliding along pavement or blunt injuries of the head and extremities result from the momentum of the victim as the body is tossed or dragged from the point of impact. Rollover injuries are generally a combination of primary, secondary, and crush injuries.

Sideswipes

Injuries caused by objects extending beyond the perimeter of a vehicle are considered *sideswipe contacts*. Pedestrians can incur sideswipe contacts from motor vehicles. In a brief contact, there may even be absence of a definite impact site. Major or minor injuries can be caused by objects affixed to the side of an automobile such as mirrors, tires, or even a roof.

Head injuries often occur from being knocked to the ground. The types of injuries described earlier as secondary impacts also pertain to falls after a sideswipe.

Bibliography

DiMaio, DJ and DiMaio, VJM. 2001. *Forensic Pathology*, 2nd ed. Boca Raton, FL: CRC Press.
Dolinak, D, Matshes, E, and Lew, E. 2006. *Forensic Pathology: Principles and Practice*. Burlington, MA: Elsevier.

Firearms Identification 12

OBJECTIVES

Upon completion of this chapter and corresponding reference material, the reader will be able to

- Discuss the history and development of firearms
- Differentiate between a rifle and shotgun
- Identify various kinds of bullets
- Identify direction of rifling from recovered bullets
- Describe two types of handguns

Firearms

History of Firearms

The first firearm was a fourteenth-century hand cannon. It was a crude weapon with a smooth, unified bore that was loaded with a variety of small hard objects like metal, rocks, or gravel. The matchlock was the standard firearm of the first settlers in North America. This firearm was named for the match, a wicked piece of material that was lit when lowered into a priming pan of loose gunpowder. The wheel lock was the first firearm to use flint and steel for lighting the primer—similar to a cigarette lighter. The flintlock fired when a flint clamped into the hammer, struck a metal plate, and sparks from the flint ignited the gunpowder. The flintlock was used from the 1600s until the 1800s.

In the early 1800s, fulminate of mercury was used as a primer in the percussion lock firearm. A small cap coated with fulminate of mercury was struck by the hammer causing a spark to ignite the gunpowder. This type of primer led to the self-contained cartridge and was an important step in the development of breech-loading (rear-loading) firearms. Rimfire and center-fire ammunition are used in breech-loading firearms. The breech-loader resulted in the ability to open and close the back of the barrel, permitting rapid firing.

Ammunition

Ammunition used in a rifle or pistol is generally called a cartridge. A cartridge contains powder, primer, and a bullet assembled in a case.

Gunpowder (propellant) drives in the bullet from the firearm as it burns. Types of powder include rolled ball, flake, lamel, and tubular. Primer usually consists of compounds of lead, barium, or antimony and is used to light the powder. It burns quickly when struck by a sharp blow of the firing pin. In center-fire ammunition, the primer is contained in a small metal cap that fits in the center bottom of the cartridge case. In rimfire ammunition, the primer is located in the rim of the cartridge case.

Common cartridges for rifle and pistol use are listed in chart form and by cartridge interchangeability. The ammunition must match the gun in which it is fired. The caliber is stamped on the head of the cartridge. Examples of caliber in inches and metric equivalent are listed in chart forms.

Forensic pathologists generally categorize projectiles into three major groups.

Rifle	Pistol	Cartridge	Can Use in
.22 Long Rifle	.22 Long Rifle	.22 Short	.22 LR, .22 Magnum
.22 Magnum	.22 Magnum	.22 Long	.22 LR, .22 Magnum
.223 Remington	.25 Auto	.22 Long rifle	.22 Magnum
.243 Winchester	.32 Auto	.32 Auto	.32 Revolvers
.270 Winchester	.357 Magnum	.38 Spl	.357 Magnum
.30–30 Winchester	.357 Magnum	.38 ACP	.38 Super
.308 Winchester	.380 Auto	.44 Spl	.44 Magnum
.30–06 Springfield	.38 Special	.44 Magnum	.45 Colt
	.40 Smith & Wesson	.45 Auto	.45 Colt (with clips)
	.44 Magnum	.410 Shotshell	.45 Colt
	.45 Auto	12 gauge	10 gauge
5.56 mm × 45 mm	6.35 mm		
7 mm × 57 mm	7.62 mm	9 mm Luger Revolvers	
7.62 mm × 39 mm	7.65 mm	.380 Auto	.38 Spl, 357 Magnum (with Tape)

1. Small caliber (.22 or .25)
2. Medium caliber (.357, .38, 9 mm)
3. Large caliber (.44)

Common Cartridge	Cartridge Interchangeability
Caliber in Inches	Metric Equivalent in Millimeters
.22	5.56
.25	6.35
.30	7.62
.32	7.65
.40	10
.45	11.43

Bullets	
Gauge	Caliber in Inches
.410	.410
28	.550
20	.615
16	.670
12	.730
10	.775

Bullets fall into two categories:

1. All-lead bullets
2. Metal-jacketed bullets

The configuration of a bullet may be

- Round nose
- Wadcutter (cylindrical)
- Semiwadcutter (a truncated cone with a flat tip and sharp shoulder)
- Hollow point
- Hydra-Shok (central post)
- Glazer round (composed of a lead core, snake shot metal pellets, and a blue Teflon plug)

All-lead bullets are constructed of lead to which antimony, tin, or both have been added to increase the hardness of the alloy. Some lead bullets are covered by a thin coating of copper or copper alloy that acts to harden and lubricate the bullet. This coating should not be confused with a copper jacket.

Metal-jacketed bullets may be either full metal-jacketed or partial metal-jacketed. As a rule, military ammunition is full metal-jacketed, while civilian ammunition is partial metal-jacketed. Jacketing usually consists of copper, although aluminum and steel (rarely) may be used. In partial metal-jacketed ammunition, the metal jacket is open at the tip to expose the core of the bullet.

Mechanism of a Firearm

With a cartridge in the chamber of a gun, the hammer falls, driving the fire pin to strike the primer at the base of the cartridge. This ignites the primer that explodes and ignites the powder. The powder burns and creates gas powder that expands in the case forcing the bullet and gas down the barrel of the gun.

Safety

Most guns have a safety. One must learn exactly how it works. The safety blocks the trigger so that it cannot be pulled. The bottom or latch that puts in on or off is located close to the action on a firearm.

The safety must always be engaged whenever a gun is loaded. The safety is released only prior to firing the gun.

Be careful! Only the safety blocks the trigger—nothing else. A hard blow in the right place can still fire the gun. Also, a safety can wear out or may not work. Never depend on the safety to prevent a gun from firing by accident.

Handgun Actions

There are four types of handgun actions:

1. Bolt action—The bolt is a firearm in which the breech closure is in line with the bore at all times; manually reciprocates to load, unload, and cock; and is locked in place by breech bolt lugs and engaging abutments usually in the receiver. The two principal types of bolt actions are the turn bolt and the straight pull.
2. Single shot—The single-shot pistol is usually a break-open action. The cartridge is loaded and ejected by hand.
3. Revolver—The name revolver derives from the action of the revolver's round magazine or cylinder; each time the trigger is pulled or the hammer is cocked, the cylinder revolves. When the chamber in the cylinder is in line with the barrel, it becomes the firing chamber. Revolvers work by single or double action. With single action,

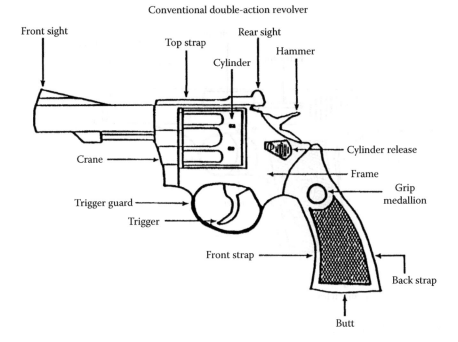

Conventional double-action revolver

Figure 12.1 The drawing depicts a revolver.

the hammer must be cocked before each shot is fired; whereas with double action, the hammer is cocked and the cylinder rotates when the trigger is pulled (Figure 12.1).

4. Semiautomatic—Most semiautomatic pistols must be cocked for the first shot. Each time the trigger is pulled, an empty cartridge is ejected and a fresh one loaded. Extra cartridges are carried in the magazine or clip (Figure 12.2).

Basic Types of Handguns

Revolvers all possess a cylinder that revolves with each cocking and firing of the weapon. Cartridges are usually of the rimmed type and are not automatically ejected during firing. Revolver mechanisms may be either single action or double action. Single-action guns are typified by the frontier-style "six shooter." These weapons all have an external hammer that must be manually cocked before the gun can be fired by pulling the trigger. The term single action refers to the fact that pulling the trigger accomplishes only one thing—release of the cocked hammer. Double-action revolvers may possess an external hammer or be hammerless. Pulling the trigger of a double-action revolver accomplishes two things—it cocks the weapon and releases the hammer (whether internal or external). Most double-action revolvers

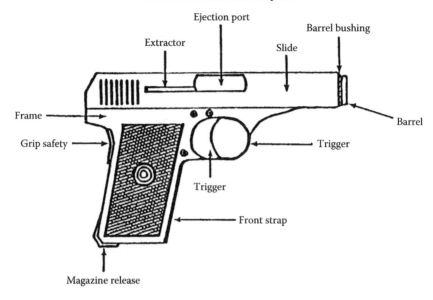

Figure 12.2 The drawing depicts a semiautomatic pistol.

with external hammers may also be operated in the single-action mode. The weight of a double-action trigger pull is always heavier than a single-action pull (typically 2×–3×).

Autoloading pistols or automatics all take cartridges from a magazine or clip located in the grip. Upon discharge, the slide moves rapidly rearward extracting and ejecting the expended cartridge as well as recocking the gun. As the slide is driven forward by an internal coil spring, a live cartridge is stripped from the magazine and loaded into the chamber. This cycle takes place with each pulling of the trigger until the ammunition supply in the magazine is exhausted. At this point, depending on the design of the particular pistol, the action may remain open with the slide held back by a latch or follower in the magazine.

Rifling

Rifles and handguns have rifled barrels. A series of parallel spiral grooves are cut the length of the interior of the barrel. The grooves are called rifling and cause the bullet to spin and travel point first. The metal between these grooves are called lands and the distance between the lands is referred to as bore diameter.

Rifle Actions

The action is the heart of the rifle. The stock and barrel are attached to the action. It includes all the small parts that load, fire, and eject the cartridge. There are five types of rifle actions:

1. Hinge action
2. Bolt action
3. Lever action
4. Pump action
5. Semiautomatic

(Figure 12.3)

A gun is usually referred to by its action; for example, a bolt-action rifle or a semiautomatic shotgun.

The single shot is the most simple type of action. A shell or cartridge is loaded by hand. Modern single shots are generally bolt actions. Many older models are lever actions. In other words, they must be reloaded by hand after each shot.

The action works by operating the bolt, lever, or pump when shooting the bolt action, lever action, or pump action, respectively. It extracts or ejects the empty shell, and then it loads a fresh shell into the chamber and cocks the gun for the next shot.

Some hunting guns are called automatics; this is not correct. They are actually semiautomatics or autoloaders. In other words, the action does most of the work by itself. It reloads by itself, but the trigger must be pressed to fire each shot.

Machine guns are true automatics. They continue to fire as long as the trigger is held back or until ammunition is depleted. Machine guns are not legal hunting guns anywhere and are only legal if registered under federal law.

Shotguns

Shotguns differ from rifled weapons in that they have a smooth bore and are designed principally to fire multiple pellets down the barrel rather than a single projectile. The term gauge is used to describe the caliber of a shotgun. This refers to the number of lead balls of the given bore diameter that weigh 1 pound. In a 20-gauge shotgun, 20 lead balls that are the diameter of the bore weigh 1 pound. The only exception to this nomenclature is the 410 shotgun, which has a bore diameter of 0.410 inch.

Shotgun barrels all have some degree of choke. Choke refers to a partial constriction of the bore of the barrel at its muzzle end to control the size of

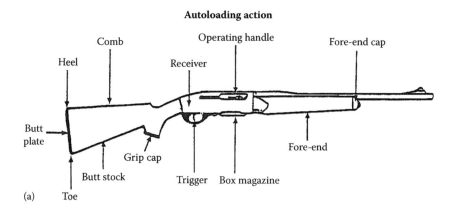

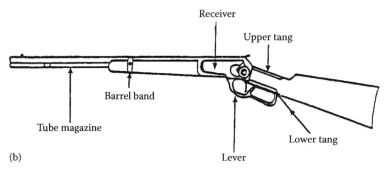

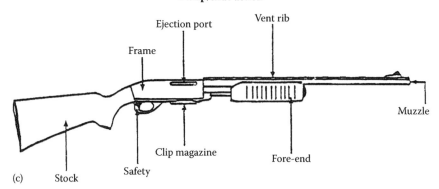

Figure 12.3 The drawing depicts different types of rifles: (a) autoloading, (b) levers, and (c) pump/slide.

the shot pattern. The choke, rather than the gauge of the shotgun, determines the size of the shot pattern at a specific distance. The tighter the choke, the smaller the pattern of pellets. Shotgun choke ranges from full choke to cylinder bore, with the tightest choke being the full choke weapon and the cylinder bore weapon having virtually no choke at all.

Modern shotgun ammunition consists of a plastic body or tube with a thin brass-coated steel or brass head, primer, powder, pellets, and wads. The end of the shell is usually closed in a wedge-shaped crimp. The only common exception to this is Federal 00 buckshot. This has a thin circular disk of plastic closing off the end of the shell that functions as an over-the-shot wad, with the edges of the mouth of the tube rolled into a crimp, holding the wad in place.

The shot loaded in shotgun shells is lead, lead with a thin copper coating, or steel. Shot can be divided into two categories—birdshot and buckshot. Birdshot is used to hunt birds and other small game. Buckshot is used for larger game and by police agencies.

Bibliography

DiMaio, VJM. 2016. *Gunshot Wounds, Practical Aspects of Firearms Ballistics and Forensic Techniques*. Boca Raton, FL: CRC Press.

Gunshot Wounds

13

Medicolegal Investigation of Firearms Injuries

Common Questions

A. Where was the person shot?
B. How many times was the decedent shot?
C. Where are the entries and reentries? Where are the exits?
D. Are there any bullets through clothes that did not penetrate the body?
E. What was the course or direction of each shot through the body?
F. What was the sequence of fire?
G. What is the mechanism of death due to gunshot?
H. What was the muzzle to target distance? Contact? Close? Intermediate? Distant? Any intermediate targets? Ricochet?
I. What was the direction of fire, especially in relation to the shooter?
J. In what position was the decedent when shot?
K. What is the estimated interval of survival between injury and death?
L. What was the capacity for movement and activity after being shot?

M. What kind of ammunition(s)?

N. What was the cause of death?

O. Any competing causes of death? (e.g., body found in water or in fire)

Mechanisms

A. Perforating vital structures and causing hemorrhage. Examples are perforations of the heart, great vessels, lung, or highly vascular solid organs.

B. Damaging organs that control vital body functions. Examples are brain injuries with swelling that interfere with breathing and cardiac control or injuries of the high cervical spine that impair breathing (Figure 13.1).

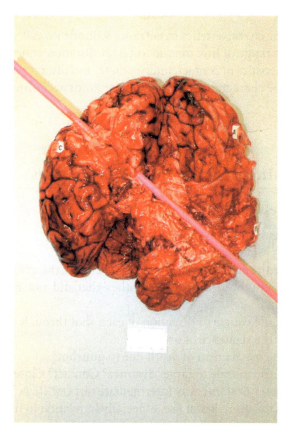

Figure 13.1 The photograph depicts a wound track through the underside of the brain with a trajectory rod in place to more clearly demonstrate the path of the missile.

C. Causing complications that result, either immediately or remotely, in death. Examples are sepsis associated with gunshot injuries to the bowel, coma-induced complications of pneumonia, seizures due to gunshot injuries to the brain, or pulmonary emboli complicating recumbency due to injury. Some complications are lethal years after the injury (such as bowel obstruction due to adhesions caused by the injury).

D. High-velocity weapons may cause lethal injury due to blast injury to adjacent organs without directly perforating them. Injuries to the neck may result in injury to the cord (contusion) or airway (soft tissue swelling) without directly perforating them. This is due to the transfer and dispersion of the kinetic energy of the bullet to tissue.

E. Sites of fatal gunshot wounds include
   1. Brain 40%
   2. Heart 25%
   3. Aorta or other major vessel 25%
   4. Solid viscera 10%

Scene and Body Exam

A. Examination at the scene of death/circumstances:
   1. Observe and obtain the following information from the investigating officer and witnesses:
      a. Who is the decedent? Is the decedent a prominent person or person at risk?
      b. Date last seen alive, when found, and by whom?
      c. How did the person come to be found?
      d. Evidence for time of injury and time of death.
      e. Where is the body? Open vs. concealed place? Known to the decedent?
      f. Is the gun present? Is it the decedent's?
      g. Where is the weapon, cartridge case, and spatter in relation to the decedent? Any bullets in walls, mattresses, chairs?
      h. In what position was the person when shot? Sitting, standing, lying down, sleeping?
      i. Any evidence of activity or motion after injury?
      j. Any evidence of struggle or sexual assault?
      k. Any evidence of forced entry? Anything missing?
      l. Photograph the above and anything that will be disturbed during transport. Coordinate photography with investigator to ensure all is covered.
      m. Bag the hands in paper bags and secure with rubber bands to preserve any residues, spatter patterns, or trace evidence.

2. Document the scene (body, gun, recovered bullets) through a scene sketch and narrative summary.

   a. Are any obvious inconsistencies apparent at the scene?

B. Examination of the clothed body and clothing.

1. Recover all clothes from any intermediate treating agency such as EMS or emergency room.
2. If received separately, examine clothes with the body.
3. Identify entrances by powder or wipe, or in driven fibers.
4. Body should be examined clothed and photographed as received. Residues present on clothing distinguish entrances from exits and indicate muzzle to target distance. Powder residues may be present but not visible, requiring rhodizonate testing by a firearms examiner to document distance. Fragments of intermediate targets such as wood or ricochet surface material may also be recovered from clothes.
5. Refrain from cutting clothing. Clothing should be retained and hung to dry.
6. Note in the record any damage or residues deposited on clothes.
7. Note any bullet holes to clothes that are not associated with injury to the body—usually tangential grazing shots.

C. Radiography.

1. Radiographs should be taken of the clothed body to avoid loss of bullets wedged between layers of clothes or within the lining of clothes.
2. Radiographs should be taken even when it appears the bullet has exited because fragments of jacket or parts of special ammunition may be lost in the track.
3. Be sure x-rays capture skin edges of the chest and abdomen to find bullets as they commonly become lodged just beneath the skin.
4. Label films carefully. X-rays may be submitted as evidence in court to document the location of projectiles in the body.
5. Radiographs may show direction of bone fragments pointed in the direction the bullet was traveling.

D. Examination of the unclothed body.

1. Order by number or letter each wound on a diagram and look at each one to characterize an entrance or exit. When tracks are sorted, label entrance and exit with the same number and "X" for projectile recovery.
2. Look for residues using a hand lens or dissecting scope. Resect and block any ambiguous wounds for microscopic examination for powder at the end of examination.
3. Examine wounds before cleaning.

4. If wounds do not clearly indicate entrance or exit, or if multiple surfaces are involved, a series of digital photographs for reference may help sort out possible tracks.

5. Hypothesized tracks need confirmation by autopsy according to the policy outlined by the death investigation system.

6. Depending on overall circumstances, other studies may be necessary before cleaning.

E. Special studies.

1. Perform gunshot residue tests and trace metal tests before disturbing or washing the hands.

2. Any tests for lead residues to distinguish blunt force injuries from grazing wounds should be performed prior to washing.

3. Alternate light source examination for trace evidence.

F. Photography.

1. Photograph body as received, clothed and unclothed.

2. Photograph hands and wounds if residues and blood splatter patterns are present or if pertinent to the case when residues and blood splatter patterns are not present, (e.g., if person is said to have "grabbed the gun").

3. Photograph body after cleansing to show wound locations.

4. Photograph individual wounds to document entrance, exit, and distance characteristics.

5. Photograph the body with trajectory rods following the autopsy and cover autopsy incision with drapes.

6. Shoot true anterior/posterior (AP) and laterals plus any other views deemed meaningful. For example, reposition and photograph the arms to show position of an entry and associated reentry or impossibility of a self-inflicted shot.

7. Photograph recovered bullets.

G. Internal examination.

1. Document each wound by diagram and narrative, recording size and wound characteristics; by measurements from top of the head and midline; and by anatomical location.

2. Trace each track recovering any trace evidence (fabric or intermediate targets) and metal.

3. Compare completeness of recovered materials with radiographs.

4. Document by measurement the location of each recovered missile.

5. Identify pathological findings pertinent to survival (such as large hemothorax or hemoperitoneum) or capacity for activity (such as transection of the thoracic spinal cord that would have precluded running or any other motion).

6. Recover any old bullets from previous injuries.

7. Handle bullets with gloved hands (never use metal forceps).
8. Correlate autopsy information with that of the investigating officer in the autopsy room to identify any inconsistencies not apparent at the scene.
9. If a fetal death occurs, document its injuries as a separate case.

H. Collection of evidence on gunshot cases—items collected include the following:
   1. Gunshot residue, trace metal, or lead tests.
   2. Bullets and bullet fragments.
   3. Material adherent to bullet.
   4. All clothing.
   5. Pertinent trace evidence such as recovered and exemplary hairs, fibers, glass, etc.
   6. Radiographs.
   7. Blood, vitreous and other body fluids, and liver for ethanol and drug testing.
   8. Blood spots for DNA testing.
   9. Hospital admission blood and body fluids, if death was delayed.
   10. Clothes for DNA typing if multiple transfused (or collect from blood bank initial hospital sample drawn for type and crossmatch).
   11. Sexual assault kits if decedent is a woman, or if circumstances or pathologic findings are suspect for recent sexual activity in a male shooting victim.
   12. If a fetus is involved, collect serological evidence—fetal and placental blood and tissue from the fetus for possible paternity testing.

Gunshot Wounds

A. Description of a wound includes
   1. Size rough indication of caliber but not infallible
   2. Shape indicator of direction
   3. Characteristics abraded, stippled, burned, lacerated, etc.
   4. Patterns of muzzles, intermediate targets
   5. Contaminants wood, glass, clothing
   6. Distance of entrance, exit, or recovery from top of head to left or right of midline front or spine
   7. Description in relation to anatomical location, for example, to the right front shoulder
   8. Its path through the body listing organs perforated
   9. Evidence of vital reaction in the form of bleeding or inflammation
   10. Location of recovery or exit

B. Entrances vs. exits

Characteristic	Entrances	Exits
Burn	Yes	No
Powder	Yes	No[a]
Stippling	Yes	No
Abrasion	Yes	No, unless shored
Laceration	Yes, if contact[b]	Yes

[a] Unless exit is close to a near shot, but margin will be free of burn and powder.

[b] Wounds to palms and soles are lacerated regardless of distance.

C. Distance ("range of fire," "muzzle to target distance").

1. Caveats on clothed body surfaces, distance is best determined by firearms examiner and examination of the clothes—especially if the shot looks distant.
2. Uncovered body surfaces.
   a. Look before washing and shaving.
   b. Photograph close up before and after any alteration if wound is doubtful or critical to interpretation of case (when there is discrepancy between wound and history).
3. Contact muzzle resting on skin +/muzzle marks (Figure 13.2).
   a. Zero to minimal powder without stippling on outside.
   b. Margin is burned black.
   c. Usually lacerated—at least a little with 22s.
   d. Gunshot wound to the skull.
      i. In tissue over bone, such as the skull, larger calibers may show stellate laceration and entry wounds may be larger than exit wounds.
      ii. Often associated with radial fractures at the entrance and sometimes at the exit.
      iii. Entrances show soot residues on the bone and dura.
      iv. Beveling of bone—inner table of entrance wound (Figure 13.3) and outer table of exit wound (Figure 13.4).
      v. Wounds to the temples are associated with fractures of the orbits and periocular ecchymoses; that is, "black eyes."
   e. If angled, residues leak out onto skin at edges that are not in contact—wound may be oval instead of round.
   f. Powder is blown into subcutaneous tissue.

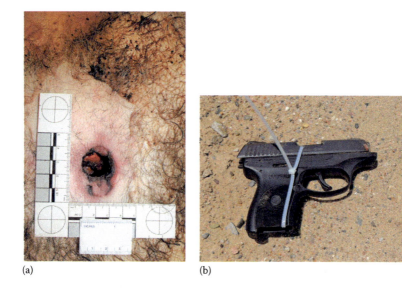

(a)   (b)

Figure 13.2 (a) Contact range gunshot wound demonstrates soot in and around the wound edges, with glide imprint at lower edge. (b) Gun used to cause muzzle imprint.

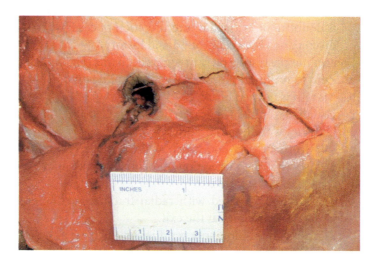

Figure 13.3 An entrance wound on the skull shows internal beveling and soot.

     g. Subcutaneous tissue may be pink due to carbon monoxide (CO) in gases combining with blood locally to form carboxyhemoglobin.

     h. Is visible microscopically as yellowish black crystalline debris on surface and in track.

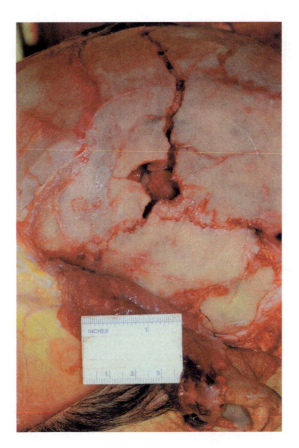

Figure 13.4 An exit wound on the skull shows external beveling.

      i. Alizarin S stain may identify residues in decomposed entrances.

      j. Difficult to determine in decomposed bodies.

      k. Powder may remain on bone in decomposed and skeletonized bodies and after skin is surgically resected.

      l. Consistent with homicides and suicides—rarely accidents.

  4. Tight "hard" contact weapon is pushing in the skin.

      a. Shows all of the above and often also a muzzle mark.

      b. Muzzle marks often indicate muzzle configuration showing sight marks, ejector rod marks, slide marks, etc. (Figure 13.5).

  5. Near contact range but not in contact; ½ inch away from skin.

      a. Entrance has wide zone of powder and burn (Figure 13.6).

      b. If angled, residue will be eccentric with the wider margin pointing toward same side where muzzle was positioned.

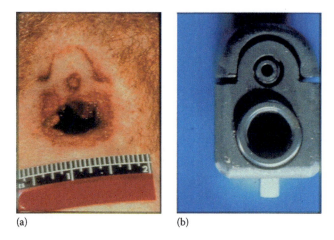

(a)　　　　　　　　　　　　(b)

Figure 13.5 (a) An imprint on the skin from a contact range gunshot wound. (b) The muzzle of a gun that can cause an imprint at contact range.

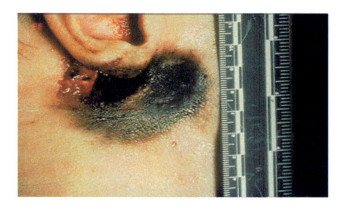

Figure 13.6 The photograph depicts soot around the wound.

      c. May not be able to distinguish from an angled contact gunshot wound.
      d. Scraping some of the residues on a cotton square may help determine the type of ammunition if no bullet or gun is available.
  6. Intermediate range (Figure 13.7).
      a. Intermediate from ½ inch to 6–12 inches.
        i. Zone of powder increases but becomes less dense with increasing distance.
        ii. Shows tattooing or stippling by powder grains with pattern and shape that reflect the type of powder and distance.

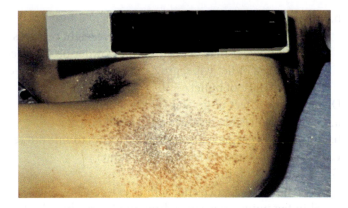

Figure 13.7 Stippling is the hallmark of intermediate range wounds.

    iii. Beyond 1 foot may not be able to see residues unless look-
ing very carefully and perhaps not even then. Will be
chemically visible on clothes.
    iv. Residues can indicate ball, flattened ball, or flake disk
(Figure 13.8).
    v. Pattern can be duplicated by firearms examiner for a closer
estimate of distance.
    vi. "Pseudotattooing."
- Fragments of intermediate target.
- Fragments of bullet shaved off by poorly fitted cylinder
to barrel.
- Fragments from bullet fragmenting after hitting
another surface (i.e., asphalt).
- Suture marks.

Figure 13.8 Different types of gunpowder are depicted: left, ball; center, flattened
ball; right, flake disc.

   b. Intermediate greater than 6–12 inches or 1 foot.
      i. Depending on weapon, may not see slight residues.
      ii. Ball powder may deposit visible powder up to 3 feet.
      iii. May see bullet wipe, grayish residues from barrel carried on surface of bullet.
7. Distant range 2 feet or greater (Figure 13.9).
   a. Usually no visible residues unless ball powder.
   b. Requires firearms examination of clothes to rule out residues.
   c. Wounds at 4 and 40 feet look the same.
8. Graze wounds (Figure 13.10).
   a. Abrasion at entrance end; split at exit.
   b. Skin tag points may show direction from which bullet came.
   c. Tears point to direction bullet traveled.
9. Atypical entrances.
   a. Reentries irregular or slits; line up with adjacent body part.
   b. Tumbling entrances elongated or cylindrical wound after hitting another surface or tissue.
   c. Irregular from semi-jacketed separating; may see two irregular holes.
   d. Foreshored entrances through belts or firm adjacent intermediate target so that entrance is widely abraded but clean except for traces of target.
   e. Palm and sole entrances are stellate regardless of distance.
   f. Star-shaped abrasions around entrance; accelerator ammunition.
   g. Stellate where skin is stretched tight over bone.

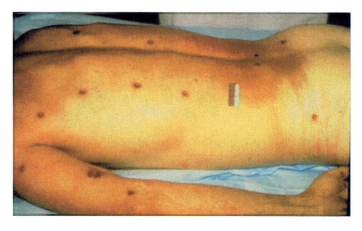

Figure 13.9 Distant wounds show no evidence of soot or stippling.

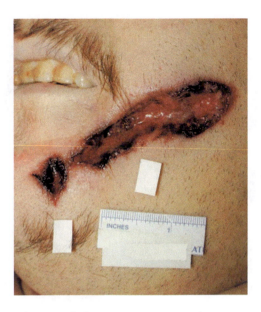

Figure 13.10 The photograph depicts a graze wound.

10. Gunshot wound exits.
   a. Slits in soft stretchy tissue areas (Figure 13.11).
   b. Stellate over tight skin of skull, chin (Figure 13.12).
   c. Shored exits abrasion caused by skin being firmly in contact with hard surface at moment of exit. May resemble a distant-range entry wound.
11. Other marks associated with gunshot wounds.
   a. Cylinder gap marks if cylinder of weapon is in close proximity to clothes or skin, residues escape from in front and sometimes from rear of cylinder to form a roughly linear deposit of residues. Distance between hold and first mark is measure of barrel length.
   b. Patterns representing shapes of intermediate targets such as zipper teeth, religious medals, or coins.

Shotgun Wounds

A. Weapons and ammunition.
   1. Fire pellets, slugs, and rarely some specialized projectiles such as flechettes.
   2. Per U.S. law, barrel must be greater than 18 inches or else is considered "sawed off" and illegal.

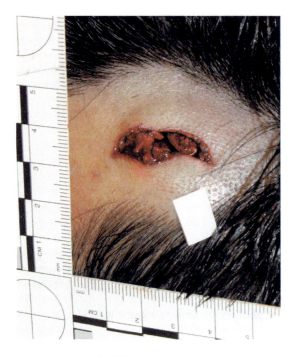

Figure 13.11 Exits are often slit-like lacerations.

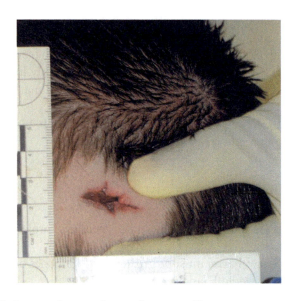

Figure 13.12 Some exit wounds may have a stellate appearance.

3. Barrel is not rifled.
4. Gauge describes caliber number of lead balls of the given bore diameter that weigh 1 pound—that is, with a 12-gauge shotgun, 12 balls of diameter 0.662 inch weigh 1 pound.
5. For 10–28 gauge shotguns, the larger the gauge, the smaller the bore (12 gauge is the most common weapon). The smallest bore size is 0.410 inch; it is not named by convention and has a 0.410 inch bore diameter.
6. Choke partial constriction of barrel at muzzle end to keep shot together longer at long distances no practical meaning in terms of most shotgun injuries.
7. Shell components and materials recovered from wounds.
   a. Birdshot.
      i. Tube, paper, or plastic with brass head
      ii. Powder
      iii. Over powder wad, cardboard and fiber filler wads, and over shot wad, +/plastic collar
      iv. +/polyethylene/polypropylene filler to cushion shot
      v. Plastic one-piece wads, "power piston," "triple plus," open to show petals
      vi. Shot the larger the number, the smaller the shot—that is, No. 12 is smaller than No. 2
   b. Shot, wads, collars, and one-piece "power piston" type wads may be recovered from contact and close wounds.
   c. Buckshot.
      i. Larger pellets S4 small; 000 largest.
      ii. Filler color may vary, white or black.
      iii. Filler marks may look like stippling; filler travels out further than powder.
      iv. Scrape off residues to differentiate black filler from powder.
   d. Slugs.
      i. Most common are Foster, Brenneke, and Cabot.
      ii. Foster is hollow grooved metal; if close, Brenneke leaves screw, cardboard, wad, and slug; Foster and Cabot may have plastic inserts to keep shape.
   e. Special loads are made for special purposes.
B. Shotgun wounds/distance
   1. Contact/close.
      a. Most devastating firearms injury at close range.
      b. Birdshot usually does not exit. Nearly all kinetic energy is expended in body.
      c. Buckshot and slugs may exit when tangential.
      d. Contact head shots fragment head.

e. Determine entrance by reconstructing skin edges; otherwise head looks the same whether shot is to back, mouth, or temple.
f. Intraoral shots may show lacerations at corners of mouth.
g. In right-handed persons, left hand may show powder or rust from steadying muzzle.
h. Contact shotgun wounds to the trunk well-defined hole with extensive internal dispersion and damage.
i. In bodies where skin surface not intact, that is, decomposed or burned degree of dispersion will be the same whether contact or several yards ("billiard ball effect").
j. Underlying soft tissue will be pink due to carboxyhemoglobin.
k. Recover pellets, plastic shotcup, and cardboard wadding from wound

2. Distant.
   a. Pellets disperse with distance axiom is: distance in yards.
   b. Inches of spread 1 (discount flyers).
   c. Margins show scalloping, then dispersion.
   d. Buckshot scalloped at 3 feet, satellite holes at 9 feet.
   e. Definitive distance determined by firearms examiner shooting the weapon in question with the ammunition in question.
   f. Dispersed buckshot may show incomplete pattern and resemble multiple bullet injuries.

3. Wad marks
   a. Power piston four petals; .410 has 3 at 1–3 feet. Wad marks out to 20 feet.
   b. Filler wad works to 15 feet.

Rifle Wounds

A. Low-velocity rifles.
   1. Entrance of contact wound may show "teardrop" burn.
   2. Fired bullet may show microgrooving indicating a rifle shot.
   3. Damage is less than higher velocity rifles.
B. High-velocity rifles.
   1. May injure structures without perforating them.
   2. Bullets are full or semi-jacketed.
   3. Military are full metal jacketed; they deform and fragment less.
C. Distance: contact, intermediate, or distant.
   1. Contact wounds to the head.
      a. Gas expansion explodes head.
      b. Entrance is at origin of radial tears.
      c. Residues may be minimal.

2. Wounds to trunk do not disrupt like head wounds.
   a. If contact, may leave muzzle mark.
   b. Organs show more disruption than handgun.
   c. Underlying tissues may be pink.
   d. Bullet more likely to tumble and fragment.
   e. Radiographs show "lead snowstorm."
   f. Entrances may show microtears.
   g. Show less powder than handguns.
   h. Exits are larger and more irregular than bullets from handguns.

Conduct after Injury

A. Only immediately incapacitating injury is gunshot wound to mid-brain or basal ganglia of brain.
B. Incapacitation does not mean death. Survival may be longer.
C. Only injuries that prevent return of fire are head shots and shots to the firing hand.
D. Behavior limited only by blood flow to brain; consciousness remains 10–15 seconds after heart/carotid disrupted.
E. Trunk shots may walk, drive, run, return fire.

Concealed Sites for Injury

A. Usually small caliber.
B. Axilla, back, nose, eye, base of skull where bullet may travel below the base and not be seen upon opening the skull or removing the neck.
C. Head and hair-bearing areas.
D. In areas already injured.
E. All orifices.
F. Always look at the back, axilla and feel through the hair for swellings, blood, and holes.

Other Miscellaneous

A. Weapons.
   1. Air guns
   2. Zip guns
   3. Nail guns
B. Bullets.
   1. Unrifled consider smooth bore weapon.
C. Ammunitions with distinctive characteristics.
   1. Glazer round copper jacket with pellets and a plastic plug, x-rays of pellets and plug show distinctive patterns.
   2. Exploding ammunition x-rays see primer cap and anvil.

   3. KTW load green Teflon coating.
   4. Nyclad black nylon coating.
   5. Shotshell cartridges, "snake shot" fine pellets, lethal at close range to temporal bones.
   6. Silvertip jacket is aluminum; jacket may be missed on x-ray.
   7. Black talon hollow point that opens and looks like a flower, black-coated.

Forensic Studies

   A. Gunshot residue tests on hands, body parts, and clothes.
   B. Distance patterns proximity patterns for range of fire.
   C. Comparison of recovered bullets with suspect weapons.
   D. Comparison of bullets to link a firearm to more than one case, especially over a period of time.
   E. Examination of bullet for
      1. Residues of intermediate targets, fabric, tissue, wood
      2. Patterns from intermediate targets such as screening
      3. Cytology or immunology on recovered tissue from a bullet to determine through whom of several persons or objects (wood) it passed
      4. Classes of weapons of origin
   F. Comparison of muzzle mark patterns with exemplars.
   G. Trigger pull.
   H. Mechanical working order and safety devices, "gun just went off."
   I. Defects that predispose gun to accident—does it go off when dropped?
   J. Reconstructions using anatomical models.
   K. Examination of gunshot residues from wounds for powder type.
   L. Elemental analysis of recovered microfragments of bullets for ammunition manufacturer.

Manner of Death

   A. Depends on correlation of all historical, scene, pathologic, and forensic science evidence.
   B. Caveats.
      1. Beware of premature assignment of accident or suicide to a shooting death until investigation is complete.
      2. True accidental shooting deaths are uncommon.
      3. Beware of "accident" while "cleaning a gun."
      4. Beware of accidental shooting while hunting.

5. Guns do not just "go off." Weapons at risk for accidental discharge upon dropping or casual handling can be determined by firearms examiners.
6. Distance, direction, and reconstruction are critical to determination of manner.
7. Measure GSWs from the heel up, and midline to side.
8. If there is concern of manner of death for a GSW or SGW, measure from the right middle finger to the entry wound.
9. Self-inflicted GSWs from "Russian Roulette" are generally ruled as suicide manner.

Bibliography

DiMaio, VJM. 2016. *Gunshot Wounds, Practical Aspects of Firearms Ballistics and Forensic Techniques.* Boca Raton, FL: CRC Press.

Natural and Accidental Deaths

III

Natural Deaths

14

MARY H. DUDLEY
LAUREN E. DVORSCAK

OBJECTIVES

Upon completion of this chapter and corresponding reference material, the reader will be able to

- Describe and define the major natural causes of death by organ system
- Describe the common cardiovascular diseases responsible for sudden natural death
- List two types of cardiomyopathy
- Differentiate between nontraumatic and traumatic subarachnoid hemorrhages
- Identify diseases of the liver and pancreas that cause death
- Compare and contrast restrictive and obstructive types of respiratory diseases

Introduction

Among the manners of death, the largest category is death from natural causes. Accurate determination of natural death is important to the family to identify familial conditions as well as to the regional and national data banks to identify causation. Funds for research, programs to change health practices, and patient education efforts hinge upon identified needs, that is, the number of people per 100,000 who die from a medical condition or its sequelae.

The distinction between accidental and natural causes is also important. This becomes particularly significant when an individual with a chronic condition becomes involved in an accident. Insurance accidental death benefits may pay double compared to a natural death benefit.

Most natural deaths handled by the medical examiner's office (MEO) are those cases where there may or may not be a prior medical history of natural disease, medical treatment, and medical care by a physician. If there

155

is a physician willing to sign a death certificate for an unattended home death and there is no sign of nonnatural circumstances of death, the MEO will decline jurisdiction. Unattended natural deaths are often sudden and unexpected in individuals without a prior medical history. The cause of natural deaths may include various organ systems including the cardiovascular system, central nervous system, respiratory system, gastrointestinal system, and others.

Cardiovascular System

The most common cause of sudden, unexpected death in the United States is due to cardiovascular disease. Cardiovascular disease includes pathology of the coronary arteries and/or the aorta, including atherosclerotic cardiovascular disease, aortic aneurysms, and myocardial bridging. Valvular disease, cardiomyopathies, and infection of the heart valves or heart muscle can also cause sudden, unexpected cardiac death.

Atherosclerotic Cardiovascular Disease

The most common cause of death from cardiovascular disease is coronary atherosclerosis. Approximately half of individuals with coronary artery disease die suddenly. At autopsy, significant obstruction of the coronary artery lumen of 75% or greater is seen in one or more vessels. Atherosclerosis may also be seen in the aorta. Corresponding cardiomegaly (enlargement of the heart) often accompanies atherosclerotic cardiovascular disease and is typically an indication of hypertensive cardiovascular disease. In some individuals with a history of hypertension who die suddenly, the autopsy shows an enlarged heart with left ventricular thickening, or hypertrophy, and no significant atherosclerosis. The mechanism of death in these cases is a cardiac arrhythmia, ventricular fibrillation.

Aortic Aneurysm

Aortic aneurysm as a cause of death may include aortic dissection and abdominal aortic aneurysm. Both conditions result in thinning of the wall of the aorta, causing weakness and eventual rupture of the aorta and eventual bleeding. Dissecting aortic aneurysm usually occurs in the arch of the aorta and is associated with hypertension, Marfan syndrome, and pregnancy. Abdominal aortic aneurysm occurs in the distal abdominal aorta, near the bifurcation of the common iliac arteries, and is associated with atherosclerotic cardiovascular disease.

Myocardial Bridging

Myocardial bridging has been noted in cases of sudden, unexpected cardiac death of young to middle-aged adults. Normally, coronary arteries lie on the surface of the heart before entering the muscle at the apex. However, at autopsy, some individuals show a variant of the coronary arteries that tunnel under the heart muscle close to the coronary ostia. This variant has been associated with sudden, unexpected death related to the length and depth of the overlying myocardial tissue bridge covering the coronary artery. Atherosclerosis is also associated with the bridging segment, as well as fibrosis or scarring distal to the segment, which may cause cardiac arrhythmia.

Valvular Disease

Mitral Valve Prolapse

Mitral valve prolapse is associated with sudden cardiac death. The abnormal mitral valve located between the left atrium and ventricle shows cupping, redundancy, and thickening of the mitral valve, sometimes with ballooning into the left atrium. The thickening is caused by a gelatinous protein material, which weakens the valve and may be a marker for additional myxomatous changes in other areas of the heart, including the vessels, the myocardial system, and/or the left ventricle, leading to arrhythmia or death.

Cardiomyopathy

Cardiomyopathy is a general term for pathology of the heart. Cardiomyopathy types include dilated, hypertrophic, and infiltrative (restrictive) forms. Dilated cardiomyopathy involves weakness, thinning, and dilation of the ventricle walls that may be secondary to alcoholism or congestive heart failure. Hypertrophic cardiomyopathy is defined by thickening of the left ventricle and interventricular septum that causes blockage of the outflow tract and restricts blood flow through the aortic valve. Infiltrative (restrictive) cardiomyopathy is caused by abnormal deposits of protein fibrosis, including conditions such as sarcoidosis or amyloidosis.

Infectious Cardiac Disease: Myocarditis and Endocarditis

Myocarditis is an infection of the heart muscle caused by bacteria, fungi, or viral organisms. Endocarditis is infection or inflammation of the heart valves and/or the inner lining of the heart that may cause vegetations to form (Figure 14.1). Endocarditis may be noninfectious or caused by a

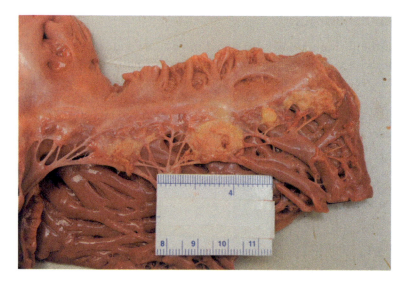

Figure 14.1 Vegetations on a heart valve in endocarditis.

variety of infectious organisms. Individuals with prosthetic heart valves, heart valve injury, or other cardiac abnormalities are at an increased risk of developing endocarditis. Subtle clues on the body may be a clue to endocarditis, such as flat or raised red lesions on the hands and feet or hemorrhages in the nails.

Central Nervous System

Sudden, unexpected natural deaths arising from the central nervous system may include seizure disorders, vascular pathology (including stroke, arteriovenous malformation, berry aneurysm, and hypertensive hemorrhage), and infections.

Seizure Disorder

Individuals that die from seizure disorders may have a history of prior head injury or epilepsy. Autopsy may show softening and discoloration of the cerebral cortex in cases of prior trauma, whereas the gross lesions are not seen in epilepsy. The circumstances of death are important, as it will affect the manner of death as homicide, accident, or natural. Death from a terminal seizure may show injury from biting the tongue. Toxicology results may show subtherapeutic anticonvulsant medication levels. The mechanism of death may include positional asphyxia or a lethal cardiac arrhythmia due to adrenalin release secondary to seizure activity.

Vascular Pathology

Vascular pathology causing sudden death includes a cerebrovascular accident (stroke) caused by narrowing of the cerebral arteries and cerebral ischemia, due to decreased blood flow to the brain. Hypertension can cause a hemorrhagic stroke of the brain. Other vascular abnormalities include a congenital weakness of the vessel wall, causing ballooning, or aneurysm, which may rupture and cause rapid death. The aneurysms are generally of a small size located at the base of the brain and termed "berry" aneurysms. Another congenital anomaly of the cerebral vessels is an arteriovenous malformation, which is composed of a webbed network of thin-walled arteries and veins. This malformation may rupture and can be diagnosed at autopsy.

Infections

Infections of the central nervous system include bacterial invasion of the brain coverings, termed meningitis, or of the brain matter, including encephalitis or abscesses. Cultures help to identify the infectious organisms.

Tumors

Brain tumors may involve the meninges or brain tissue. Occasionally, an individual may die suddenly or unexpectedly from an undiagnosed primary or metastatic brain tumor. The mechanism of death includes seizures and increased intracranial pressure from the space-occupying lesion.

Respiratory System

Diseases of the respiratory system are another potential source of unexpected deaths due to natural causes. Significant causes of death due to respiratory diseases include infections, restrictive diseases such as pulmonary fibrosis or obstructive diseases such as asthma, and emphysema or chronic obstructive pulmonary disease.

Infections

Bacteria, viruses, and fungi may infect the upper and lower respiratory tract. The upper respiratory tract consists of the airways above the vocal cords. Significant infection of the upper airway, such as laryngeal abscesses or inflammation of the epiglottis, can obstruct the airway and cause death by a lack of oxygen delivery to the lungs. The lower respiratory tract consists of the airways below the vocal cords. Pneumonia is a significant infection of the lower airways in the lungs that can be a result of bacteria or viruses. Pneumonia may also be a result of aspiration of oral or gastric contents into the airways. This may happen for a variety of reasons and it is important to determine whether an individual had a history of difficulty swallowing, seizures, or any significant history that may predispose him or her to aspiration. Chronic pneumonia may lead to inflammation of the lung lining, pleurisy.

Restrictive Lung Diseases

Restrictive lung diseases ultimately decrease the ability of the lungs to expand properly. The overall lung volume becomes decreased over time and the work of breathing becomes increased. Often, in restrictive lung diseases, fibrosis or scarring of the lung is the end result. Scarring of the lungs can arise from a variety of causes and has been associated with allergic reactions to inhaled particles, a consequence of drug toxicity, long-term exposure to dust particles such as asbestos, and infections such as tuberculosis, among many others. Pulmonary fibrosis, or lung scarring, however, frequently has no known cause.

Obstructive Lung Diseases

Obstructive lung diseases are those that result from a blockage of the airways. Individuals with obstructive lung disease have problems exhaling, often due to collapse of the smaller airways and/or inflammation of the airways. Examples of obstructive lung diseases include asthma, emphysema, and chronic bronchitis.

Asthma

Asthma is a reactive airway disease where swelling and abundant mucous production are triggered by a variety of environmental or genetic factors. Swelling of the airways can cause significant obstruction and inhibit gas exchange. Autopsy may reveal hyperinflation of the lungs as a result of air trapping in the lower airways. On cut sections, the lungs may demonstrate abundant mucous plugs and prominent bronchioles as a result of smooth muscle hyperplasia.

Chronic Obstructive Pulmonary Disease

Chronic obstructive pulmonary disease encompasses chronic bronchitis and emphysema, which are chronic, progressive diseases that affect the lungs. The most common cause for development of these diseases is cigarette smoking, although other environmental and genetic factors may also play an important role. Exposure over time to airway irritants causes the lung tissue to become thin and dilated. Autopsy may reveal grossly dilated alveoli and blebs on the surfaces of the lungs, which may rupture into the chest cavity. The mechanism of death in these cases is a result of air trapping in the lower airways, which hinders efficient gas exchange.

Gastrointestinal Tract

Common natural diseases of the gastrointestinal tract that can cause death include cirrhosis of the liver, gastrointestinal ulcers, and pancreatitis.

Cirrhosis

Exposure of the liver to toxins such as alcohol or infections such as hepatitis causes repeated cycles of liver injury and regeneration. Over time, the pattern of injury and regeneration causes scarring of the liver, resulting in nodularity, or cirrhosis, seen at autopsy (Figure 14.2). Cirrhosis is an end-stage liver disease, where the liver can no longer function properly. The liver serves many purposes, such as filtering toxins, producing blood clotting factors, synthesizing proteins, and producing bile for digestion. When the liver is significantly damaged, bile flow may become blocked, toxins may buildup in the bloodstream, and blood may not clot properly. Death may be due to a variety of mechanisms including hepatic encephalopathy (toxic ammonia buildup in the bloodstream and brain) or gastrointestinal bleeding. An important clue to significant liver disease

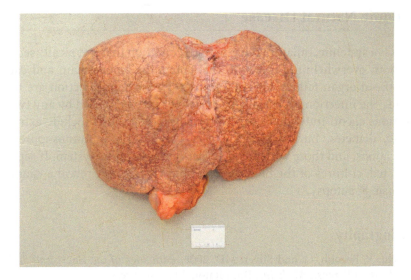

Figure 14.2 Pale, cirrhotic liver due to a combination of hepatitis C and chronic alcohol abuse.

during death investigation is yellowing of the skin and eyes, termed jaundice of the skin and scleral icterus.

Gastrointestinal Ulcers

Ulcers in the gastrointestinal tract may be secondary to a variety of causes but are commonly a result of toxins, infections, or chronic irritation of the lining of the esophagus, stomach, or intestine. Ulcers may also be secondary to reflux of stomach acid into the esophagus or, more rarely, a tumor breaking through the inner lining of the gastrointestinal tract. Significant ulcers may cause death by eroding through a blood vessel to cause gastrointestinal bleeding.

Pancreatitis

Pancreatitis is a painful inflammatory condition of the pancreas that can be caused by infection, obstructing gallstones, high lipid levels in the blood, or toxins such as alcohol. When severe, inflammation of the pancreas may cause significant leakage of pancreatic enzymes into the surrounding tissues or blood vessels to cause hemorrhage or fat necrosis that may be seen at autopsy. Rare signs of pancreatitis may be seen on the external surfaces of the body and include hemorrhage under the skin of the left flank or around the umbilicus.

Systemic Natural Disease

Sepsis is a systemic, inflammatory, natural condition that is typically secondary to an overwhelming infection that enters the bloodstream and causes widespread organ failure. Original sources for such an infection are widespread. The infection is typically bacterial but may be caused by any type of infectious agent. Individuals at risk for developing sepsis include extremes of age, diabetes, burn victims, cancer patients on immunosuppressant medications, and those with any disorder of the immune system. If sepsis is suspected, cultures of the blood and various tissues may reveal a causative organism at autopsy.

Bibliography

Fineschi, V, Baroldi, G, and Silver, MD. 2006. *Pathology of the Heart and Sudden death in Forensic Medicine.* Boca Raton, FL: CRC Press.
Kumar, V, Abbas, A, Fausto, N, Robbins, S, and Cotran, R. 2005. *Robbins and Cotran Pathologic Basis of Disease.* Philadelphia, PA: Elsevier Saunders.

Asphyxial Deaths

15

OBJECTIVES

Upon completion of this chapter and corresponding reference material, the reader will be able to

- List five causes of extrinsic asphyxia
- Describe the pathological findings associated with asphyxial deaths
- Discuss asphyxia as a cause of death
- Describe evidence that may be gathered at the scene of a death by asphyxia
- Differentiate between death by hanging and by carotid hold
- Discuss three key points associated with drowning deaths

Asphyxial Deaths

Asphyxia refers to any condition in which the body or any vital part of the body is deprived of oxygen by any means. The act of producing asphyxia is called "suffocation."

Extrinsic causes of asphyxia include choking, toxic gases, exhaust gas (such as carbon monoxide), electric shock, drugs, anesthesia, crushing injuries of the chest, compression of the chest, injury to respiratory nerves, and decrease in environmental oxygen. Intrinsic causes include hemorrhage, foreign bodies in the throat, swelling of air passages, obstructive diseases of air passages, ruptured aneurysm, pulmonary edema, cardiac insufficiency, and obstructive tumors. Other common causes of asphyxia are paralysis of the respiratory center or muscles, pneumothorax, narcotic drugs, electrocution, and child abuse.

The primary cause, however, is usually obstruction of arterial blood to the brain or of venous blood leaving the brain, which results in unconsciousness, coma, and death. In unnatural causes of death, there is rarely obstruction of the airway without evidence of struggle. Asphyxia caused by a broken neck is rare except in judicial hangings where death is instantaneous.

Manner of Death

Suicide comprises the majority of asphyxia as a manner of death. Ten to twenty percent of suicides are by hanging. Asphyxia as homicide is rare. The victim is generally a child or frail elderly adult or an adult incapable of struggle because of drug or alcohol influence. Legal (judicial) hangings are also uncommon. Lynching is hanging by mob action and, although historically common, is relatively rare.

Accidental asphyxia occurs primarily in industrial or farm accidents when clothing is caught in machinery and the victim cannot be released. Infants and children sometimes die when they become caught between crib rails or while playing. Accidental strangulation or asphyxial deaths may occur during autoerotic activities. Victims are almost exclusively male and are either completely naked or have the penis exposed when the body is discovered. Evidence of sexual activities and fantasy including pornography, bondage, ritualism, and transvestism is frequent. The scene of death is often a mirrored room with an apparatus to cause anoxia. A noose is commonly padded and the escape mechanisms fail when accidental death occurs.

Types of Asphyxia

Forensic pathologists commonly classify asphyxia into three types:

1. Compression of the chest or neck
2. Obstruction of the airway
3. Exclusion of oxygen

Compression of the chest must be sufficient to prevent adequate respiratory movements. However, compression of the neck can occur with or without blockage of the airway as with hanging or strangulation (throttling).

Smothering, aspiration of foreign material, and swelling of the respiratory lining membranes all cause airway obstruction. Allergic reactions and inflammatory responses can cause sufficient swelling to incur death. Oxygen depletion, replacement by other gases (carbon monoxide or carbon dioxide), and chemical interference (cyanide poisoning) are forms of asphyxia.

Asphyxia as Cause of Death

Cyanosis and petechial hemorrhages about the face, eye sclera, pleura, and epicardium indicate death by asphyxia. Ligature marks on the neck might lead to confirmation of causation, although all of these findings—individually or together—can be seen in conditions other than asphyxia. However, in practice, the majority of cases do not show all of the findings; indeed, many do not show any of the classical stigmata.

Scene investigation is an important adjunct to diagnosis of cause. Plastic bags near the body, postural asphyxia, or body position give additional clues to the cause of death. Presence of a noose is suspect for a death by hanging. The noose should be photographed in the position found at the scene and again after removal by cutting away from the knot. Nooses can be of almost any material—wire, rope, cord, belt, towel, bedding, clothing, or woven dental floss (with some prison deaths). Hanging can occur in almost any position such as vertical with feet either on or off the ground. Kneeling, sitting, crouching, supine, and prone positions can also be used. Hanging can be accidental or premeditated as homicide or suicide.

Choke or Carotid Holds

Choke holds or carotid sleeper holds are intended to produce transient cerebral ischemia and unconsciousness. The arm and forearm, a baton, large metal flashlight, or other devices are used to compress the neck. Compression can also be done by hand if the person applying the hold is strong and is able to reach both carotid arteries on the victim's neck with the thumb and index finger. Military and police officers are taught these holds as a technique to control the enemy or criminal, or as a means of self-defense.

In a choke hold, the forearm compresses the neck to occlude the upper airway. In this hold, the forearm is placed straight across the front of the neck. The free hand grips the wrist and pulls the wrist back. Loss of function is due to collapse of the airway and carotid arteries, subsequently decreasing oxygen to the brain. If too much force is used, the larynx or hyoid bone can be fractured. The resulting hypoxia sensitizes the heart to arrhythmias. Stimulation of the carotid sinus by pressure on the neck causes bradycardia (slowed heart rate) and a decrease in arterial blood pressure. Release of catecholamine ensues. The victim is immobilized, confused, and controlled.

The carotid hold is known as a sleeper hold. Symmetrical force is applied by the forearm and upper arm to the sides of the neck in a way that only the carotid arteries and jugular veins are compressed and not the trachea. The arm is placed about the neck with the antecubital fossa or crook of the arm centered at the midline of the neck. The free hand grips the other wrist and pulls it backward, creating a pincer effect. Compression of the carotid arteries causes loss of consciousness in approximately 10–15 seconds. A carotid sleeper hold can easily and unintentionally become a choke hold on a violently struggling individual.

There is rarely any finding of trauma to the structure of the neck with pathological examination. Compression of the carotid arteries with decreased cerebral blood flow can precipitate a stroke in an individual with atherosclerotic disease. The pressure of the hold may dislodge an atherosclerotic plaque, and an air embolus causes the stroke. Neck compression may also cause stimulation of the carotid sinus with resultant bradycardia.

Pathological Findings

External, internal, and neck examinations make up the autopsy focus in a suspected death by asphyxia. External examination shows congestion or engorgement of the face and eyes. The tongue is usually protruding, dry, dark, and swollen. Bloody mucus is often dried at the nose and/or mouth and petechiae, small pinpoint hemorrhages, show on mucus membranes, eye sclera and conjunctiva, and scalp (Figure 15.1). Depending upon the position, dependent portions of the body may be engorged (hands, feet, or genitalia). A groove around the neck will indicate the presence and nature of a noose. Grooves are asymmetrical—that is, high in the back or beneath the ear and under the chin ("V"-shaped). Skin folds about the neck in obese adults or babies may resemble noose marks.

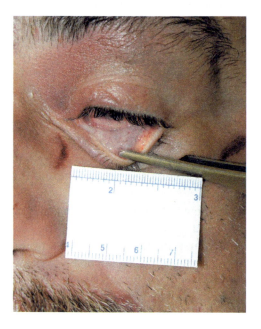

Figure 15.1 Petechial hemorrhages on the lower eyelid, pulled downward with a hemostat.

The internal examination may demonstrate little evidence of injury to the subcutaneous tissue immediately beneath the skin. Middle ear hemorrhage and petechiae are common. There is persistent fluidity of blood and edema of the brain. Rarely, thoracic and abdominal injuries are present, although right ventricular dilation and visceral congestion are evident.

Dissection of the neck should not begin until the chest cavity and cranial vault have been removed and examined. The strap muscles of the anterior neck should be examined in a layered fashion from outer to inner muscle groups. Adequate exposure is required and the skin incision should extend up the posterolateral aspect of the neck. Careful removal of the larynx, hyoid bone, base of the tongue, and upper trachea is performed en bloc with adjacent soft tissues, leaving the blood vessels of the carotid sheath.

Differences exist between strangulation by ligature (usually a homicide) and hanging.

Strangulation

- Horizontal neck pressure abrasion is seen.
- Neck mark is commonly below the level of the thyroid cartilage.

Hanging

- Neck mark passes upward toward the knot—it may be horizontal as with strangulation if the hanging occurs while lying.
- Hanging mark is at or above the level of the thyroid cartilage.
- Fractures seldom occur with hanging, except with a long drop or in the elderly.

Drowning Fatalities

Jim L. Caruso

Epidemiology

Nearly 9,000 drownings occur in the United States each year (the third most common cause of accidental death) with an estimated 80,000 near drownings.

North Carolina averages 150–200 drowning deaths each year. Most common victim is male, ages 10–19; male/female ratio is 10:1; 90% are accidental, 10% are suicide. Boating accidents account for 17% of accidental drownings.

Half of all drownings occur May–August; two-thirds occur in freshwater. Alcohol and other drugs are frequently factors.

Key Points

1. Drowning is a diagnosis of exclusion. Prior to arriving at this conclusion, one must rule out other causes of death (e.g., trauma, natural disease processes, drug overdose, disposal of a homicide victim in water). Therefore, a complete autopsy including toxicology is always indicated.
2. A drowning death is death by asphyxiation with subsequent hypoxemia and cerebral anoxia. The amount of water inhaled is variable and, in 10%–15% of cases, laryngeal spasm can result in dry drowning.
3. Absorption of large amounts of water—which especially occur in cases of freshwater drowning—was once thought to cause serious electrolyte abnormalities and potential fatal dysrhythmia. This is no longer assumed to be the case as it is likely that a healthy heart and kidneys would compensate for the increase in volume, and electrolyte abnormalities do not seem to play a large role.
4. The "break point" is defined as the time when a person can no longer voluntarily breath-hold. This occurs in response to blood levels of carbon dioxide (CO_2) and oxygen (O_2). The person breathes regardless of his or her immersion status and if submerged, continued inhalation of water occurs.
5. The type of water inhaled—fresh or saltwater—usually has little bearing on survival. Freshwater drowning usually results in larger amounts of fluid absorbed and more damage to pulmonary surfactant. This may become clinically important if the victim survives. Saltwater drowning usually results in greater pulmonary edema, pleural effusions, and hemoconcentration.
6. Near drowning is defined as resuscitation of a submersion victim with subsequent survival of at least 24 hours regardless of whether or not death occurs after this period.
7. No definitive diagnosis of drowning can be made based on autopsy findings alone. The circumstances, autopsy findings, and toxicology results are combined to arrive at the cause of death. Nonspecific autopsy findings in drowning deaths may include edema fluid in the airways, large and bulky lungs filled with fluid, water in the stomach, right ventricular dilation, cerebral edema, and hemorrhage in the petrous or mastoid bones.
8. External findings that may occur prior to or after death include "washerwoman palms" (wrinkled skin), "gooseflesh," and bites from animals living in the water.
9. Because drowning victims usually struggle, rigor mortis sets in earlier and rapid cooling slows the decomposition process. Immersion leaches blood from wounds, so determining antemortem or postmortem wounds may be difficult. Animal bites may occur prior to or after death.

10. Various chemical tests—especially electrolyte studies—have been proposed to aid in the diagnosis of drowning or in determining freshwater vs. saltwater drowning. None has proved consistently useful and most are of no value.

11. Diatom analysis has long been a favorite and controversial topic when discussing drowning deaths. Diatoms are ubiquitous, microscopic, unicellular algae with a silica skeleton in the shape of two valves. Because these organisms are found everywhere, their presence in the body could be due to inhalation, ingestion, or aspiration. Laboratory glassware and water may contain diatoms. Various techniques for evaluation include ultrasonic or acid digestion of the tissue. Often a part of the body less likely to be exposed to postmortem diatoms (e.g., bone marrow, solid organs) is examined. One attempts to find diatoms in the decedent that are specific to the body of water from which the body was recovered. Of course, there have been drownings in water where the victim regularly swam, eliminating the usefulness of this technique.

Basic Investigation

- Review past history, clinical history, and resuscitation efforts.
- Scene investigation and circumstances of the death; evidence.
- External exam and evidence of injury, x-rays, paying special attention to the head/neck.
- Autopsy to include thorough cardiovascular, respiratory, musculoskeletal exam.
- Sinuses and middle ear exam may be useful.
- Toxicology.

Bibliography

DiMaio, DJ and DiMaio, VJM. 2001. *Forensic Pathology*, 2nd ed. Boca Raton, FL: CRC Press.

Dolinak, D, Matshes, E, and Lew, E. 2006. *Forensic Pathology: Principles and Practice*. Burlington, MA: Elsevier.

Reay, DT and Eisele, JW. 1982. Death from law enforcement neck hold. *Am J Forensic Med* 3:253–258.

Reay, FT and Holloway, GA. 1982. Changes in carotid blood flow produced by neck compression. *Am J Forensic Med* 3:199–202.

Spitz, W and Fischer, R. 1993. *Medicolegal Investigation of Death: Guidelines for the Application of Pathology to Crime Investigation*. Springfield, IL: Charles C. Thomas Press.

Environmental Deaths

16

OBJECTIVES

Upon completion of this chapter and corresponding reference material, the reader will be able to

- Name the criteria for hypothermia and hyperthermia as causes of death
- Identify environmental factors that contribute to thermal deaths
- Discuss problems with collecting evidence related to a hyperthermia death
- List medical conditions that predispose an individual to death by heat
- Describe organs in a hyperthermia death compared to a hypothermia death

Fatal Accidental Hypothermia

Introduction

Exposure deaths are common in rural New Mexico. A review was done of more than 300 cases of exposure deaths in a 10-year period from environmental circumstances, demographic characteristics, autopsy findings, toxicology results, and postmortem chemistry to develop a profile of the at-risk individual in New Mexico (Dudley, 1992). Since there are no diagnostic anatomic abnormalities exclusive to hypothermia, determination of exposure as the cause of death depends on recognition of associated—but no diagnostic—anatomic findings coupled with circumstantial evidence and toxicology results.

Hypothermia deaths result from several circumstances. The most common circumstance surrounding exposure deaths is exposure while intoxicated. This is by far the largest group, particularly in New Mexico. The elderly have been found to wander away from home or a nursing home and die of hypothermia. Elderly individuals at home in poorly heated homes and an increasing number of homeless individuals die of "exposure." Another category includes individuals trapped by severe winter storms or other natural disasters such as flash floods. The final category of exposure deaths is outdoor sports enthusiasts—skiers, hikers, and participants in water sports who miscalculate their exposure and get caught by a change in weather.

This study reviewed the demographic data of exposure deaths, including age, sex, race, and presence of alcohol. It found that the incidence of "exposure" was evenly spread over all age groups—85% were male and 62% were Native Americans, although less than 10% of the New Mexico population are Native Americans. Seventy percent of the cases showed blood alcohol levels exceeding 0.10%.

Findings

Most hypothermia deaths occurred in the northwest corner of New Mexico in the Native American population. There are more hypothermia deaths per year in this region of New Mexico than anywhere else in the United States. Most deaths of this type are associated with alcohol. Alcohol is prohibited on the Native American reservation; thus, many Native Americans leave the reservation to go to the nearest town to drink and are caught without shelter on cold evenings. Vans pick up intoxicated individuals on cold nights; this may help reduce the high numbers of hypothermia deaths.

Since there are no diagnostic anatomic abnormalities characteristic of hypothermia, a determination of exposure as cause of death depends on the recognition of associated—but not diagnostic—anatomic findings coupled with circumstantial evidence and toxicology. It is important to exclude other causes of death such as trauma, blunt force injury, or asphyxia (including drowning). Fatal drug and alcohol intoxication as well as natural disease must be excluded.

The autopsy yields external and internal findings that contribute to the diagnostic criteria of hypothermia as cause of death. External manifestations include careful inspection for appropriate clothing for weather conditions, paradoxical undressing, or wet frozen clothing. Evaluation of the skin surface for abrasions, contusions, or lacerations is necessary. A characteristic bright pink to red lividity is seen with a cold body.

It is important to distinguish postmortem cold artifacts from injury. Sometimes previous evidence of hypothermia such as frostbite or absence of digits may suggest an at-risk individual.

Internal manifestations include reduced core temperature. Gastric ulcers and hemorrhagic pancreatitis are seen—especially in those individuals who live 24–48 hours. Microinfarct of major organs may be noted. We have noticed an enlarged right atrium of the heart in our cases in New Mexico, which may be due to internal bradycardia and congestive heart failure. Another finding is pulmonary congestion.

Classic gastric ulcers are often seen in hypothermia deaths. The surface ulcerations have a "punched-out" appearance and are called Wischnevsky's gastric lesions.

Toxicology and postmortem chemistries may be helpful in evaluating hypothermia cases. Alcohol and other drugs such as phenothiazines, opiates, and central nervous system depressants (barbiturates) are contributing factors to hypothermia deaths. John Coe reported high vitreous glucose levels in hypothermia deaths. We analyzed vitreous electrolyte and glucose levels on 15 fatal hypothermia cases, and all but two cases had low glucose levels. In reviewing the cases with low glucose levels, most of these deaths occurred relatively fast at extremely cold temperatures.

The two individuals with higher glucose levels had longer survivals. We concluded that the longer survival period allowed for a stress response reflected by the higher glucose levels. A study of iatrogenic hypothermia during cardiopulmonary bypass surgery suggested that hypothermia blocks insulin secretion. The numbers studied in the two cases are quite small for determining the relevance of glucose levels and merit further study.

Case Studies

The following two case studies are typical of cases often seen in rural New Mexico:

1. The first case is of an 86-year-old male who was found lying near a railroad track on coarse gravel. Apparently, the decedent wandered away from a boarding home 2 miles away. He had a history of confusion and disorientation. He was inappropriately dressed for the cold weather. The head showed blood on the forehead, raising the question of an accident; perhaps he had been hit by a train or foul play may have been involved.

   However, once he was cleaned up, the injury was only a superficial laceration of the forehead. His knees had contusions and abrasions—probably obtained while crawling around on the rocky surface before he died.

2. The second case was of a 59-year-old Native American male who was found near a drainage ditch. He was dressed inappropriately for the extremely cold weather conditions. He had been walking in the water in the ditch where his shoes were stuck in the mud. He was found wearing only his socks. The scene of investigation showed that he had attempted to crawl up the embankment before he died. He had a high blood alcohol level and died of hypothermia.

Conclusion

One of the difficulties in evaluating hypothermia cases is distinguishing between postmortem cold artifact and trauma. The uniform dark pink livor patterns over the face, lips, and tongue show postmortem drying artifacts in contrast to relatively preserved skin from a pressure pattern where the individual had been lying on his face. The cold artifact could be misinterpreted as abrasions.

Hypothermia is a diagnosis of exclusion. Therefore, to determine hypothermia as a cause of death, one must evaluate environmental circumstances, anatomic findings, and toxicology results.

Hyperthermia Deaths

The temperature of the human body is approximately 98.6°F (37°C), generally regardless of the environmental temperature. A lack of thermoregulation because of exercise, illness, or disease can be deadly to a segment of the population. Extreme summer heat waves in Philadelphia (1993) and Chicago (1995) resulted in many deaths attributable to hyperthermia.

Classic hyperthermia is manifested by a core body temperature greater than 105.8°F (41°C), hot and dry skin, and dysfunction of the central nervous system. Recent research during the Philadelphia heat wave (1993) used antemortem temperatures greater than 103°F (39°C). Victims of classic heat stroke are primarily elderly, debilitated persons in epidemic fashion during a period of prolonged high external temperature and accompanying humidity. Other risk factors include alcoholism, urban residence, poverty, residence on upper floors of buildings, and use of major tranquilizers. Obesity and cardiovascular or neurological disease have also played a factor in death due to hyperthermia. Persons who decreased physical activity, use air conditioners, and can provide self-care are low risks for heat stroke and subsequent death.

Pathologic changes from heat stroke involve primarily the central nervous system and cardiovascular system. Included in neurological changes are cerebral edema, petechiae, and gross hemorrhage. Cerebellar signs of neuronal degeneration and necrosis can be evident. Some victims may show evidence of seizure activity.

Additional findings related to cardiovascular changes include signs of fluid volume deficiency, decreased vascular resistance, and myocardial degeneration. Some victims are in varying stages of decomposition when discovered; others have died of heat stroke, but the external temperature has cooled and reduced the core temperature. Consequently, some findings may be unclear. Environmental findings during the investigation contribute to the determination of the cause of death.

Preexisting natural disease might be attributed as the primary cause of death when the criteria for heat-related death are not met and the victim dies during a heat wave. In such instances, exposure to the hot environment is listed as a contributing cause of death.

The manner of death in hyperthermia is usually cited as "accidental." There are cases where children have died in closed, hot automobiles when left there by a parent. Homicide may then be the manner of death if abuse and neglect enter the investigation.

Because epidemic heat stroke occurs in a predictable manner during a period of sustained high outdoor temperatures, the public should be informed of the prevention measures. In smaller communities, the ME/coroner may take the initiative to inform people if the public health agency has not done so.

Reference

Dudley, MH and Zumwalt, RE. 1992. Hypothermia deaths: Diagnostic criteria. Abstract presentation at *AAFS National Meeting 1992*, New Orleans, LA.

Bibliography

DiMaio, DJ and DiMaio, VJM. 2001. *Forensic Pathology*, 2nd ed. Boca Raton, FL: CRC Press.

Dolinak, D, Matshes, E, and Lew, E. 2006. *Forensic Pathology: Principles and Practice*. Burlington, MA: Elsevier.

Mirchandani, HG and McDonald, G. 1996. Heat-related deaths in Philadelphia-1996. *Am J Forensic Med Path* 17(2):106–108.

Todd, KH. 1994. Environmental emergencies, bites, and stings. In Stein, JH, ed., *Internal Medicine*, 4th ed. St. Louis, MA: Mosby.

Fire Deaths

17

MARY H. DUDLEY
LAUREN E. DVORSCAK

OBJECTIVES

- Identify four forensic issues in fire-related deaths.
- List five common causes of house fires.
- Differentiate between positive scientific means of identification and unreliable identifiers.
- Describe the possible causes and manners of fire-related deaths.
- Discuss the various components of a complete death investigation of fire-related deaths.
- Compare the pertinent autopsy findings to artifactual findings in fire deaths.

Introduction

In 2014, over 1 million fires were reported in the United States (National Fire Protection Association, 2016). Approximately 2200 deaths in the United States per year are attributable to burns or injuries sustained in destructive fires (National Safety Council, 2015). A significant amount of fires occur in the home, and the most common lethal fires are attributable to smoking in the home (National Fire Protection Association, 2016). Other causes of residential fires include defective electrical wiring, improper use of electric heaters, kitchen and cooking accidents, and children playing with matches.

Deaths attributable to fire may be immediate or delayed. Immediate mechanisms causing death in fires include thermal burns and inhalation of products of combustion (importantly, carbon monoxide). Delayed deaths are typically a result of burn complications, such as fluid and electrolyte losses through damaged skin, chronic respiratory failure from thermal lung injury, or sepsis and subsequent shock from infections that can complicate thermal burns.

Death investigation in fires includes the careful assessment and determination of the scene in conjunction with additional agencies such as law enforcement and the fire department. Forensic issues in fire-related deaths not only involve determination of the cause and manner of death but often involve severely disrupted and damaged remains, making accurate identification an important issue for the investigator. Additionally, the determination of whether the decedent was alive or dead at the time of the fire is of significant importance. Fires may not only be the result of accidents but may be set intentionally by the decedent or another party in an attempt to destroy evidence. Radiography, therefore, can play an important role in fire-related deaths, not only as an aid in identification of remains but to determine additional injuries, such as retained missiles from gunshot wounds, or other foreign bodies. If arson is suspected, clothing should be preserved and tested for the presence of accelerants. Volatile analysis may also be done on soil or carpet under the body. Samples are collected and placed into airtight containers made of glass or metal to be sent in for analysis. Plastic bags are never used for this purpose.

Contributory conditions in fire deaths must also be considered. If it seems as though the decedent could have escaped the fire, other factors may have played a role in the death. For example, drug or alcohol intoxication, young or advanced age, significant underlying natural disease, hyperthermia/heat exhaustion, and trauma are conditions that increase the likelihood of fatality in a fire.

Forensic examination of the remains includes a complete external and internal examination. External examination should include an estimation of the percent surface area burned and the degree (depth) of thermal injury. It is also important for the investigator to be aware of artifacts that may occur in fire deaths. The forensic autopsy continues the examination in greater depth. Internal examination of the organs involves special attention to the upper and lower airways, microscopic examination of the organs for thermal injuries, and collection of toxicology samples.

External Examination

Complete external examination will determine the percentage and degree of thermal injuries. The percentage of body surface area burns is based on the "Rule of Nines" as follows:

- Head—9%
- Chest—18%
- Back—18%
- Upper extremities—9% each
- Lower extremities—8% each
- Groin—1%

This formula is typically used for adults and does not correlate well to the body surface area in children, due to their relatively large head, which accounts for approximately 18% of the surface area in a child. The percentage of burns can predict survivability by adding the percentage burned to the age of the victim. If that number is near 100, the mortality rate is significantly high. For example, a 60-year-old adult with approximately 50% of the body burned has a very poor survival rate when compared to a 5-year-old child with 60% of the body burned.

Degree of thermal burns is assessed by thickness, or tissue depth, and may be designated first, second, or third degree. First-degree burns involve the skin surface, causing redness and pain. Sunburns are a typical example of first-degree burns. Second-degree burns cause blistering of the epidermis or outer layer of the skin. These burns are considered partial thickness. Third-degree burns involve full skin thickness and require emergent medical attention and may require skin-graft surgery. In the forensic external examination, it is important to document the degree of burns sustained and the extent of underlying tissue such as muscle or bone that is exposed.

Fire deaths may be due to thermal burns, smoke inhalation, or carbon monoxide toxicity. A common external observation associated with co-toxicity is cherry-pink lividity due to carboxyhemoglobin.

Artifacts of Thermal Injuries

Artifactual changes from heat may be evident on examination and may be unrelated to trauma. Artifacts encountered in extreme heat injury include a characteristic, pugilistic posture of the body. Pugilistic posturing resembles a fencing or fetal body position. The arms and legs may be flexed and contracted due to intense heat that causes fractures of the extremities. The wrists may be bent and digits may be missing. Skull or facial fractures may also be secondary to intense heat. Charring of the external body surfaces, clouding of the corneas, splitting of the skin, and variable exposure of the internal organs unrelated to trauma are common findings on external examination of fire deaths.

Another artifactual finding seen at autopsy is epidural hemorrhage, unrelated to trauma. Congealed blood in the epidural space may be an artifact of heated blood and bone marrow from the thin bones of the skull (Figure 17.1).

Dental restorations may undergo changes under intense heat, such as vaporization or deposition of metal in the facial soft tissue. These metal deposits can mimic fragments of missiles from gunshot wounds. Any intact skin should be evaluated for discoloration. In particular, a cherry-red appearance of the skin or tissue may indicate significant carbon monoxide exposure.

Postmortem injuries may also be uncovered on examination as a result of falling fire debris or recovery efforts and may be unrelated to antemortem injuries.

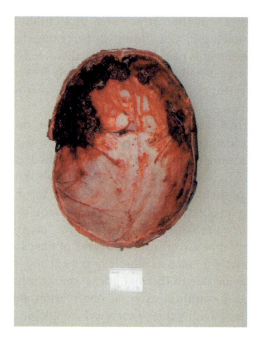

Figure 17.1 One example of thermal artifact is a thermal epidural blood collection, caused by leeching of the bone marrow into the epidural space due to intense heat.

Identification

Positive identification of fire death victims is difficult secondary to disruption of the body tissues by thermal injuries. Thermal injuries obscure presumptive identifying features, such as scars, marks, or tattoos. A visual identification or comparison to a photo may not be possible in severely burned remains. Additionally, charring or loss of the digits in the fire often precludes adequate identification by fingerprints. Other means of identification for victims of fire can include postmortem x-rays for comparison of intact bone features, identifying prosthetic implants, or comparing facial sinus cavities. Dental examination and comparison of records are also an important avenue for identification of disrupted remains. DNA samples can also be compared to antemortem data or family members for identification purposes.

Internal Examination

A complete autopsy rules out trauma and natural diseases in fire-related deaths. It is important to establish if the subject was alive at the time of the fire or dead prior to the fire. This is determined by examining the upper

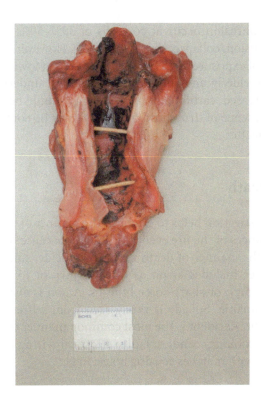

Figure 17.2 Soot in the airways indicate that an individual was breathing at the time of a fire.

and lower airways, including the trachea and lungs. If the individual was breathing at the time of the fire, soot and burns may be seen in the trachea (Figure 17.2). Microscopic sections of the lung can show dark, foreign material consistent with soot in the alveoli, or air sacs, which supports smoke and soot inhalation.

Toxicology

Blood, urine, and vitreous fluid samples are collected for toxicology analysis. Of particular interest are drugs, alcohol, and carbon monoxide (CO) levels in the blood. CO is colorless, tasteless, and extremely deadly with an affinity to bind with hemoglobin 200 times that of oxygen. Increased blood levels of carbon monoxide, typically above 20%–30%, are also indicative that the individual was alive at the time of the fire. Smokers in particular may have higher resting levels of carbon monoxide, typically less than 10%. There are no symptoms of co-toxicity at levels up to 10%. Levels from 10% to 30% may cause headaches, fatigue, or loss of attention. Severe headaches, nausea, vomiting, and confusion occur at co-levels of 30%–50%. Levels over 50% may cause convulsion, collapse, coma, and death. However, death may occur within minutes of exposure to CO with blood levels at lower concentrations, especially in the elderly and those individuals with underlying disease. If significantly increased, carbon monoxide toxicity should be listed as a cause of death. The presence of drugs and/or ethanol may be contributory factors to the cause of death.

Manner of Death

The scene of investigation helps to establish the manner of death determined by the circumstances of the fire event. Although the cause of death is related to fire injuries, the manner of death may be homicide, suicide, or accident. Homicide manner includes arson as direct injury or to conceal gunshot wounds, blunt injury, or sharp force injuries. Arson is also seen for profit, revenge, or pyromania. Suicide is rarely seen from self-emulation or incidental entrapment. Accident is the most common manner of death related to adults smoking, cooking, candles, faulty electrical wiring or equipment, or children playing with matches causing house fires.

Firefighter Fatalities

Firefighter fatalities occur related to work-related deaths from failure of protective equipment, CO toxicity, smoke inhalation, blunt injury, hyperthermia/heat exhaustion, and natural causes. Also, delayed, work-related deaths include respiratory failure and exposure to harmful particulates causing various cancers.

References

National Fire Protection Association. February 14, 2016. Fires in the U.S. Website accessed at http://nfpa.org/researcg/reports-and-statistics/fires-in-the-us.
National Safety Council. 2015. *Injury Facts*, 2015 ed. Itasca, IL: National Safety Council.

Bibliography

Dolinak, D, Matshes, E, and Lew, E. 2006. *Forensic Pathology: Principles and Practice*. Burlington, MA: Elsevier.

Electrical Deaths

18

Death by Electrocution

Electrocution as a cause of death is an infrequent event. However, it is the fifth leading cause of occupational injury in the United States. Approximately 4000 injuries occur annually nationwide, but only 1000–1500 deaths occur (Taylor et al., 2002). The causes of electrical deaths are high-voltage current, lightning, and low-voltage current. Accidental electrocution is the most commonly seen death by electrocution. Suicide by electrocution is rare and homicide is even more uncommon. Alternating current (AC) is more commonly encountered than direct current (DC) because humans are four to six times more sensitive to AC than to DC.

Electrical Terms

Electrical terms are described as volts, amperes, and resistance. Ohm's law states that resistance equals voltage divided by amperage ($R = V/A$). Amperes are calculated by dividing volts by resistance ($A = V/R$). Hertz (Hz) refers to 1 cycle/second or the frequency of polarity change/time. AC alternates polarity 60 times/second or 60 Hz. Any investigation of a scene should contain as much information as possible about the circuitry to enable further calculations.

Low voltage refers to less than 1000 V of AC, while high voltage is over 1000 V and can be either AC or DC. Currents within a United States household are 120 V for most appliances and 220 V for clothes dryers, stoves, and some washing machines. A typical urban or suburban power line supplies approximately 7,500 V; transcontinental cable supplies roughly 100,000 V.

Commonly used outlet plugs have two or three slots for appliance cords. Plugs have a hot wire, neutral wire, and a ground. The two-prong plugs have an internal ground.

Types of Outlets/Receptacles

Electrical current runs from the point of contact to the point of grounding and follows the shortest path. This also applies to current that enters the body. Electrical burns are found at the entry and exit sites in approximately half of low-voltage electrocutions and essentially all high-voltage electrocutions. The time when the burn was caused—antemortem or postmortem—is difficult if not impossible to differentiate. Minute metal particles may be deposited at the entry or exit site.

Electrical Deaths

Low-Voltage Electrocution

Low-voltage electrocution requires direct contact with the electrical circuit. The amperage is the most important electrical measurement for damage assessment. Fatal ventricular fibrillation can be caused by 70 mA of electricity. Involuntary muscle contractions are caused by as little as 15 mA, commonly known as "shock." Dry calloused skin presents a higher resistance than moist skin. Less than 2 A can cause ventricular arrest although when the current is turned off, the heart should begin a normal sinus rhythm.

High-Voltage Electrocution

Direct contact with a hot wire is not necessary with high-voltage electrocution because the current can arc or jump across a distance. With 1000 V, the electric arc is but a few millimeters. However, a current of 100,000 V can arc about one yard. High voltage can cause irreversible electrothermal injury where the temperature generated can be as high as 4000°C (7232°F). There is usually damage to the medulla of the brain stem that affects respiration.

Lightning

Lightning strikes are high-voltage DC. The strike can occur directly, by a side flash, or by conduction through another object. Death is due to cardiopulmonary arrest and/or electrocution injuries. An arborescent (fernlike) pattern remains on the skin at the entry site.

Autopsy Findings

At autopsy, nonspecific gross findings may resemble an asphyxial death in appearance. The skin and blood vessel walls may show gross microscopic changes from the electrical burn. Morphologic changes in the heart are manifested by a contraction band necrosis in the sinoatrial and atrioventricular nodal areas and widespread focal contraction band necrosis in all four chambers. Finally, focal degeneration of the media of coronary vessels is evident.

Skin changes at the area of electrical contact show a targetoid burn appearance with central brown or black necrosis (skin destruction) surrounded by an area of clearing or pallor and an outside rim of hyperemia (redness) (Figure 18.1).

Investigation of Electrocution

A large number of electrical deaths are discovered at the scene. Any electrical death scene poses a danger to the first people to reach the scene.

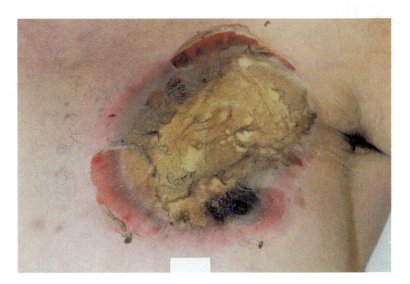

Figure 18.1 A large electrical burn with erythema around the edges.

The immediate action when an electrical death is suspected is to shut off the cause of the current. The local power company is summoned to provide the exact location of the suspected electrical problem and to shut off the power. The possibility of electrocution exists when wires or electrical appliances are evident, electrical repairs or installation is in progress, or an unusual situation occurred such as "He yelled and then became unconscious."

Investigators of electrical deaths and injuries should possess basic skills regarding testing and electricity. These include basic testing techniques for hot and ground wires, altered wiring, and correct installation of ground lugs. Investigators should also be able to test the amount of current available. Investigators should be certified as electricians to enable them to provide testimony as expert witnesses.

Investigators are able to answer numerous questions related to electrocutions:

How much current was available? Is this common practice? Was it possible for the decedent to be a conductor of electricity? What were the circumstances that made this possible? How was the electrical wound caused (from scene information and autopsy findings)?

Safety of the investigator and prevention of a second fatality is of the utmost priority. If an electrical death is suspected, the scene must be secured and the faulty appliance removed and later tested.

Bibliography

DiMaio, DJ and DiMaio, VJM. 2001. *Forensic Pathology*, 2nd ed. Boca Raton, FL: CRC Press.

Dolinak, D, Matshes, E, and Lew, E. 2006. *Forensic Pathology: Principles and Practice*. Burlington, MA: Elsevier.

Spitz, W and Fischer, R. 1993. *Medicolegal Investigation of Death: Guidelines for the Application of Pathology to Crime Investigation*. Springfield, IL: Charles C. Thomas Press.

Taylor, A, McGwin, G, Valent, F, and Rue, LW. 2002. Fatal accidental electrocutions in the US. *Inj Prev* 8:306–312.

Wright, RK and Gantner, GE. 1990. Electrical injuries and lightning. In Froede, RC, ed., *Handbook of Forensic Pathology*. Northfield, IL: College of Forensic Pathologists.

Drug and Alcohol Deaths

19

OBJECTIVES

Upon completion of this chapter and corresponding reference material, the reader will be able to

- Describe external findings and long-term complication of intravenous drug abuse (IVDA)
- Discuss the major drug categories and drug effects on the body
- Estimate blood alcohol levels from number and type of alcoholic beverages ingested over an identified period of time
- List individual variables that affect the levels of alcohol in the body
- State the blood alcohol level for legal definition in the state where you live or where you work of "driving under the influence of alcohol," "driving while intoxicated," "drunk driving," or other reference to operating a motorized vehicle while drinking
- Discuss the difference between vitreos and blood alcohol levels
- Describe the impact of putrefaction on blood alcohol content

Death from Drug Abuse

Illegal drug use causes accidents and is often the cause of homicides. Opiates, stimulants, volatiles, and sedatives or tranquilizers are major drug categories associated with fatalities. Ingestion, inhalation, and injection are usual routes of drug abuse.

Intravenous drug abuse (IVDA) carries complications related to both the drug itself and to the route of administration. Sudden death can occur from overdose. Systemic infections including HIV/AIDS, hepatitis, tetanus, and bacterial sepsis are common from shared needle use and contaminated supplies. Intravenous drugs (IVDs) are frequently "cut" with a substance to reduce the toxicity of the dose or "fix." Strychnine, talc, starch, or arsenic can be involved as an adulterant.

Indications of IVDA are needle punctures over veins. Puncture marks may be visible on the arms, hands, legs, feet, or neck. Sites between the toes or along the bones may evidence inflammation. Tattoos frequently conceal puncture sites. Needle "tracks" over veins are the result of scarring from repeated needle punctures; these represent long-term drug abuse. Cutaneous "skin pop" ulcers result from injection of nonsterile drug preparations into the subcutaneous tissue. This can be purposeful or accidental if a vein is missed. Ulcers heal as round or oval pressed scars. Skin popping is the last resort of IVD abusers who run out of accessible veins.

In the emergency room or with ambulance crews, it is important to circle any existing puncture sites before or immediately after intravenous (IV) infusions are started. Then document the existing sites and site of the IV. It can be confusing at autopsy to differentiate between attempts to insert a therapeutic IV and needle track marks.

Opiates

Opiates provide pain relief with feelings of euphoria. The most common disadvantage of opiates for analgesia is respiratory depression.

Morphine and codeine are derived from the opium poppy. Semisynthetic variations are heroin, oxycodone, and hydromorphone. Completely synthetic preparations are meperidine (Demerol), propoxyphene (Darvon), pentazocine (Talwin), and methadone. Opiates can be inhaled, ingested, or injected. Some forms are available orally for long-term pain control.

Heroin and codeine are metabolized to morphine and are central nervous system depressants. Heroin is generally injected into peripheral veins. Chronic use causes scarring of the veins and surrounding soft tissue, resulting in "needle track marks" generally found in the arm or hand veins. Occasionally, the marks are covered by elaborate tattoos in an attempt to conceal the injection sites. Fatalities can occur when packages of morphine are transported in condoms in the gastrointestinal tract of an individual. Sometimes they leak into the blood stream causing fatal drug overdose.

Stimulants

Cocaine, amphetamines, and hallucinogens are classified as stimulants. As with opiates, swallowing, "shooting up," and snorting are the usual methods of use. Amphetamines come in a variety of forms including crystal, crack, crank, and prescription drugs commonly used for behavioral control such as Dexedrine or Ritalin. Lysergic acid, peyote, mushrooms, and phencyclidine are common hallucinogens. The common response of all stimulants is euphoria, agitation, hallucinations, hyperthermia, and tachycardia.

Cocaine is the most commonly abused stimulant with the highest prevalence in the United States in the Northeast and West Coast. Homicides related to trafficking are higher in urban centers; one report from Connecticut cited 38% of homicide victims with positive toxicologic specimens.

Cocaine is extracted from the leaves of the Erythroxylon coca plant and the alkaloid. Cocaine hydrochloride results from dissolving the alkaloid in hydrochloric acid to produce heat-labile white crystals. Freebase or crack is made from the cocaine hydrochloride crystals and can be smoked.

The pharmacologic action of cocaine affects every body system. Seizures, deliriums, fevers, hemorrhages, and changes in hematological makeup are frequent. Cocaine is metabolized by the liver rapidly (half-life of 30 minutes) into benzoylecgonine, norcocaine, and ecgonine methyl ester. Concurrent use of ethanol and cocaine produces the product cocaethylene, which has toxic properties by itself in addition to its two components. Cocaine can be consumed by chewing, snorting, smoking, or IV injection. With progressively increasing blood levels, "skin popping" is another method of administration. Cocaine is a vasoconstrictor and chronic snorting can cause perforation of the nasal septum resulting from repeated nasal inhalation. Erosion of dental enamel occurs with nasal inhalation into the mouth.

Body packers try to carry cocaine in plastic bags or balloons by swallowing the balloons or inserting them into the rectum or vagina. The "mule" can die if a bag leaks. Similar in properties to cocaine, methamphetamine is also a stimulant with a half-life of 3 hours. It is metabolized by the liver to amphetamine.

In any case of drug overdose where the patient dies in the emergency room or hospital, it is important to keep everything connected to the patient in place. This means that all IV lines are sent intact as well as all fluids in urine or nasogastric collectors. Antemortem specimens are helpful in determining the cause of death. All hospital specimens should be saved. Too often an initial specimen is collected (blood or urine) and forgotten during the course of treatment or when the patient dies.

Volatiles

People like to sniff paint; sometimes they actually spray paint on their hands or faces. Volatiles are usually suspected at autopsy as a result of the scene of death. Blood is collected and placed into a volatile container that traps fumes. Blood levels, however, are not very helpful. Blood must be collected properly or the volatiles will vaporize and there will be no sample.

Samples can be obtained at autopsy from solid organs—liver, lung, brain, and kidney. A larger tissue section is used to ensure complete examination.

Sedatives/Tranquilizers

Sedatives and tranquilizers, sometimes known as "sleeping pills" or "hypnotics," belong to a number of drug classifications. Many of these drugs are prescribed reluctantly because of low therapeutic index and high addiction liability. Barbiturates, known as "blues," "yellows," or "reds," and phenobarbital are available by prescription and often on the illegal market.

Drugs taken for sedation and sleep disorders can result in a longer period of sedation than anticipated, related to the dose and potency of the drug. This can lead to accidental overdose. Coupled with alcohol, the effects can result in a deadly overdose. The ME/coroner's office must determine whether the overdose was intentional or accidental.

Tranquilizers are generally ingested. Therefore, stomach contents, vomitus, pills, or bottles at the scene assist in determining the cause of death. Blood samples and solid organ tissue are examined at autopsy to determine if alcohol was associated with the drugs.

Alcohol Deaths

Introduction

Forty-two percent of the general population abstain from drinking alcohol or rarely drink alcohol. Thirty-one percent consider themselves to be light drinkers; that is, they have an average of less than one drink per day. Eighteen percent are classified as moderate drinkers who drink one or two drinks daily, and approximately 9% of the population are heavy drinkers who consume more than two drinks per day.

A "drink" is a 12-ounce can of beer (4% alcohol), 4-ounce glass of wine (12% alcohol), or 1 ounce of 100-proof liquor (50% alcohol). Each drink increases blood alcohol levels by 0.02% depending on a number of variables that affect the rate of alcohol absorption through the stomach and upper small bowel. Most alcohol is absorbed in 1 hour, but the rate of absorption depends on

- Concentration and total quantity of alcohol in the stomach
- Nature of food already in the stomach
- Length of time stomach contents remain in the stomach
- Permeability of the stomach and intestinal membranes

In most states, blood alcohol level for intoxication for driving is 0.08%–0.10%. Five drinks of any substance within an hour will enable almost anyone to become legally drunk, using the current 0.1% level. If the body metabolizes alcohol at 0.02% an hour, the measured blood level still varies individually primarily due to body weight.

Alcohol is absorbed unaltered through the gastrointestinal tract and its presence is detected in the blood within 5 minutes. The maximum concentration is within 30–90 minutes. Alcohol is metabolized in the liver to carbon dioxide and water and is excreted by the kidneys and lungs. Alcohol absorption begins immediately in an empty stomach. However, absorption is delayed when the stomach is full.

Blood levels of ingested alcohol cause different mental and physical responses. Mild euphoria and relaxation occur with less than 0.05% ethanol in the blood. Deterioration of judgment and control of inhibitions begin at 0.05%–0.15%. Emotional liability, crying, or outbursts of anger occur at 0.15%–0.25%. Mental confusion leading to stupor, coma, and death occur at 0.25%–0.35% blood level. Translated to the ability to drive a motor vehicle, probable impairment and poor judgment begin after the first drink at 0.05%. The driver shows decreased reflexes and impaired coordination from 0.05% to 0.1%. Severe impairment occurs after 0.1% blood alcohol level, and the person is "legally drunk."

Blood alcohol concentration affects clinical symptoms as follows:

Blood Alcohol Concentration (g/100 mL)	Stages	Symptom
0.01–0.05	Subclinical	Little effect
0.03–0.12	Euphoria	Beginning sensory/motor impairment
0.09–0.25	Excitement	Impairment, incoordination, drowsiness
0.18–0.35	Confusion	Disorientation, lethargy
0.25–0.40	Stupor	Impaired consciousness
0.35–0.50	Coma	Possible death

In the laboratory, samples are measured on the gas chromatogram and the various volatiles represent a peak on a graph depending on time of release from the "head space" of the specimen.

Alcohol is distributed to various tissues in proportion to the water content of the individual tissues. Tissues with low water content have low alcohol content. Equilibrium is usually reached within 1 hour after drinking. The relative concentrations of alcohol in body fluids and tissues are

- Whole blood, 1.0%–1.15%
- Urine, 1.2%–1.4%
- Cerebral spinal fluid (CSF), 1.10%
- Vitreous humor, 1.15%
- Brain, 0.85%–0.90%
- Air in the lung, 1/200% (one volume of blood contains the same amount of alcohol as 2100 volumes of air from the lung)

Alcohol is eliminated from the body through the liver, urine, perspiration, and exhalation. The liver metabolizes 90%–95% of alcohol. Liver disease interferes with metabolism and delays elimination from the body. Some drugs compete with alcohol for liver function and excretion. Excretion from other pathways totals 5%.

Blood and Vitreous Alcohol Levels

Vitreous alcohol levels trail behind blood alcohol levels during alcohol consumption until equilibrium is reached, but then vitreous levels are higher than blood levels once drinking ceases. Ordinarily, the vitreous fluid alcohol value lags behind the blood value by approximately 1 hour. That is, the vitreous level is lower during the preabsorption state and higher during the postabsorption state. Therefore, both vitreous and blood alcohol levels should be obtained to determine if an individual has just started or stopped drinking.

Postmortem vitreous alcohol levels may be more accurate than blood alcohol levels in hospitalized trauma cases. For example, blood alcohol can be diluted if the patient is given transfusions of IV fluids. Blood alcohol levels may also vary if the patient has bled profusely due to depletion factors.

Postmortem Changes and Generation of Ethanol

Postmortem changes do not cause increase or deterioration in blood alcohol concentrations until putrefaction starts. Putrefaction may cause increase, decrease, or no change in blood alcohol levels. Analysis of vitreous humor or urine in decomposing bodies helps the ME/coroner determine whether alcohol found in the blood was ingested before death or formed after death.

Ethanol may be generated through the action of microbes on sugars in the blood during the postmortem period—both in situ and during specimen storage. Reports indicate that one-half to two-thirds of blood specimens taken at autopsy contain microbes—primarily yeast and *Escherichia coli*—that are capable of producing alcohol through fermentation. This fermentation requires sugar (glucose) and is promoted by elevated temperatures. In this regard, blood glucose may increase to values exceeding 500 g/dL during the immediate postmortem period. Heart blood has particularly high glucose values immediately after death, probably due to agonal glycogenolysis.

If the body is placed at 4°C within a few hours of death and if the collected specimen is adequately preserved (1% sodium fluoride), fermentation is inhibited and the alcohol value measured in the collected specimen reflects the immediate premortem value. An exception may be for low alcohol values such as 0.05% or less. Such values must be interpreted with caution because fermentation during the postmortem period can easily produce such low levels of alcohol.

The vitreous specimen is somewhat protected from postmortem ethanol production by bacteria. Thus, vitreous ethanol levels may be more accurate than blood levels in decomposed, severely traumatized, embalmed, or burned bodies. Vitreous fluid behind the lens of the eye can be a very accurate measurement, especially if decomposition has occurred and blood alcohol is higher as a result of postmortem ethanol production. Blood ethanol levels may be falsely elevated in decomposition up to 0.20 g% as observed in studies by Zumwalt et al. (1982) when no alcohol consumption occurred. However, if the eye is intact and the vitreous humor is clear, vitreous ethanol levels may be quite accurate.

Collection of Samples for Alcohol

The ME/coroner is often asked to testify in court as to the condition of the person at the time of an accident or death: "How many drinks did the person have?" That is difficult to determine because the exact length of time the person was drinking is often unknown—all that may be known is the blood alcohol level. As noted earlier, the concentration could be 1% in the blood and higher in the urine. Sometimes, there is no ethanol in the blood, but there is a very high level in the urine due to metabolism over time. The levels are never equivalent, and it is sometimes hard to determine alcohol levels.

Proper collection of blood alcohol samples during autopsy is important in determining both cause and manner of death. Studies have shown significant differences in blood alcohol concentrations between blood samples taken from different parts of the body. Collection of postmortem blood samples for alcohol concentrations can also cause inaccuracies or errors. For example, drawing heart blood through the chest wall may result in contaminated samples—especially if there are internal injuries. Blood levels should be substantiated by analysis of vitreous humor, urine, CSF, and bile for ethanol content.

The first consideration is whether collection from the heart is as adequate as collection from a peripheral site such as the femoral vessels. When collection is carefully performed, alcohol results from these two sites are not significantly different. However, if pericardial fluid is included in the collection from the heart, the alcohol value may be falsely elevated due to postmortem diffusion of alcohol from the stomach. This is especially true in cases of decomposition and trauma where the usual barriers to diffusion from the stomach may be more easily breached during the postmortem period. In studies of alcohol diffusion from the stomach, alcohol values up to 0.23% were found in pericardial fluid at the same time that carefully collected heart blood was negative for alcohol. In cases where the integrity of the blood specimen is in question, a vitreous fluid specimen may be useful in corroborating the blood alcohol value.

Conclusion

In the toxicology laboratory, cocaine, methamphetamine, and morphine are detected by direct method (radioimmunoassay) or through the gas chromatogram–mass spectrometer that breaks the compound into its molecular components that can be charted on a graph and compared to a computer match. Heroin is detected from a urine sample by the presence of 6-monoacetylmorphine (6-MAM).

Alcohol and drugs are found in many forensic-related deaths such as motor vehicle accidents, homicides, and suicides. Alcohol and drugs may also be the sole cause of death by intoxication. Unless otherwise supported by scene investigation, an illicit drug death is generally classified as an accidental manner of death. The cause of death is generally "acute drug intoxication." Two or more drugs are classified as "mixed drug intoxication." A death involving drugs and alcohol is signed out as a "combined drug and ethanol intoxication."

Legal medications can be used in illegal ways. Consequently, both legal and illegal drug use can result in accident, suicide, or homicide. Scene investigation and complete toxicology evaluation and autopsy findings are needed to provide complete information in the death investigation.

Reference

Zumwalt, RE, Bost, RO, and Sunshine, I. 1982. Evaluation of ethanol concentrations in decomposed bodies. *J Forensic Sci* 27(3):549–554.

Bibliography

Baselt, RC. 1995. *Disposition of Toxic Drugs and Chemicals in Man*, 4th ed. Foster City, CA: Chemical Toxicology Institute.

Baskin, SI. 1991. *Principles of Cardiac Toxicology*. Boca Raton, FL: CRC Press.

Cravey, RH and Baselt, RC. 1981. *Introduction to Forensic Toxicology*. Davis, CA: Biomedical Publications.

Dolinak, D. 2013. *Forensic Toxicology: A Physiologic Perspective*. Calgary, Alberta, Canada: Academic Forensic Pathology, Inc.

Karch, SB. 1996. *The Pathology of Drug Abuse*, 2nd ed. Boca Raton, FL: CRC Press.

O'Neil, MJ. 2013. *The Merck Index*, 15th ed. Cambridge, UK: Royal Society of Chemistry.

Workplace Deaths

20

CHERYL L. POZZI

OBJECTIVES

Upon completion of this chapter and corresponding reference material, the reader will be able to

- List five areas of concern in the workplace where lack of information regarding forensic issues can have serious consequences
- Identify six components of a basic accident/investigation plan for the workplace
- Describe the need for proper occupational and safety forensic techniques in the workplace
- Discuss proper use and function of components of the forensic evidence kit for the workplace
- Describe the purpose and differences among close-up, mid-range, and distance photography used in scene investigation in the workplace

Occupational and Safety Forensic Techniques

Introduction

Occupational health and safety personnel are frequently involved in accident investigations. These personnel include occupational health nurses or physicians, industrial hygienists, company-trained safety investigators, internal security personnel, fire protection personnel, and hazardous management personnel. Any of these people may be the first called to an accident scene or may be called in at a later time for additional investigations. There may also be a designated company emergency response team that responds to emergencies. This team may be comprised of employees with various skills who "volunteer" their expertise during a crisis. To respond to accident scenes is not necessarily part of their job duties or descriptions.

Companies are often concerned with the safety and welfare of employees as well as visitors, neighboring companies and citizens, and the environment. They may have a communication and action plan in place with the regional fire and police departments depending on the types of chemicals used and potential hazards. The local fire department and/or the internal safety/security or fire department may be responsible for conducting periodic evaluations to determine if various safety regulations set forth by the National Institute for Occupational Safety and Health and Occupational Safety and Health Administration (OSHA) are being met. They may also perform duties during crises such as

- Identifying hazardous substances
- Evacuating people
- Securing the premises
- Neutralizing chemicals
- Properly disposing hazardous materials
- Testing for safety before allowing reentry to the environment

During an accident, there may be injured persons requiring treatment or possible fatalities. In the occupational setting, it is imperative to know the following:

- The plant layout
- Hazardous substances with which employees work
- Locations of any hazardous processes or equipment
- Typical signs and symptoms of exposure to any of those hazards

An investigator or health professional responding to the accident scene could easily be disabled by toxic gases, electricity, or other hazards. As critical as forensic investigations are, additional fatalities or injuries are unnecessary and preventable. Outside investigators should employ a communication force with company safety personnel to better understand substances involved and potential consequences.

Violence in the workplace has become the second leading cause of death in the workplace and the first leading cause of death in the workplace for women. Some incidents have not been as blatant as gunshot wounds. Incidents have been known to include drowning in vats of poisonous chemicals, use of high-powered machinery, parking lot rape, poisoning with hazardous chemicals, sabotage of personal protective equipment, alterations of warning devices, arson, and tampering with hazardous exposure meters.

It is important for occupational personnel to understand forensic techniques. Issues where lack of information about forensic techniques can create serious consequences include

- Destruction or loss of evidence
- Improper documentation
- Lack of or poor photography
- Breaking chain of evidence rules
- Improper investigative procedures

The best measures that safety or occupational personnel can take are to be informed about proper forensics techniques and then to develop accident plans that incorporate these skills. Good communication with other professionals that may be involved is also necessary.

Investigation Plan

Develop a basic accident/investigation plan. Start with the basics to build an investigation system and team as knowledge and resources increase. This plan should recognize all important persons who may be involved from different disciplines. It should also define roles so that each job is defined without redundancy or confusion. There should be internal investigators within the scene; external investigators who may interview witnesses; and another group who represents the command center for filtering information, directing personnel, etc. The basic plan should include methods to correlate all information. Someone should be assigned to deal with the media, internal and external legal personnel, internal security, external law enforcement agencies, medical investigators, OSHA, and any other officials who either become involved or require notification.

Develop a checklist so that during the crisis everyone is fully aware of each step and procedure. This ensures that proper equipment is available, everyone has been notified, and details are not overlooked.

Forensic Evidence Kit

Create an internal evidence kit. Law enforcement agencies may have their own systems. During smaller incidents where external law enforcement may not be necessary, proper supplies are critical. The following is a list to start developing a company evidence kit:

- Envelopes and self-sealing plastic bags ranging from sandwich to garbage bag sized with means of permanent marking and sealing (to identify evidence without damage).
- Absorbent cotton or gauze (for drying wet evidence inside paper bags).

- Identification tags labeled to include date, time, location description, and investigator's name. These should be completed and attached to evidence and then collated with a master list.
- Paper bags from sandwich to grocery store sizes (for some organic evidence that cannot be sealed in plastic bags due to moisture concerns).
- Wide-mouthed, plastic containers with screw-on lids in various sizes up to 1 gallon (to protect fragile or other evidence that should be in a closed, rigid container).
- Flashlights and extra batteries.
- Auxiliary lighting for outdoor situations. A portable generator with extension cords are helpful and are essential at remote sites or during power outages.
- Digital camera, flash unit, and extra batteries.
- Camcorder with a tripod and auxiliary lighting, several fresh tapes, and extra batteries. The camcorder taping provides a visual and audible record and can be used to record interviews.
- Permanent marker fine enough to write on evidence tags.
- Pen that will not bleed onto fabric.
- Chain of evidence form. (No one touches, observes, or photographs evidence without signing, dating, and noting the appropriate time on the forms.)
- Personal protective gear including gloves, masks, eye wear, clothing, and shoes appropriate for the area. Blood-borne pathogens are always a potential hazard.
- Designated vehicle if the accident is at a remote site or not within walking distance. (Four wheel drive or golf carts may be appropriate.)
- Crime or accident scene tape, traffic cones, barricades, etc.
- Voice-activated, handheld tape recorder with extra batteries and tapes.

Record basic information when the accident is reported. The tape recorder is the easiest and best means of documentation. Perform a voice test prior to proceeding. Note time of day, weather conditions, lighting, if the surface of the flooring was previously wet with another substance, if construction is taking place in the area, etc. Capture all pertinent information. Use the tape recorder to interview witnesses and document all findings. After returning to your office, transcribe the recorded tape as soon as possible and duplicate the master tape. Store these as permanent records in two secure locations.

Conduct an initial survey of the scene. Determine whether hazardous conditions persist. Is it safe to proceed with the investigation? Notify ancillary support if necessary for protection or evacuation. Determine the need for health-care assistance. Can the company health department manage the level of injuries or is the situation more extensive with greater numbers of victims requiring additional support?

Rope off the scene for evidence protection. Privacy screens may also be required. Protect evidence from destruction by the environment, people, insects, or animals.

Photography

Photograph the scene. Photographs should include distance shots to record the complete perspective, midrange shots, and close-up, detailed shots. Use of a ruler or scale in the photographs may be necessary for accuracy. A bold pocket rod as used by surveyors is ideal in photographs. Date notation can be helpful. Permission need not be obtained when photographing persons involved in an accident. Consider photographing groups of bystanders who might have witnessed the accident. There can never be too many photographs. Label and keep photographs with the case file.

Collect and label all appropriate evidence items. These should be photographed before collection. Transfer of these items should always follow the chain of evidence rules. If they must be stored, ensure they are kept in a locked area. Do not forget to write a detailed report to accompany all this work. This should be done immediately before details fade from memory.

Conclusion

Safety and occupational health personnel must realize their jobs are critical. The victim may have a legal claim against the manufacturer of a vehicle, tooling product, office chair, or chemical substance. The company may have to prove that they were not negligent in supplying proper safety instruction or devices to employees who subsequently hurt themselves on the job. An employee may have a legal suit against the company for lack of warning about hazardous materials. There might be a workplace violence situation with a resulting death or injury. This might involve investigation from various perspectives. Accurate documentation of these incidents can assist those involved. Occupational health and safety professionals must strive to provide a competent and complete investigation.

Bibliography

US Department of Labor Occupational Safety and Health Administration. February 10, 2016. Website accessed at https://www.osha.gov.

Child Fatalities and Domestic Violence

IV

Domestic Violence

21

MARY H. DUDLEY

OBJECTIVES

Upon completion of this chapter and corresponding reference material, the reader will be able to

- Discuss the incidence of crimes against women—nationally and in your community
- Describe physical injuries seen with domestic violence
- Discuss major components of the domestic violence protocol
- Identify the role and responsibility of the sexual assault nurse examiner and discuss the incidence of elder abuse

Responsibilities of the Health-Care System

Although the Joint Commission on Accreditation of Healthcare Organizations has mandated standards for identification of victims and collection of evidence, surveys conducted have shown that many victims are unreported (Black et al., 2011). Hospitals may fail abuse victims as a result of the following:

- Time constraints.
- Lack of training.
- Reluctance of health-care workers and victims to talk about domestic violence.
- The health-care system also fails victims as a result of lack of recognition of the problem.
- Acts such as keeping victims waiting in emergency rooms.
- Derogatory medical notes and records.
- Blaming victims for their condition.

Crimes against Women

Physical assault is a major cause of injury sustained by women, and sexual assault is a significant proportion of those crimes. Women are much more likely to be injured in an assault than men, and more than half of rape victims are less than 18 years of age at the time of an assault (Tjaden and Thoennes, 2006). In particular, intimate partner violence is cited as a cause of injury for nearly 4 out of every 1000 women (Catalano, 2012). Households comprised of multiple female children and an unmarried adult were 10 times more likely to experience violence than households comprised of married adults with children (Catalano, 2012).

Index of Suspicion

- Be suspicious of repetitive patterned injuries.
- Be suspicious of facial injuries (e.g., bruises).
- Be suspicious of bite marks because of their potential association with sexual abuse.

Domestic Violence Protocol for Primary Care Setting

1. Obtain/document.
    a. Incident history (quotes) from battered woman
    b. Address of occurrence
    c. Name/relationship of person she states caused injury/injuries
2. Perform complete physical/neurological exam.
    a. Document injuries (body map/trauma sheet, sites of injuries). Indicate old/new injuries.
    b. Identify presence of bruises, cuts, lacerations, burns, abrasions, etc.
    c. Determine extent or type of injuries inconsistent with patient's explanation.
    d. Assess multiple injuries in different stages of healing.
    e. Document problems during pregnancy, specifically preterm abortion, bleeding, intrauterine growth retardation, and hyperemesis.
    f. Document other related problems.
        i. Evidence of alcohol/drug abuse.
        ii. Eating disorders.
        iii. Vague or nonspecific physical or psychological complaints (fatigue, anxiety, rage, loss of appetite, dissociation, chronic irritable bowel syndrome, pelvic inflammatory disease, ulcers).
        iv. Repeated use of emergency services.
        v. X-ray if indicated (to determine old/new fractures).

3. Mental health exam.
  a. Assess emotional abuse.
  b. Look for other related problems.
    i. Depression, sleep disturbances, nightmares, and social problems.
    ii. Suicidal ideation, suicide attempts/threats, patient and/or partner.
  c. Determine treatment/referral mental health department if indicated.
4. If the victim has been sexually abused or raped, do a physical exam or refer to sexual assault response team/emergency department. Also collect forensic evidence.
  a. Assess safety of patient/children
5. Informed consent (photography) make copy of consent for chart.
  a. Photograph injuries (multiple photographs).
  b. Determine wound size with ruler—include in photograph.
  c. Include patient's name and date of birth, date, photographer's name with all photographs.
6. Rights/access to medical records.
  a. Inform battered woman of her rights to her medical records and how to access them in case of future medical and/or forensic needs.
7. Referrals.
  a. Domestic Violence Center.
  b. Child Protective Services (CPS) child abuse.
  c. Children's Advocacy Center sexual abuse.
8. Call 911 report domestic violence crime.
9. Reporting.
  a. Health-care provider should discuss reporting requirements and solicit cooperation of the patient. However, the patient's consent is not required to make a report—patient's safety must be considered at all times.
  b. Information reported to a law enforcement agency should not include the complete medical record but should be limited to information that is necessary for the agency to respond.
10. Documentation.
  a. SOAP format is one that may be used to record information from the patient's description of the incident.
    i. Subjective: quote the patient as much as possible. Record the patient's description of the incident.
    ii. Objective: record objective findings, information must be accurate. In a court of law, the medical records are presumed to be correct when there is a discrepancy between the chart and the patient's testimony. Complete a body map.

        iii. Assessment: assess the situation for immediate safety of the patient and lethality of the situation (lethality checklist and danger assessment tool).

        iv. Plan: make a report when appropriate, provide resources, aftercare actions, and consider immediate safety issues. Document police involvement to include the police department called/responded and name of the officer to whom information/evidence was given.

    b. Document information given for referrals to counseling crisis centers, safe houses, etc.

11. Treatment.

    a. Treat medical injuries as indicated. Use caution in administering/prescribing medications, especially if the patient is returning home and the abuser has not been determined or apprehended; medication may make the patient unable to avoid assault.

12. Aftercare.

    a. Assess immediate safety of patient/children, respecting the victim's evaluation of the situation; determine if she feels safe.

    b. Assess lethality; inform patient if her situation is potentially lethal.

    c. Remind her that battering is a crime and that she is protected by law.

    d. Ask her what help she would like to receive.

    e. Furnish her with a list of area shelters and crisis lines.

    f. Explore available options for the patient/children.

    g. Can patient/children stay with family/friends?

    h. Does patient need or want immediate access to a shelter?

    i. Provide copy of a safety plan if needed.

    j. Contact Child Protective Services (CPS) for child safety issues.

References

Black, MC, Basile, KC, Breiding, MJ, Smith, SG, Walters, ML, Merrick, MR et al. 2011. The National Intimate Partner and Sexual Violence Survey (NISVS): 2010 summary report. Atlanta, GA: National Center for Injury Prevention and control, Centers for Disease Control and Prevention.

Catalano, S. 2012. *Intimate Partner Violence, 1993–2010*. Washington, DC: Bureau of Justice Statistics, National Crime Victimization Survey.

Tjaden, P and Thoennes, N. 2006. *Extent, Nature, and Consequences of Rape Victimization: Findings from the National Violence against Women Survey*. Washington, DC: Department of Justice.

Sexual Assault

22

OBJECTIVES

Upon completion of this chapter and corresponding reference material, the reader will be able to

- State the legal definitions of rape, consensual sex, and statutory rape
- Describe the process of investigation of a victim of sexual assault
- Identify pathological evidence of assault and identify the functions of sexual assault nurse examiners (SANE)

Sex-Related Deaths and Crimes

Deaths related to sexual activity and crimes involving sexual assaults make up a significant proportion of deaths encountered by medicolegal death investigators. Approximately 1 in 5 women and 1 in 71 men report experiencing rape (Black et al., 2011). Along with the increase in crimes, there is an increase in demand for investigation and pathologic examination of specimens and victims of sex-related crimes.

Sex-related deaths can be classified into numerous entities and involve several manners of death. Occasionally, the sudden death of a male involved in sexual activity can be attributed to natural causes; the cause of death is usually cardiovascular disease including atherosclerosis, cardiomyopathy, and berry aneurysm. It is important to note that fecal soiling and fluid discharge from the penis can be seen normally as a postmortem change and should not be misinterpreted as evidence of sexual activity in an otherwise natural death.

Accidental deaths and injuries sometimes result from sexual activity. Death scenes involving naked or partially clothed bodies and the presence of sexually explicit literature should be documented. Scene investigation is very important in autoerotic asphyxial deaths.

Sexual assault is associated with homicides where the cause of death is from head trauma, strangulation, or suffocation. Bite marks are associated with sexual assaults and leave important forensic evidence to identify the suspect.

Rape

Sex-related homicides frequently involve rape. Rape is defined as the unlawful carnal knowledge of a person against the will or without the consent of the person. The first element—carnal knowledge—is sexual intercourse and involves genital penetration of any degree with or without erection, ejaculation, orgasm, or trauma to the hymen. The second element—consent—depends on circumstances of the event; its definition may vary in different jurisdictions and from case to case. The definitions of consensual sex and statutory rape also vary between jurisdictions. Consensual sex generally means that both parties involved willfully consented to intercourse or the sexual act in question. Statutory rape is typically defined as an adult engaging in a sexual act with a minor, or an individual younger than legally defined in the particular jurisdiction's statute.

Epidemiological studies of rape show that victims are usually female, although there is much less careful documentation of male victims with regard to homosexual rapes. Female rape victims are usually in their late teens or early 20s, although there is a wide range of ages (Centers for Disease Control and Prevention, 2012). According to national survey results, nearly 40% of women are first raped between the ages of 18, but approximately 42% reported experiencing their first rape before the age of 18 (Black et al., 2011).

Rape is most frequent in areas where income is low and unemployment rate is high (Black et al., 2011). Rape is perpetrated in a context of violence rather than passion.

Profiles of Rapists

There is no single stereotypical rapist. General typologies of sex offenders may include compensatory, sadistic, power/control, and opportunistic (Robertiello and Terry, 2007). Even though the motivation behind rape is varied, there are some similarities between types of offenders. Many offenders have personalities that identify with masculinity, condone violence, have negative views of the opposite sex, have substance abuse problems, low self-esteem, and have not found an alternative outlet to manage aggression (Robertiello and Terry, 2007). At some point, these individuals lose control of their thoughts and act on their plans.

Rape murderers have also been divided into two types that display different behaviors and characteristics, according to Federal Bureau of Investigation criminal profiles:

1. Organized offenders are more apt to plan, use restraints, commit sexual acts with live victims, show or display control over their victims, and use vehicles to transport themselves to and from the crime scene.
2. Disorganized offenders are more apt to leave a weapon at the scene, position the dead body, perform sexual acts on the dead body, keep the dead body, try to depersonalize the body, and not use a vehicle.

Theories have been proposed to explain the behaviors of rapists; these include psychodynamic, behavioral, and biologic factors.

Investigation

Pathological investigation of sex-related deaths, including rape homicides, begins at the crime scene. Look for and document evidence of forced entry or struggle, preserve fingerprint evidence on things like cigarette butts, beer cans, and other objects. Look for weapons or instruments. Note stains from blood, semen, feces, or saliva that may be used for serological analysis. Search the premises for paraphernalia and possibly collect soil or vegetation evidence. Be aware that an otherwise seemingly innocent death scene may really be the scene of a rape homicide.

Examination of the victim, whether living or deceased, involves collection of evidence, description of clothing and injuries, and documentation of findings. The ultimate goal of the examination is to properly interpret the findings and reconstruct the events that occurred around the time of the death.

Clothing should be examined while on the body to document the degree of disarray and which parts of the body, if any, are exposed. The presence of obvious tears should be noted for possible correlation with injuries on the body. Trace evidence such as fibers and hairs should be sought.

Nail clippings and scrapings are usually routines in homicide cases. Consider the use of "Super glue" fumes to develop latent fingerprints on the body. Finally, use an ultraviolet lamp to examine the body for seminal fluid stains and swab suspicious areas. Be aware that pus, urine, and milk can cause false positive fluorescence.

The external examination of the rape homicide is no different than that of any other forensic case. Areas of particular concern are the genitals, anus, and breast where abrasions, lacerations, contusions, and bite marks could be present. Hands and arms could show defensive type wounds such as broken fingernails, and the lower extremities could show marks related to forcible restraint. The neck should be inspected for ligature or finger marks and the mouth and eyes may show signs of asphyxia.

Internal examination should not proceed until specimens have been collected from the vagina, anus, and mouth. This process is facilitated by the use of a "sexual assault kit" because it involves collection of evidence that may indicate recent sexual activity. Both smears and swabs are collected along with blood for serology and hair from various parts of the body. A mechanism for the maintenance of a "chain of custody" is usually provided in commercially prepared kits.

Pathological Evidence

Smears can be examined for the presence of sperm, and a wet smear can be evaluated for the presence of motility. Sperm usually retain their motility for ½–2 hours after intercourse but lose their ability to move due to exposure to the acid pH of vaginal secretions.

Morphologically recognizable sperm have been reported in approximately half of women who have had intercourse within the preceding 24 hours, but that percentage drops significantly as time passes (Hazelwood and Burgess, 2009). Sperm may be identified in samples taken from women who have showered, bathed, douched, or used various barrier methods of birth control. In the deceased victim, there are reports of recognizable sperm in samples taken weeks after death. A negative examination does not exclude recent sexual activity because a negative result may be due to the normal dissolution of sperm over time or sterility of the male partner.

Swabs, fluids, and stains can be tested for acid phosphatase activity. The level of acid phosphatase activity decreases over time but is an unreliable indicator of the time of ejaculation. Vaginal fluid zinc levels are also elevated after intercourse but are not a reliable indicator.

DNA Analysis

The newest development in the examination of sexual assault victims is the use of deoxyribonucleic acid (DNA) "fingerprinting." Studies have shown that even minute quantities of DNA can produce usable DNA fingerprints for comparison.

Other Sexual Deaths

Deaths related to homosexual activity among males can have unusual features. A promiscuous homosexual male can become exposed to violent and/or sadistic subcultures. Additionally, the incidence of suicide among homosexuals has increased since the outbreak of the HIV/AIDS epidemic.

Sex-associated asphyxia from hanging in autoerotic asphyxia associated with solitary masturbation is usually accidental. Death results from constriction of the carotid arteries during orgasm for the purpose of increasing the perceived pleasure. This can result in direct brain anoxia or cardiac arrhythmias when the usual escape mechanism fails. It is thought to be exclusively a male phenomenon. Other associated findings are evidence of repeated behavior, secluded location, sexually explicit literature at the scene, padded ligatures, binding of the limbs, an escape mechanism, and sometimes, crossdressing (transvestitism).

Sexual Assault Nurse Examiners

The use of sexual assault nurse examiners (SANE) to collect evidence from live victims in emergency rooms began in the early 1990s. Prompt collection and preservation of evidence has increased the conviction rate of sex offenders. Forensic nurses can provide necessary psychological support for sexual assault victims and are trained in legal issues to testify as expert witnesses in court.

References

Black, MC, Basile, KC, Breiding, MJ, Smith, SG, Walters, ML, Merrick, MR et al. 2011. The National Intimate Partner and Sexual Violence Survey (NISVS): 2010 summary report. Atlanta, GA: National Center for Injury Prevention and control, Centers for Disease Control and Prevention.

Centers for Disease Control and Prevention. 2012. *Sexual Violence Facts at a Glance.* Atlanta, GA: National Center for Injury Prevention and Control, Division of Violence Prevention.

Hazelwood, RR and Burgess, AW. 2009. *Practical Aspects of Rape Investigation: A Multidisciplinary Approach.* Boca Raton, FL: CRC Press.

Robertiello, G and Terry, KT. 2007. Can we profile sex offenders? A review of sex offender typologies. *Aggress Violent Behav* 12(5):508–518.

Child Abuse and Infanticide

23

OBJECTIVES

Upon completion of this chapter and corresponding reference material, the reader will be able to

- Define child abuse and infanticide
- Identify state legislation related to reporting child abuse and/ or neglect
- Discuss the pathological finding of abusive head injury
- Discuss five types of nonaccidental trauma
- Compare and contrast Resnick's five basic classifications of infanticide

Child Abuse (Nonaccidental Injury)

Definition of Child Abuse

Child abuse is the purposefully inflicted injury of a child through physical, chemical, or emotional assault or neglect.

Incidence

- Approximately 9 in 1000 children are victims of maltreatment (Centers for Disease Control and Statistics, 2013).
- An estimated rate of 2 per 100,000 children die from maltreatment (Centers for Disease Control and Statistics, 2013).
- Most child fatalities that are a result of maltreatment occur prior to the age of 4 (Centers for Disease Control and Statistics, 2013).

Features and Types

- Failure to thrive psychological trauma.
- Neglect often appears dirty and cachectic.
- Battered child with multiple injuries of various ages.
- Single-episode abusive head injury.
- Munchausen syndrome by proxy.

External Features

- Mainly blunt-force injuries.
- Abrasions often patterned.
- Contusions of different ages.
- Lacerations occasionally.
- Fractures or deformity.
- There can be internal injuries without external manifestation.
- Burns and scalds.
- Scalds from hot water may be deliberate or accidental.

Twelve criteria used to confirm suspicion of nonaccidental inflicted injury:

- Multiple bruises/scars.
- Concurrent injuries/neglect.
- History of prior hospitalization.
- Delay in seeking medical treatment for injury.
- Injury appearing older than alleged.
- Account of injury incompatible with age.
- No witness to the "accident."
- Relative vs. parent transports child.
- Injury attributed to sibling.
- Injured child is excessively withdrawn, submissive, and polite and does not cry during painful treatment.
- Scalds of hands and feet, symmetrical full thickness or isolated burns of the buttocks.
- The history of how the injury occurred does not match the injury noted on examination.

Epidemiology

One in seven children in the United States is estimated to experience some form of maltreatment in their lifetimes (Centers for Disease Control and Statistics, 2013). Most children are victims of neglect; however, approximately

20% of those abused experience some sort of physical violence (Centers for Disease Control and Statistics, 2013). Children under 1 year of age have the highest rates of victimization, and approximately 1/3 of those abused are under the age of 3 (Centers for Disease Control, 2013).

Characteristics of Abusers

Although any person can be an abuser, some characteristics have emerged. Females are more likely to be the abusers in nonfatal situations, whereas males outnumber females in fatal cases. Abusers were frequently victims of abuse from their own parents or by other adults. Abusers are often young, immature people with emotional disturbances and sociopathic personalities. Psychoses are rare in abusers. Regardless of social class, stress is a factor, although more abuse is seen in lower socioeconomic classes.

Forms of Fatal Abuse

Abuse takes many forms. Trauma, poisoning, and neglect result in fatalities.

Physical Trauma

Types of physical trauma include single or multiple battering with fists or hands, which is called blunt trauma. Asphyxia by smothering, strangulation, or drowning is more frequent than hanging. Burns, stab wounds, firearm injuries, and sexual abuse comprise the most common types of abuse to children.

Nonaccidental Head Trauma

Nonaccidental head trauma (abusive head injury), formerly known as shaken baby syndrome, occurs in infants, often to quiet a crying baby. Subdural and retinal hemorrhages are common results but are not diagnostic of injury. If the injuries are not fatal, the infant is left severely brain damaged and blind. Soft tissue and epidural hemorrhages of the neck, cerebral edema, cerebral contusion, and axonal (white matter) injuries are sometimes seen.

Neglect

Neglect is the failure to provide food, shelter, protection, and medical care as required by law. The types of neglect therefore include starvation (malnutrition), dehydration, exposure to dangerous environments, and failure to provide medical care.

Burns

Burns account for a high number of hospitalized children. Burn injuries occur in approximately 10% of child abuse cases, and 10% of hospital admissions are the result of child abuse (U.S. Department of Justice, 2001). Burns can be described as contact or scald. Contact burns are the result of the skin coming in direct contact with a hot object. Objects are usually metal such as irons, stove tops, heater grates, or curling irons (Figure 23.1). Scald burns are caused by hot liquid or steam. Tap water is the most frequent cause of abusive burns. As water temperature increases over 130°F, the rapidity of scalding increases dramatically. (Consider that in most therapeutic treatments using water, the temperature range is between 105°F and 120°F.)

Abusive tap water burns can be distinguished from accidental burns when the following characteristics are seen:

- Clear immersion lines
- Absent "splash" marks
- Stocking and/or glove pattern on the hand(s) or feet (Figure 23.2)

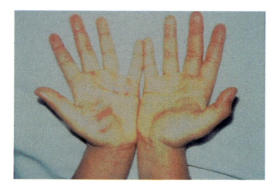

Figure 23.1 Contact thermal patterned burn.

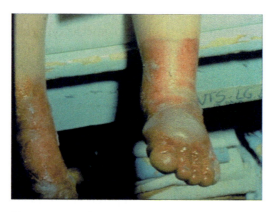

Figure 23.2 Scalding injury of child's feet.

- Protected flexion areas at the elbow, knee, and groin
- Absent "downward flow" pattern, as when a child pulls a container of hot liquid upon himself/herself from a height

Anatomic/Historic Discrepancies and Characteristics of Abuse

Delays often exist when seeking care for a child after an abusive injury. When questioned about the injury, blame is attributed to self-inflicted injury related to the child's naughty behavior. Siblings are also blamed for causing injury. Whatever explanation is given, the cause sounds implausible to explain the effects.

Child Homicide

Historically, there have been few laws governing child abuse. While child labor laws were passed in the 1800s, the extent of fatal child abuse in this country was not fully appreciated either medically or publicly until the 1960s.

In 1961, Adelson published an article in the *New England Journal of Medicine* on fatally abused children called "The Slaughter of the Innocents."

In 1962, Kempe published a radiological study of infants having multiple bone fractures in various stages of healing and postulated that these were due to repeated assaults. In this article he coined the term "battered baby syndrome."

In response to these medical studies and increased public awareness, by 1968, all states had enacted laws concerning child abuse that required all physicians and medical personnel to report suspected cases of abuse.

Epidemiology

Approximately 2 in 100,000 children died from child abuse in 2011 (Centers for Disease Control, 2013).

Characteristics of Child Abusers

Child abuse cuts across cultural, intellectual, and socioeconomic boundaries, but there are some well-known parental characteristics of child abusers. Abusing parents or guardians often have emotional disturbances and sociopathic personalities but seldom are psychotic. They are often young and immature and frequently were abused children themselves. Dependency, age inappropriateness, sadomasochism, egocentricity, and narcissism have been described. When seen in a clinical situation, abusive parents may be impulsive, demanding, withdrawn, depressed, or angry. There is often a stressful precipitating event. Since the precipitating event is often financial, it could explain the higher instance of child abuse among lower socioeconomic classes. More females than males abuse children, probably due to increased access to the children. Males, however, are more frequently involved in cases of fatal child abuse.

Physical Abuse

Physical abuse should be suspected when there is any inflicted injury on a child requiring medical therapy, where there are inflicted bruises or abrasions on an infant, or where there are inflicted bruises or injury to the face of a child.

Sexual Abuse

Sexual abuse is probably the most underreported form of child abuse, often occurring in the home and involving another family member. Approximately 9% of abused children have been victims of sexual abuse (Centers for Disease Control, 2013). Accidents, bruising, and abrasions generally occur over bony prominences.

Physical Neglect

Physical neglect occurs when there is failure to act where the law imposes the duty to provide food, shelter, clothing, and medical care. Emotional abuse and neglect is probably the largest area of child abuse, and while it is hard to estimate numbers, this is the iceberg sitting beneath the tip of physical abuse. Children suffering from any of the aforementioned forms of child abuse may show learning disabilities, developmental lags, and inappropriate or abrupt changes in behavior and mood. Bite marks can be associated with sexual abuse.

Physical Injuries as Evidence of Child Abuse

Time of Injury

Determining the time of injury can be instrumental in eliminating or including a suspect in child abuse. Unfortunately, there is no known way to determine the age of an injury with scientific certainty. Among the uncontrollable variables that affect the speed of healing are size and location of the injury, whether the injury is contaminated or clean, and individual factors such as age and nutritional and immunological statuses.

Bruises

Fresh bruises may be red, purple, blue, brown, or various combinations of those colors. The color of a bruise depends on its size and depth, density of hemorrhage, and normal pigmentation of the skin. The normal process of healing generally leads to color changes through yellow and green. Determination of age of a bruise by its color is variable and unreliable.

Abrasions

Abrasions or scraping away of the outer skin surface can occur after death and can appear identical to an injury sustained before death.

Only after a number of hours of survival following an abrasion will there be microscopic evidence that the abrasion occurred before death.

Fractures

Bones heal in a logical sequence, but the speed of healing is variable and depends on the age of the individual, location of the fracture, stability of the fracture, and individual characteristics. The healing changes can be seen microscopically as early as 24–36 hours after injury. Calcification of the healing fracture is seen within 5–7 days microscopically but cannot be seen by x-ray until after 7 days at the earliest and usually not until 10–20 days.

Degree of Force in Head Injuries

In fatal and nonfatal child abuse cases that involve severe head injuries, the most common question asked is, "What is the degree of force necessary to cause the injury?" This question is often raised as a variation of, "Could the injury have been sustained by a fall of three feet onto a carpeted floor?" Such a question seems simple and straightforward, but it is impossible to answer with certainty. For obvious reasons, no reliable experimental data are available on the amount of force necessary to cause a skull fracture or other serious head injury in a normal living human child.

Whether or not a serious injury will result from a fall or blow depends on the exact point of impact, whether or not the head is moving or stationary at impact, and unknown individual factors. Certainly, if short falls onto ordinary surfaces routinely caused severe injuries, few children would survive the toddler years. However, that does not mean that in some situations a seemingly short fall onto an ordinary surface cannot cause a severe injury.

Forms of Child Abuse

Battered Baby Syndrome

This syndrome is characterized by a child or infant who has suffered repeated assaults over a period of time and usually has injuries in various stages of healing. Use of x-rays is invaluable in helping to identify this syndrome (Figure 23.3).

Single Episode Fatality

Child abuse death as a result of a single abuse episode occurs as frequently as battered baby syndrome.

Subtle Fatal Child Abuse

Subtle fatal child abuse occurs when a child or infant is willfully killed or seriously injured in such a way that there are few or no anatomic findings that would explain the death or debility or in such a way that the death, illness, or injury appears to be the result of an accident or natural disease. The small size and delicacy of infants and small children render them vulnerable to death and serious injury by a variety of subtle mechanisms.

Causes of subtle fatal child abuse can generally be classified under

- Physical assault
- Chemical assault
- Negligence

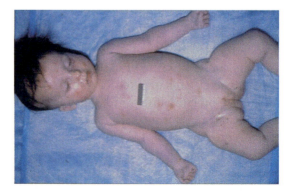

Figure 23.3 Multiple injuries in a child.

Physical Assault

There are a number of ways that fatal physical assault can occur without causing demonstrable anatomic evidence. Most of them are asphyxial. A lack of suspicion in approaching these cases can obscure recognition of their willfully inflicted nature.

Smothering of an infant may be accomplished without causing anatomic injury. Likewise, placing a foreign object down the throat of an infant may cause death with no demonstrable evidence if the obstruction is removed prior to examination. Manual or ligature strangulation and compression of the chest (traumatic asphyxia) can be accomplished without leaving marks.

Blunt impacts to the head may cause concussions in children with the rapid onset of cerebral edema and death. Anatomically, cerebral edema may be the only finding. Shaking impact syndrome may cause severe cerebral damage or even death. Autopsy findings may be limited to retinal hemorrhages and a scant bilateral subdural hematoma.

A willfully inflicted minor injury that would not cause significant morbidity in a healthy infant or child but which hastens or contributes to the death of a child severely debilitated by disease or congenital defect should result in determination of a homicidal manner of death rather than natural.

Drowning of an infant or child may leave no specific anatomic findings. If the child is removed from the water and the fact of immersion is concealed, the child may appear to be the victim of sudden unexpected infant death. Even if the immersion is apparent, the death may appear accidental.

The diagnosis of homicidal drowning requires suspicion; thorough investigation of the circumstances; and an autopsy directed toward confirmation of immersion, evaluation of any survival interval, and identification of any injury.

Deliberate drowning of infants and small children invariably is unwitnessed and occurs in the home. Parents often fit the usual sociopathologic profile of abusing guardians and there may be a precipitating stress event. Most deliberate immersions are probably unplanned and the result of uncontrolled rage. The child may be held under water until unconscious. The result may be a period of survival after removal from the water (near drowning). The pathologist should seek evidence of survival (postimmersion syndrome), aspirated foreign material, especially if the immersion may have occurred in something other than tap water, and evidence of any bruises or abrasions of the face suggesting forceful submersion of the head.

As many as one-quarter of all tap water scald burns in infants or small children are the result of abuse or neglect.

The following are the circumstantial factors suggestive of abuse:

- Medical care is delayed.
- An adult is present, but the victim is brought for medical care by someone else.
- The adult turns on the water.
- There is a major family disruption or stress.

Anatomic factors suggestive of abuse include

- Mirror image burns
- Extensive full thickness burns
- Burns on palms and soles
- Clear-cut immersion lines

The developmental age, strength, and coordination of the child should also be taken into account in determining willful vs. accidental scalding. Maximum water temperature should be checked to determine the length of exposure needed to cause the burn.

Increasingly frequent, there is survival of severely injured children—usually with head injuries—who receive aggressive medical care. These children survive their injuries only to be severely handicapped. Many are institutionalized or bedridden and prone to repeated infection, seizure disorders, or other life-threatening complications. When these children die, one cannot ignore that immediate cause of death is inseparable from the original injury, which is the appropriate proximate cause of death. One must explore the circumstances of the original injury and apply the correct manner of death even if the original injury occurred years or decades earlier.

Chemical Assault

Chemical assault is a less common form of child abuse than physical assault. When it does occur, it is extremely difficult to detect and prove. Few drugs or poisons produce pathognomonic or even characteristic lesions. Thus, a correct diagnosis usually requires prior suspicion. The offending agent need not be a classic poison or drug because almost any substance is potentially dangerous to an infant or child if taken in sufficient quantity. The assault may be a deliberate attempt to kill the child or an attempt to quiet or discipline the child.

Negligence

Child abuse through negligence can result not only from an overt act such as physical or chemical assault but also as a result of failure to act when duty is imposed by law. Therefore, the law places responsibility on the parents or guardian to provide food, shelter, protection, and medical care for their children. Death or injury resulting from willful failure to provide such care should be considered child abuse.

Munchausen Syndrome by Proxy

A distinctly unusual form of subtle child abuse is Munchausen syndrome by proxy. The Munchausen syndrome itself deals with patients who lie about their physical conditions or alter bodily fluids or specimens in order to be hospitalized or otherwise gain sympathy and attention. These patients undergo numerous hospitalizations, multiple diagnostic procedures, and often needless operations. The Munchausen syndrome by proxy occurs when parents or guardians cause numerous hospitalizations for their children either through repeated physical or chemical assaults, by falsifying medical history, or by altering diagnostic tests to gain sympathy and attention. The child may undergo numerous hospitalizations with numerous harmful hospital procedures and may even die from complications of the physical and chemical assault.

Infanticide

Infanticide, the killing of infants and newborns, dates back to ancient Greece. Historically, infanticide involved disposing of deformed or sickly infants. The female infant was valued less than the male. However, the practice continues in many contemporary cultures—including our own—of disposing of unwanted but otherwise healthy infants and children.

Infanticide has been condemned by the church and the state, but little was done in the way of prosecution of offenders until the sixteenth century in England and New England. In the United States today, there are no separate statutes that deal exclusively with infanticide and filicide (specific term used when the offender is a parent of the child). Neonaticide, by strict definition, is the murder of a newborn within the first 24 hours of life. Charges vary from state to state. In ancient Rome, the father had the right to kill his children.

Several research studies are aimed at possible causation and prevention. Resnick's classification system includes five basic categories of infanticide and filicide. Twice as many mothers, compared to fathers, killed their infants. Mothers who kill their children are generally 16–38 years of age. Less than 20% of them are married and the majority are not seen as being psychotic or depressed. Many of these young women are poor and have concealed their pregnancy and then killed and disposed of the infant secretly.

The most common methods used to kill the infants are asphyxial (strangulation, smothering, or suffocation), which leaves little physical evidence on the body and is difficult to prove. Infants are frequently delivered into toilets and allowed to drown. Occasional cases involve significant blunt force injuries to the head. The most dangerous time for a child is during the first 6 months of life. This is the time period when postpartum depression and psychoses may be encountered.

In 1969, Phillip Resnick published a study on children murdered by parents. He reviewed world literature from 1751 to 1967 and found 155 case reports (24 neonaticides were excluded from the study).

According to Resnick, the five basic classifications of apparent motive are

1. Altruistic, involving association with maternal suicide, the need to relieve real or imagined suffering, and twin infanticide
2. Acute psychoses, usually postpartum depression and psychoses, delirium, or hallucinations
3. Unwanted child of either a married or an unmarried mother or involving "secret pregnancies"
4. "Accidental" deaths, which include a violent single outburst, chronic child abuse, and neglect
5. Spouse revenge, also called the Medea complex

Altruistic child murders include those when a parent kills the child as a prelude to committing suicide. Possible explanations are that the mother projects her own identity onto the child or has concerns regarding who will care for the child after the parent is dead. The second type of altruistic filicide is committed to put the child out of imagined or real suffering such as chronic, debilitating illness. Twin infanticide occurs when a parent is unable to provide adequately for both twins and feels compelled to sacrifice one twin.

Resnick's second classification describes the parent under the influence of hallucinations, delirium, or postpartum depression. Emotional responses range from the "baby blues" that nearly all new mothers experience to deeper depressions and finally to massive psychotic reactions. The mother's relationship with the child is affected and can result in death of the child.

Unwanted child filicides are those that occur when the child is not wanted or was not planned. Unmarried teenage mothers frequently hide their pregnancies and will occasionally kill the child at birth, delivering the child alone in secrecy and disposing of the body as though the pregnancy never happened. Married women may kill a child that is illegitimate or was unplanned and presents a financial burden for the family.

"Accidental" filicides are not accidents but are unplanned, unintentional deaths of children during violent outbursts. They are accidental in that homicidal intent is absent. The mother may not have an active role in the abuse; she may merely stand by and watch her husband or boyfriend abuse the child. At other times, the mother is the one who has been abusing the child and causes the death. Deaths due to maternal neglect also fit into this category. Many cases of neglect are the result of poverty, ignorance, and chemical dependency. Munchausen syndrome by proxy is the unintentional death of a child that results from the actions of the mother inducing illness or reporting symptoms of disease, which she has caused in order to get sympathy. One common practice is to smother the child until the child stops breathing and loses consciousness. Sometimes there is a miscalculation and the child dies.

Resnick's last category includes children who are killed by one parent in an attempt to punish the spouse. This is the classic Medea complex named after Medea, Jason's wife, who killed his sons to punish him for his infidelity.

Skull Fractures: Child Abuse or Accident?

Introduction

Force related to skull injury and loss of consciousness relates significantly to the outcome of head injuries in infants and young children. Kempe (1962) studied 280 children who fell out of bed and found that only three children sustained skull fractures with no loss of consciousness or serious sequelae. Hobbs (1984) and Duhaime (1992) also studied children with falls and skull fractures, but neither examined fatal vs. nonfatal cases comparing accidents and abuse.

Abused children are often brought into emergency departments with unusual explanations for somewhat common injuries. Explanations often have elaborate reasons for "accidents." There is limited information available on skull fractures in children, although extensive military studies are available on adults with skull fractures. Consequently, a research question was developed to ask, "Is there a difference in the findings of skull fractures between accidental death and child abuse in children under two years?"

A retrospective review of 97 clinical and autopsy cases of children under 2 years old correlated data between head injury and forces involved (Dudley, 1993). Fracture characteristics provide clues in determining the cause and manner of death between accidents and child abuse. Using hospital cases over a 5-year period (1989–1994) and 15 years of autopsy records, deaths attributed to accident and injury of children under 2 years old were reviewed. Autopsy reports, police reports, scene photos, x-rays, MRIs, and CT scans were reviewed. Pediatric radiologists provided consultation on skull x-rays to verify autopsy reports and x-ray findings.

Body diagrams showing the site of injury and length and extent of the fracture were constructed for each case. Biomechanical factors identified the amount of force, direction and type of force, and environmental impact surface. Other variables included age, location and extent of injury, time lapse before treatment, loss of consciousness, and rescuer action.

Physics was applied to calculate the force of the fall or impact from the height of the fall, weight of the child, and type of surface, which indicated the dissipation of force. In motor vehicle accidents, whether the child was restrained or unrestrained was important. If the child was a pedestrian, it was important to know if the child was thrown or run over.

Four groups established for analysis included fatal and nonfatal accidents and fatal and nonfatal child abuse. Of 97 children studied (75 accident related and 23 abuse), 72 deaths occurred. Fractures from airplane accidents, occipital dislocation, and neonatal forceps delivery were excluded from the study.

Fatal Accident

The fatal accident group showed mainly complex skull fractures. Most were stellate or biparietal, 20% were depressed, 10% were growing fractures, and half of the number examined crossed the suture line. All 53 children had external and internal head injuries and loss of consciousness. Crush and rotational force injuries were common to fatal accidents.

Nonfatal Accident

Eighteen children were involved in nonfatal accidents. This includes falls, motor vehicle accidents, and one child kicked by a horse (impacted by an object). Linear fractures predominated in this group, followed by stellate (2) and depressed (3) fractures. Only half of the fractures crossed the suture line. Most cases (16) had external head injury, but only three of this group had brain trauma. One child presented with other body injury. Four cases lost consciousness initially. Rotational force injuries were present in nonfatal injuries, and crush force occurred more frequently in fatal situations.

Fatal Abuse

In both fatal abuse and nonfatal abuse injuries, all children were under a year old. Sixteen cases of head injury resulting from child abuse were fatal. Abuse victims represented a younger population, 14 days to 11 months old, whereas the accident group ranged from 3 weeks to 2 years. Skull injuries included nine complex and seven linear fractures. All cases had external head injury, brain injury, and immediate loss of consciousness. Within the study group, the fractures were more often biparietal, stellate, or growing. No depressed fractures were found and only one fracture crossed the suture line. Other body injuries consistent with child abuse were present in 14 children. Crush force injuries were present in 33% of the cases.

Nonfatal Abuse

Nonfatal child abuse subjects (7) included two linear and five complex fractures including two biparietal, two stellate, and three depressed. Of these, two were diastatic and two crossed the suture line. Half of the victims had external head injury and half had subdural hemorrhage. None experienced initial loss of consciousness. Only one had other body injury. Crush force injury appeared to be a factor in two cases.

Discussion

Skull fractures were characterized as linear, a thin fracture line, or complex. Complex included multiple (at least two fractures), diastatic (a fracture wider than a thin line), bilateral or depressed (an indentation of the bony cortex). There were fracture characteristic differences between abuse and accident cases, with abuse cases showing more complex, stellate, diastatic, and biparietal fractures.

Force

Force to a child's head was determined in 33 cases when sufficient information was available for calculations. Force calculations for a fall require the weight of the child, the distance of the fall, and type of impacting surface. Speed of the motor vehicle is needed when a motor vehicle is involved. Force categories included crush (compression between two solid objects), rotational (a moving head impacting a fixed object), and translational (fixed head impacted by another object) injuries. Fatal accident cases with high force calculation accounted for severe craniocerebral injuries and immediate loss of consciousness, similar to injuries seen in fatal abuse cases.

In summary, our findings concur with other studies that accidental falls from low heights rarely cause severe intracranial injuries or death in infants. An analysis of over 15 years of head injuries in children under 2 years old showed only three fatal falls. Nonfatal skull fractures from falls had fewer long-term sequelae than nonfatal abuse cases. Careful investigation of circumstances surrounding the head injury can help to verify the account of how the injury occurred.

References

Centers for Disease Control and Statistics. 2013. *Child Maltreatment: Facts at a Glance*. Atlanta, GA: National Center for Injury Prevention and Control, Division of Violence Prevention.

Dudley, MH, Zumwalt, RE et al. 1993. Skull fractures under the age of 2 years— Accident vs. child abuse. Abstract presentation at *AAFS National Meeting 1993*, Boston, MA.

Duhaime, AC, Alario, AJ et al. 1992. Head injury of very young children: Mechanisms, injury types, and ophthalmologic findings in 100 hospitalized patients younger than 2 years of age. *Pediatrics* 90(2pt1):179–185.

Hobbs, CJ. 1984. Skull fractures and the diagnosis of abuse. *Arch Dis Child* 59:246–252.

Kempe, CH, Silverinan, FN et al. 1962. The Battered Child Syndrome. *J Am Med Assoc* 181:17–24.

United States Department of Justice. 2001. *Burn Injuries in Child Abuse: Portable Guides to Investigating Child Abuse*. Washington, DC: United States Department of Justice.

Bibliography

Adelson, L. 1972. The battering child. *JAMA* 222:159–161.

Ayoub, C and Pfeifer, D. 1979. Burns ad a manifestation of child abuse and neglect. *Am J Dis Child* 133:910–914.

Beals, RK and Tufts, E. 1983. Fractured femur in infancy: The role of child abuse. *J Pediatr Orthop* 3:583–586.

Bennett, HS and French, JH. 1980. Elevated intracranial pressure in whip-lash shaken infant syndrome detected with normal computerized tomography. *Clin Pediatr* 19:633–634.

Calleno, H and Oppenheim, WL. 1982. The battered child syndrome revisited. *Clin Orthop Relat Res* 162:11–19.

DiMaio, DJ and DiMaio, VJM. 2001. *Forensic Pathology*, 2nd ed. Boca Raton, FL: CRC Press.

Dolinak, D, Matshes, E, and Lew, E. 2006. *Forensic Pathology: Principles and Practice*. Burlington, MA: Elsevier.

Norman, MC, Newman, DE, and Smialek, JE. 1984. The postmortem examination on the abused child: Pathological, radiography, and legal aspects. *Perspect Pediatr Pathol* 8:313–343.

Weber, W. 1984. Experimental study of skull fractures in infants. *Z Rechtsmed* 92:87–94.

Zumwalt, RE and Hirsch, CS. 1980. Subtle fatal child abuse. *Hum Pathol* 11:167–174.

Sudden Unexpected Infant Deaths

24

MARY H. DUDLEY
LAUREN E. DVORSCAK

OBJECTIVES

Upon completion of this chapter and corresponding reference material, the reader will be able to

- Define sudden unexpected infant death (SUID)
- Discuss the components of a thorough SUID investigation (SUIDI)
- Describe the reasons for the change in terminology by medical examiners from sudden infant death syndrome (SIDS)
- List the risk factors for unsafe sleep conditions
- Identify the preventative aspects for parent education to reduce unsafe sleep conditions

Introduction

The classification "sudden infant death syndrome" was created from a National Institutes of Health consensus committee who recognized that some infant deaths shared similar features and were otherwise unexplained. The SIDS classification is assigned to infant deaths that cannot be explained after a thorough investigation, autopsy, and review of the clinical history (Willinger et al., 1991). The term was originally intended to place sudden unexpected deaths of infants into a category of exclusion to facilitate case tracking and research. In practical use, the classification became a diagnosis, and implied that SIDS was due to underlying natural disease processes. However, as scene investigation improved, forensic pathologists have realized that this is a far more heterogeneous group of infants, consisting of cases of undiagnosed natural diseases, accidental suffocations associated with unsafe sleep environments, and even covert homicides.

Further recommendations by the National Association of Medical Examiners attempted to update the original SIDS classification and recommended the term "sudden unexpected infant death." The SUID cause of death classification came into effect in 2006 and is used to describe any sudden and unexpected infant death, including deaths previously classified as SIDS. SUIDs can be attributed to a variety of different causes, such as suffocation, asphyxia, or entrapment, associated with the infant sleep environment (Moon, 2011). Forensic death investigators play an important role in the evaluation of SUIDs by conducting death scene investigations, doll reenactments, and interviews to obtain vital information to assist the medical examiner in determining the cause and manner of death (Shapiro-Mendoza et al., 2006).

The incidence of SIDS experienced a major decline following the 1992 American Academy of Pediatrics recommendation that infants be placed for sleep in a nonprone position (Kattwinkel, 1992). This was followed by a plateau until the introduction of the SUID classification, after which deaths attributed to SIDS appeared to decline again. However, this recent decline is most likely attributable to a diagnostic shift away from terminology like SIDS in the field of forensic pathology and may not accurately represent a continued decline in infant mortality (Senter et al., 2011).

Research at the University of New Mexico Office of the Medical Examiner in Albuquerque, New Mexico, has supported a collaborative effort in the study of reclassification in infant death and how this has impacted appropriate coding and standardization of these cases, particularly taking the diagnostic shift in manner of death into account (Dvorscak et al., 2015). Standardization in approaching infant death necessitates that medical death investigators are familiar with the changing classification scheme and the implications for statistical tracking. In order to determine how much of an impact the changing classification scheme has had in a statewide medical examiner system (New Mexico), greater than 100 infant deaths from 2006 to 2011 were reanalyzed by a group of nine pathologists. The pathologists were blinded to the original diagnosis. After review of the relevant scene, autopsy findings, ancillary testing, and supplementary photographs, each pathologist granted a cause and manner of death for the cases based on current conventions. When compared to original certification, a diagnosis of SIDS was not rendered by any pathologist in the study, accurately representing a diagnostic shift in the field. Particularly, all cases originally coded as SIDS were classified to alternatives such as suffocation/strangulation or undetermined, with rare exceptions. The study into infant death in New Mexico confirmed that the practices of certifying SUIDs have shifted significantly over time, which may account for a large proportion of the decline in deaths certified as SIDS (Dvorscak et al., 2015). This study demonstrates the importance of consistency in the approach to investigating and ultimately certifying unexplained infant deaths.

Sleep Environment

In the United States, unintentional suffocation is the leading cause of injury death among children less than 1 year of age, with a fourfold increase in accidental suffocation and strangulation in bed since 1984. Although unsafe sleeping conditions are recognized as a major contributor to accidental infant death, a discrepancy within the literature exists concerning the risk attributed to the sleep environment. Although programs and public safety campaigns have addressed preventable infant death, the danger of the infant sleep environment remains largely unpublicized and misunderstood (Mitchell et al., 1992).

Infant death due to an unsafe sleep environment is postulated to be due to unsafe sleep surface, overlay, positional asphyxia, hyperthermia, suffocation, and/or wedging/entrapment. These conditions may be exacerbated by bed-sharing (infant sleeping on the same surface as another person). Although unsafe sleep environments are recognized as a contributing factor to infant deaths, it is apparent that further clarification is needed in order to avoid preventable infant mortality.

To address these issues, a retrospective study was conducted to review unexpected deaths of infants up to 1 year of age that presented to Jackson County, Missouri, Medical Examiner's Office during 1998–2010 (Dudley et al., 2011). This office serves the Missouri counties of Cass, Clay, Jackson, and Platte, which includes Kansas City, Missouri's, most populous community. All reports prior to 2007 were assessed to determine whether there was sufficient information regarding unsafe sleep conditions and whether that information might have led to a different cause of death under SUID criteria. Particular attention was paid to bed-sharing. From 2007 through 2010, SUID criteria were employed by the Medical Examiner's Office.

In cases where bed-sharing was implicated, the following variables were extracted from the death record: death classification as accidental or natural, infant sleep position, sex, age, race, and sleep surface. Chi-square tests were used to assess the differences of bed-sharing for each demographic and risk factor variable. In addition, a time period table was created based on pre- or postimplementation of the SUID criteria. Logistic regression analyses were conducted, where the outcome variable was bed-sharing and the independent variables were the demographic and risk factor variables. All analyses were conducted using the statistical significance level of $p \leq 0.05$ (PASW Statistics Version 18.0 by SPSS, Chicago, IL, USA).

In addition, the Medical Examiner's Office had conducted two convenience surveys of mothers attending the 2006 and 2010 Kansas City Well Baby Fairs. Mothers were surveyed on their behaviors, including sleep position, exposure to secondhand smoke, and sleep surface and environment, such as the presence of bumper pads. Mothers were also quizzed on infant sleep practices. The participant responses relevant to this study were how many times a week bed-sharing occurred when their baby was less than 6 months of age as well as the circumstances surrounding bed-sharing.

In the 1998–2010 time frame, 203 unexpected infant deaths were referred to the Jackson County Medical Examiner's Office. Fifty-eight percent of the deaths occurred within the first 5 months of life. Blacks, per 1000 live births, were 3.4 times more likely to be decedents than whites.

For the 12-year period, 41.9% of unexpected infant deaths occurred on a bed, 25.6% in a crib, 16.7% on a couch, and 15.8% on other sleeping surfaces. Infant deaths varied with sleep position: 11% of deaths occurred with side sleep position, 35% occurred in the prone position, and 29% occurred in the supine position. In 25% of the cases, sleep position was unknown. Bed-sharing information was recorded in only half of all unexpected infant deaths.

SIDS was listed as the cause of death for 111 (77.1%) of the 144 cases between 1998 and 2006 and for 8 (13.6%) of the 59 cases between 2007 and 2010. The decline in SIDS diagnoses following adoption of the SUID criteria was very highly significant ($p < 0.001$).

From 1998 to 2006, 47.6% of SIDS cases involved unsafe sleep environments. This declined to 12.0% in 2007 with the adoption of SUID and to 0% in subsequent years. Prior to 2007, there was a high correlation of SIDS and bed-sharing ($r^2 = 0.79$, $p < 0.01$). The logistic regression analyses on bed-sharing showed that sleeping in a bed (OR 7.66, CI 3.43, 17.10), accidental death (OR 6.46, CI 2.20, 18.95), black race (OR 2.68, CI 1.25, 5.76), and age less than 3 months (OR 2.18, CI 1.02, 4.65) were significant factors for unexpected infant deaths.

More than 80% of infant deaths due to asphyxia/overlay were associated with bed-sharing. Bed-sharing in a bed was documented more than twice as often as on a couch or chair. Bed-sharing cases occurring in cribs, recliners, and other surfaces accounted for only 10% of deaths related to bed-sharing. Of infants who died while bed-sharing, one-third had been sleeping with their mothers.

Of the 77 mothers who participated in the convenience samples, 72% reported that their infant under 6 months of age never shared a bed. While 11.8% reported that their infant slept in an adult bed, when asked about their future intentions, 22% indicated that they do plan on using an adult bed for infant sleep. Of mothers who bed-shared, half reported doing so three or fewer times per week. The reasons for bed-sharing were stated as follows: parent/child bonding—32.4%; parent and child fell asleep while breastfeeding—17.6%; parent fell asleep with the child on a chair, couch, or air mattress—17.6%; no crib/bassinet available—11.8%; temporary sleeping arrangement while visiting—11.8%; and lack of sleeping surface for the entire family—8.8%.

Discussion

Recent studies have demonstrated a decrease in the incidence of SIDS as deaths due to accidental asphyxia associated with bed-sharing increased (Li et al., 2009). Yet, proponents of the practice postulate that bed-sharing actually reduces the incidence of SIDS as it allows a parent to respond to a distressed infant. They propose that the practice of bed-sharing has resulted in the recent reduction of SIDS cases, although no evidence supporting these claims exists. Additionally, there are studies that suggest bed-sharing actually increases unexpected infant deaths.

Proponents of bed-sharing agree that sleeping with an infant on a surface other than a bed is dangerous. Bed-sharing proponents contend evidence regarding infant death can be attributed to unsafe sleep practices such as sleeping on a couch, tobacco smoke, and low socioeconomic status rather than bed-sharing (Kattwinkel et al., 1994). Although low socioeconomic status, minority race, low education, tobacco smoke, and couch sleeping are associated with an increased incidence of infant death, it is clear that the variable of bed-sharing alone (without other risk factors) significantly increases the risk of sudden death.

The study at the Jackson County Medical Examiner's Office in Kansas City, Missouri, has shown that sleeping with infants regardless of the surface may result in sudden, unexpected death and that the majority of these deaths occurred in bed. These findings support current literature that has provided similar evidence.

The most common scenario involving bed-sharing deaths included an adult, sibling, and an infant sleeping together. This may suggest families do not have a crib; however, it has been demonstrated in previous studies that a crib is in a home in 61% of bed-sharing cases (Li et al., 2009). While several studies conclude that adult–infant bed-sharing may be a significant risk factor for sudden death in infants, there is also evidence to suggest infant–sibling and infant–infant bed-sharing may be a significant risk factor for infant death. Person et al. (2002) found that 15% of dead infants were found in a crib with a twin, and in the current study, 20% of the bed-sharing associated deaths involved an infant sleeping with a sibling, without an adult present.

Several distinctions between deaths related to SIDS and unsafe sleep were observed. Previous findings show a male predominance in SIDS. Although the total percent of female infants in the study was 41%, the number of those cosleeping was 52%. This suggests that there is no predilection based on sex for infant deaths associated with bed-sharing. Rather, this observation is consistent with the idea that bed-sharing deaths are caused by external physical forces leading to positional asphyxia. Additionally, others had found a strong risk factor for SIDS to be the prone sleep position. With the unsafe sleep environment deaths reported to the Jackson County Medical Examiner's Office, there was a higher incidence of supine and side sleep positions. In bed-sharing cases, the specific cause of death is postulated to be due to unintentional overlay leading to asphyxia or re-breathing of carbon dioxide (Bolton et al., 1993).

Research indicates the frequency of bed-sharing for infants ranges from 14% to 24% of the time; thus, children do sleep alone more often than bed-sharing (Ruys et al., 2007). This suggests that the risk of infant death is three to seven times greater while bed-sharing. Data also found that infant mortality during bed-sharing at 1 month of age was nine times greater than those infants sleeping alone (Ruys et al., 2007).

The data presented showed that the percentage of infant deaths related to unsafe sleep ruled as SIDS prior to the implementation of SUID criteria dropped precipitously after the adoption of the new criteria. Thus, many cases once ruled SIDS were associated with an unsafe sleep environment. This is further evidence supporting that the diagnostic shift in forensic pathology confounded the apparent decrease in SIDS deaths.

There are several theories as to risk factors and causation of unexpected infant deaths during sleep. Early studies suggest a triple risk model associated with SIDS, which included vulnerability of the infant, exogenous stressors, and a critical development period (Trachtenberg et al., 2012). These same risk factors may help explain the increased risks associated with infant deaths in an unsafe sleep environment. The vulnerable infant less than 6 months of age may be more subject to environmental stressors of heat or hypoxic conditions, both of which may be present during co-sleeping, bed-sharing, positional asphyxia, prone sleeping position, or wedging and entrapment. The highly vulnerable infant, such as the low-birth-weight or premature infant, may be more susceptible to a hostile external sleeping environment.

Autopsy findings described in SIDS deaths as incidental observations may be physiological findings of hypoxia or stress. Tissue markers of hypoxia have been described to include extra-medullary hematopoiesis in the liver and brain stem gliosis. Autopsy findings of persistence of fetal hemoglobin and raised hypoxanthine values in postmortem vitreous samples may indicate perimortem hypoxia (Berry, 1989). Neuropathology findings of delayed myelination and maturation of dendrite spines may explain a link between antemortem factors such as smoking and SUID (Berry, 1989). Also of interest are the findings of petechial hemorrhage in many of these infant deaths. One study concluded that a significant increase in thoracic petechiae in SUID and extension below the diaphragm were associated with hypoxemia and other conditions (Goldwater, 2011).

Unsafe sleep conditions, such as asphyxia and hypoxia, may cause overheating and hypothermia. One study found that 90% of SIDS cases were exposed to one or more exogenous stressors near the time of death. Expression of heat shock protein was also found as a biomarker for overheating in the overwhelming majority of SIDS cases. Minor inflammation in the respiratory tract in 60% of SUID cases was also notable (Berry, 1989). If the infants had a fever associated with infection, they are more at risk in a hot environment due to immature cooling mechanisms. To this end, it has been postulated that a fan may reduce the risk of infant death in adverse sleep environments. The use of a fan may be beneficial not only to cool the infant, but to circulate the air in the child's sleep environment.

Asphyxia, prone sleeping, and hyperthermia all play a role in infant death related to unsafe sleep environments. The underlying mechanism is likely multifactorial, similar to heart disease in adults, but may be also related to additional unknown intrinsic risk factors. However, awareness of the external, preventable risk factors may be significant in reducing the number of infant deaths related to unsafe sleep environments. Ruling an infant death as positional asphyxia or suffocation based on scene investigation and autopsy findings with an accidental manner is often a more accurate classification. To rule the death as SIDS or SUID with a natural or undetermined manner fails to accurately state the known findings of an unsafe sleep environment for the importance of education and preventability of many infant deaths.

The Kansas City study provides clarity and confirms findings of previously published data and distinguishes the processes of SIDS- and unsafe sleep environment–associated deaths. In this 12-year retrospective study, the trend of a decline in SIDS listed as the cause of infant death is associated with changes in classification and certification of these deaths by medical examiners. In reviewing all infant deaths in a 12-year period, the total number of infant deaths remained constant, while SIDS declined, and asphyxial deaths increased.

Conclusion

The study showed significant differences in the infant sleeping environment, position, and sex between infant deaths associated with unsafe sleep environment and those variables independent of the sleep environment. In the logistic regression analyses, age, race, manner, and cosleeping in a bed were significant independent variables. Blacks had bed-sharing rate twice that of whites. The study showed the decreased incidence of SIDS was due to, at least in part, to careful death scene investigations and procedural changes. The cause of death and exclusion of natural disease is revealed during a complete forensic autopsy, including review of medical history, cultures, x-ray, toxicology, metabolic studies, and histological findings. The manner of death is based upon the circumstances at the death scene determined by a thorough scene investigation, doll reenactment, and interviews. Deaths related to unsafe sleep environments are ruled as accidental and may be preventable.

References

Berry, PJ. 1989. Pathological findings in SIDS. *J Perinatol* 9:180–183.

Bolton, DP, Taylor, BJ, Campbell, AJ, Galland, BC, and Cresswell, C. 1993. Rebreathing expired gases from bedding: A cause of cot death? *Arch Dis Child* 69:187–190.

Dudley, MH, Hensley, ST et al. 2011. Infant death and unsafe sleep environment. Poster presentation at NAME meeting 2011, Seattle, WA.

Dvorscak, L, Lathrop, S, and Pinckard, JK. 2015. Reclassification of sudden infant deaths in New Mexico. Abstract presentation at *AAFS National Meeting 2015*, Orlando, FL.

Goldwater, PN. 2011. Intrathoracic petechial hemorrhages in sudden infant death syndrome and other infant deaths: Time for re-examination. *Pediatr Dev Pathol* 11:450–455.

Kattwinkel, J. 1992. Positioning and SIDS. *Pediatrics* 89:1120–1126.

Li, L, Zhang, Y, Xielke, RH, Ping, Y, and Fowler, DR. 2009. Observations on increased accidental asphyxia deaths in infancy while co-sleeping in the state of Maryland. *Am J Forensic Med Pathol* 30:318–321.

Mitchell, EA, Taylor, BJ, Ford, RP, Stewart, AW, Becroft, DM, Thompson, JM et al. 1992. Four modifiable and other major risk factors for cot death: The New Zealand Study. *J Pediatr Child Health* 28(Suppl 1):S3–S8.

Moon, RY. 2011. SIDS and other sleep related infant deaths: Expansion of recommendations for a safe infant sleeping environment. *Pediatrics* 128:1030–1039.

Person, TL, Lavezzi, WA, and Wolf, BC. 2002. Cosleeping and sudden unexpected death in infancy. *Arch Pathol Lab Med* 126:343–345.

Ruys, JH, de Jonge, GA, Brand, R, Engelberts, AC, and Semmekrot, BA. 2007. Bed-sharing in the first four months of life: A risk factor for sudden infant death. *Acta Paediatrica* 96:1399–1403.

Senter, L, Sackoff, J, Landi, K, and Boyd, L. 2011. Studying sudden and unexpected infant death in a time of changing death certification and investigative practices: Evaluating sleep related risk factors for infant death in New York City. *Matern Child Health J* 15:242–248.

Shapiro-Mendoza, CK, Tomashek, KM, Davis, TW, and Blanding, SL. 2006. Importance of the infant death scene investigation for accurate and reliable reporting of SIDS. *Arch Dis Child* 91:373.

Trachtenberg, FL, Haas, EA, Kinney, HC, Stanley, C, and Krous, HF. 2012. Risk factor changes for sudden infant death syndrome after initiation of back to sleep campaign. *Pediatrics* 129:630–638.

Willinger, M, James, LS, and Catz, C. 1991. Defining the sudden infant death syndrome (SIDS): Deliberations of an expert panel convened by the National Institute of Child Health and Human Development. *Pediatr Pathol* 11:677–684.

Bibliography

Kemp, JS, Unger, B, Wilkins, D, Psara, RM, Ledbetter, TL, Graham, MA et al. 2000. Unsafe sleep practices and an analysis of bedsharing among infants dying suddenly and unexpectedly: Results of a four year, population based, death scene investigation study of sudden infant death syndrome and related deaths. *Pediatrics* 106:E41.

Shapiro-Mendoza, CK, Kimball, M, Tomashek, KM, Anderson, RN, and Blanding, S. 2009. US infant mortality trends attributable to accidental suffocation and strangulation in bed from 1984 through 2004: Are rates increasing. *Pediatrics* 123:533–539.

Elder Abuse

25

ROSS E. ZUMWALT

OBJECTIVES

Upon completion of this chapter and corresponding reference material, the reader will be able to

- List characteristics of potential abusers of the elderly
- Describe the potential victim of elder abuse
- Discuss five types of elder abuse
- Differentiate between signs of abuse and signs of neglect
- Evaluate the death investigation of an elderly person

Introduction

Awareness of the problem concerning elder abuse and the limited response to it are relatively recent. In 1980, the U.S. Senate Special Committee on Aging estimated the incidence at 500,000–2,500,000 occurrences per year. It is estimated that only one in six cases is actually reported.

Indications of elder abuse include

- Psychological depression, anxiety, withdrawal, timidness, hostility, excessive willingness to please
- Emotional death wishes, change in appetite, disinterest
- Physical unexplained injuries, implausible explanations
- Neglect dirt, odor, soiled bedding, poor skin hygiene, sensory deprivation (no glasses, hearing aids, etc.)

Geriatric Pathology in Death Investigation

Clearly, it is expected that old people will die, and when they do, it often comes as no surprise. Because the death is not unexpected, it is generally concluded that the cause of death is from natural causes. This can be a dangerous assumption for those involved in medicolegal death investigation. Old people can be injured as well as be ill. In fact, many old people are particularly vulnerable to injury because of their frailty, confusion, or unsteady gait. A minor injury that would be inconsequential to a healthy young adult might be fatal to an old person. Therefore, the investigation into deaths of the elderly requires more care, rather than less, in seeking history of prior injury or environmental exposure of an injurious agent. It may also require more care in the examination of the body for evidence of injury.

Common mistakes made in the investigation of deaths of the elderly are similar to those made in the investigation of decomposed bodies. The examination of the scene may be unpleasant—the elderly may be soiled with urine or feces, and the environment may be dirty and squalid. Consequently, a superficial examination of the scene and the body may be made. The body may be examined in poor light, uncleaned, and partially clothed.

The elderly are not immune to common forms of violent death, such as gunshot wounds and motor vehicle accident trauma, and their injuries correspond to those seen in the younger population. In addition, the elderly are susceptible to fatal injuries not usually seen in the young.

Accidents

Simple falls may trigger fatal complications. A fall from standing height may result in a fractured hip or ribs. The pain and immobility from the injury may aggravate underlying natural disease or provide the setting for pulmonary emboli or bronchopneumonia. When these natural disease complications result in death, the underlying cause of death remains the injury; the manner of death depends on how the injury occurred.

The elderly frequently take prescription medications. There is a great potential for fatal drug reactions and true overdoses among the elderly because of their ages, their frequently altered mental states, and the number and amount of medications often prescribed. The death investigator must be mindful of the need for careful documentation of medications at the death scene as well as careful review of medical history and whether or not prescribed medications are listed in an inventory of the deceased's medications.

Hypothermia and hyperthermia are two conditions that may result from environmental exposure that can cause death in the elderly. The manner of death in these situations is unnatural and depends on the circumstances of the exposure. Careful scene investigation including environmental temperature is important.

Suicide

Old people can and do commit suicide. A soft ligature around the neck, hanging from a seated position, or placing a plastic bag over the head may cause death with few or no marks on the face or neck. If the scene has been altered by relatives, the investigator must be particularly attentive to detail to detect the violent nature of the death. Similarly, accidental asphyxia in the elderly may be hidden by caretakers.

Homicide

There are several categories of murder of elderly persons that are not generally seen in younger adults. Much attention has been directed to serial murders in medical institutions such as hospitals and nursing care facilities. The idea of a health-care worker as an "avenging angel" who poisons or otherwise kills the chronically ill, often moribund patients, is a common profile. The death investigator must take seriously any rumor that such activity is occurring so that deaths at that institution are monitored.

Isolated euthanasia is occasionally suspected but seldom confirmed. Assisted suicide and medical euthanasia are currently widely discussed. In situations where life-support equipment is inexplicably disconnected or too much pain medication is taken, the distinction between accident, suicide, and homicide becomes blurred and depends on an elucidation of the circumstances of death and not the autopsy findings.

Elder Abuse

Elder abuse is a social problem with many similarities to child abuse and spouse abuse. These forms of family or domestic violence are common and involve all cultures and economic levels. Public awareness of child abuse began in the 1960s. Studies of spouse abuse followed in the late 1970s. By the end of the 1990s, a great deal of attention focused on elder abuse. Elder abuse may take the form of physical abuse, sexual abuse, psychological abuse, neglect, and material abuse.

Physical abuse is the willful physical assault on an old person and may take the form of beating, slapping, shoving, or forcible restraint by tying. Psychological, emotional, or mental abuse is often represented by repeated insults or threats. Other forms of psychological abuse include confinement to small spaces, isolation from human contact, or humiliation.

Physical neglect is the failure of a clearly designated caregiver to meet the needs of an elder. The failure can result from conscious intention of the caregiver (active neglect) or can occur unintentionally (passive neglect). Physical neglect may take the form of inadequate food, housing, clothing, or medical care. Material abuse is the theft or misuse of an elder's money or other assets.

Incidence

The National Center on Elder Abuse reported that 7%–10% of adults suffer from some form of abuse (2015). Elder abuse is more difficult to identify than child abuse because of lack of professional and public awareness, relative isolation of the victims, and reluctance of the elderly to report abuse. One study estimated that only 1 in 14 cases of elder abuse comes to the attention of authorities (National Research Council, 2003).

The reasons for elder abuse are complex and rooted in the intricate interactions within families and cultures. Maladaptive families can resort to abuse during times of stress. Alcoholism, substance abuse, mental illness, mental retardation, and a history of violent intrafamily behavior can trigger overt abuse.

Characteristics of Victims

No group of the elderly is immune to the possibility of abusive behavior. However, the following characteristics make old people especially vulnerable to abuse.

Female

There are more older women than older men, and women are less likely to resist abusive behavior.

Impairment

Many studies report that abuse correlates with the extent and severity of physical or mental impairment. This produces greater demands and responsibilities for the caregiver, which can result in stress and frustration.

Provocative Behavior

Individuals who are overly demeaning, ungrateful, or otherwise unpleasant can aggravate already stressed and overburdened caregivers.

Past Abuse

Older persons who have been abused in the past are candidates for further abuse when they display increasing impairments and dependency. As with child abuse, the parent who abuses his own child teaches the child a behavior pattern and may be abused by that adult child.

Substance Abuse

An older person who is a problem drinker or drug abuser is susceptible to abusive behavior due to an inability to care for or tend to himself, particularly if he lives with an alcoholic caregiver.

Social Dependence

The elderly person who depends on his caregiver for all social interaction is more vulnerable to abuse.

Financial Dependence

Economic dependency can result in hostility by a caregiver.

Characteristics of Abusers

The following characteristics, singly or in combination, are helpful to identify caretakers at risk for abusing the elderly.

Problem Drinker

A problem drinker may act out in hostility under the influence of alcohol.

Drug Abuser

The drug abuser may not only overtly abuse an elderly person, but he may also be unaware of the consequences of poor care.

Confusion/Senile Dementia

Some caregivers are themselves physically or psychologically impaired and cannot provide needed care.

Mental or Emotional Illness

A caregiver with mental illness may be unable to care for a frail, older person.

Caregiving Inexperience

It cannot be assumed that all individuals know how to care for an elderly person. Such persons can be ineffective or hostile in their roles as caretakers.

Economically Troubled

If a caretaker views the older person as a financial drain on limited resources, he may develop hostility and become an abuser.

Economically Dependent

In some cases, the abuse may result from resentment from being economically dependent upon the older person.

Abused as a Child

Adult children who were abused as children are more likely to abuse the elderly through learned behavior or unconscious hostility.

Socially Isolated

A caretaker unengaged outside of the home may not have family or friends from whom he can receive emotional support.

Personality Disorders

Individuals with personality problems such as lack of understanding, lack of sympathy, and being hypercritical and chronic blamers often have unrealistic expectations about their roles in caregiving.

Fatal Elder Abuse

Fatal elder abuse occurs when death follows complications of injury or neglect received from caretakers. This definition excludes premeditated murder of competent independent elderly persons because of rage or for financial gain.

Investigation of possible fatal elder abuse requires a detailed account of the circumstances of the death and a thorough medical and psychosocial history.

History of the circumstances of the death should be elicited from as many informants as possible—caregiver, other family members, neighbors, EMS, police, and others. If different histories are given, documentation of what is said by each informant is important.

In discussing the case with caretakers, ask them to describe a typical day for the deceased. Ask for a history of any injuries. Listen for clues that the caretaker feels overwhelmed, particularly when the patient cannot perform such tasks as toileting, bathing, or feeding himself. Be on the lookout for inconsistencies in the explanations. Specific questions to ask about the deceased include the following:

- Was he or she intellectually or severely mentally impaired?
- Does he or she need help bathing, dressing, or eating?
- Was he or she incontinent or needed help toileting?
- Does he or she depend on the caretaker for all social interactions?
- Does he or she have or have no friends or social interactions outside the home?
- Was he or she demanding or authoritative to the caretaker?

Scene Investigation

If a body has been transferred to a hospital for pronouncement of death, try to go to the home to check for potential evidence of abuse. What is the condition of the home? Is it dirty? Is it adequately heated? Is there sufficient food and medicine on hand?

Abuse and Neglect

Signs of abuse might be seen in head injuries, absence of hair, hemorrhage below the scalp, broken teeth, or eye injuries. Unexplained bruises about the face, lips, mouth, back, or buttocks and bruises that are in various stages of healing, clustered, or form patterns are all causes for suspicion. Unexplained burns that look like cigar or cigarette burns, immersion burns, or friction burns from restraints should be investigated.

Neglect can be seen in dehydration, malnutrition, inappropriate or soiled clothing, poor hygiene, inappropriate care, decubiti, or injuries that have not been treated.

As average life spans increase, the opportunity and motivation for elder abuse increase. Medical examiners, death investigators, and others should be alert to distinguish death from natural causes from death by elder abuse.

References

National Center on Elder Abuse Administration on Aging. 2015. Statistics/Data: Elder Abuse: The Size of the Problem. Website Accessed December 2015, at http://www.ncea.aoa.gov/library/data/index.aspx. Washington, DC: Department of Health and Human Services.

National Research Council. 2003. *Elder Mistreatment: Abuse, Neglect, and Exploitation in an Aging America*. Washington, DC: The National Academies Press.

Index